The
Insurance
Fact Book

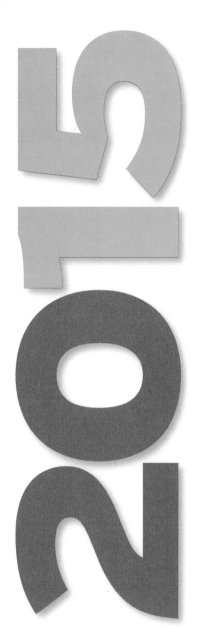
2015

**INSURANCE
INFORMATION
INSTITUTE**

TO THE READER

Since its inception more than 50 years ago, the Insurance Information Institute Insurance Fact Book has provided information to help reporters, businesses, regulators, legislators and researchers understand the trends and statistics shaping the insurance industry.

As always, the book provides valuable information on:

- World and U.S. catastrophes
- Property/casualty and life/health insurance results and investments
- Personal expenditures on auto and homeowners insurance
- Major types of insurance losses, including vehicle accidents, homeowners claims, crime and workplace accidents
- State auto insurance laws

The I.I.I. Insurance Fact Book is meant to be used along with the Institute's website, www.iii.org, which features information for consumers, researchers, public policymakers and businesses alike. The I.I.I. remains a vital source for the media, which rely on the I.I.I.'s spokespersons, Fact Book, Insurance Handbook, videos and other materials for creditable, timely information. Social networks are another way to stay in touch with the I.I.I. We welcome you to "like" our Facebook page at www.facebook.com/InsuranceInformationInstitute and follow us on Twitter at twitter.com/iiiorg.

As always, we would like to thank the many associations, consultants and others who collect industry statistics and who have generously given permission to use their data.

In conclusion, I would like to dedicate the 2015 edition of the I.I.I. Insurance Fact Book to Neil Liebman, who for more than 20 years served the Institute, its members, subscribers, media and countless others by providing accurate and timely information about this critical industry. Neil has been a key member of the Fact Book team for many years (including the 2015 edition) and has spearheaded countless other publication projects while also serving as the editorial force behind the Institute's flagship newsletter, the I.I.I. Daily. There is no question that Neil's legacy will be one that benefits future generations of insurance professionals, regulators, students and others who will rely on his work to aid in their understanding of this industry's rich history. We wish Neil the very best in his retirement.

Robert P. Hartwig, Ph.D., CPCU
President, Insurance Information Institute
@Bob_Hartwig

The I.I.I. Insurance Fact Book is published by the Insurance Information Institute, a primary source for information, analysis and referral on insurance subjects. The Fact Book contains material from numerous sources. Because these sources define and collect data in various ways, and moreover, are constantly refining the data, differences among similar data may occur.
©2015 Insurance Information Institute. ISBN 978-0-932387-72-1

Contents

- The U.S. insurance industry's net premiums written totaled $1 trillion in 2013, with premiums recorded by life/health (L/H) insurers accounting for 54 percent and premiums by property/casualty (P/C) insurers accounting for 46 percent, according to SNL Financial.

- P/C insurance consists primarily of auto, home and commercial insurance. Net premiums written for the sector totaled $481.2 billion in 2013.

- The L/H insurance sector consists primarily of annuities and life insurance. Net premiums written for the sector totaled $560.3 billion in 2013.

- Health insurance is generally considered separate. The sector includes private health insurance companies as well as government programs. P/C and L/H insurers also write some health insurance.

- There were 6,086 insurance companies in 2013, including P/C (2,623 companies), life/annuities (904), health (835), fraternal (87), title (58), risk retention groups (256) and other companies (1,323), according to the National Association of Insurance Commissioners.

- Insurance carriers and related activities accounted for $413.1 billion, or 2.5 percent of U.S. gross domestic product in 2012, according to the U.S. Bureau of Economic Analysis.

U.S. P/C AND L/H INSURANCE PREMIUMS, 2013

($ billions)

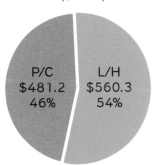

P/C $481.2 46%

L/H $560.3 54%

Source: SNL Financial LC.

- The U.S. insurance industry employed 2.4 million people in 2013, according to the U.S. Department of Labor. Of those, 1.4 million worked for insurance companies, including life, health and medical insurers (812,100 workers), P/C insurers (597,100 workers) and reinsurers (27,000 workers). The remaining 943,200 people worked for insurance agencies, brokers and other insurance-related enterprises.

- Total P/C cash and invested assets were $1.5 trillion in 2013, according to SNL Financial. L/H cash and invested assets totaled $3.5 trillion in 2013. The majority of these assets were in bonds (63 percent of P/C assets and 75 percent of L/H assets).

- P/C and L/H insurance companies paid $17.4 billion in premium taxes in 2013, or $55 for every person living in the United States, according to the U.S. Department of Commerce.

- P/C insurers paid out $12.9 billion in property losses related to catastrophes in 2013, compared with $35.0 billion in 2012, according to ISO. There were 28 catastrophes in 2013, compared with 26 in 2012.

World Life and Nonlife Insurance in 2013

Outside the United States, the insurance industry is divided into life and nonlife, or general insurance, rather than life/health and property/casualty. World insurance premiums rose 1.4 percent in 2013, adjusted for inflation, following a 2.5 percent inflation-adjusted increase in 2012, according to Swiss Re's latest study of world insurance. Nonlife premiums rose 2.3 percent in 2013, adjusted for inflation, following 2.7 percent growth in 2012. Life insurance premiums grew by 0.7 percent after inflation in 2013, down from 2.3 percent inflation-adjusted growth in 2012.

In 2013 life and nonlife insurance premiums (excluding cross-border business) accounted for 6.3 percent of world gross domestic product (GDP). Premiums accounted for 17.6 percent of GDP in Taiwan, the highest share in the Swiss Re study, followed by 15.4 percent in South Africa, 13.2 percent in Hong Kong, 12.6 percent in the Netherlands and 11.9 percent in South Korea. Premiums represented 7.5 percent of GDP in the United States, the 10th highest share in the study.

TOP TEN COUNTRIES BY LIFE AND NONLIFE DIRECT PREMIUMS WRITTEN, 2013[1]
(U.S. $ millions)

Rank	Country	Life premiums	Nonlife premiums[2]	Total premiums Amount	Total premiums Percent change from prior year	Total premiums Percent of total world premiums
1	United States[3,4]	$532,858	$726,397	$1,259,255	-1.1%	27.13%
2	Japan[5,6]	422,733	108,773	531,506	-15.2	11.45
3	United Kingdom[6]	222,893	106,750	329,643	2.4	7.10
4	P.R. China[4]	152,121	125,844	277,965	13.3	5.99
5	France[7]	160,156	94,598	254,754	7.2	5.49
6	Germany[7]	114,349	132,813	247,162	6.3	5.33
7	Italy[4]	117,978	50,576	168,554	17.1	3.63
8	South Korea[5,6]	91,204	54,223	145,427	-4.9	3.13
9	Canada[6,8]	52,334	73,010	125,344	0.6	2.70
10	Netherlands[4]	26,005	75,135	101,140	5.5	2.18

[1]Before reinsurance transactions.
[2]Includes accident and health insurance.
[3]Nonlife premiums include state funds; life premiums include an estimate of group pension business.
[4]Provisional.
[5]April 1, 2013-March 31, 2014.
[6]Estimated.
[7]Life premiums are estimated; nonlife premiums are provisional.
[8]Life premiums are net premiums.

Source: Swiss Re, *sigma*, No. 3/2014.

World Premiums Per Capita

Swiss Re's latest world insurance study is based on direct premium data from 147 countries, with detailed information on the largest 88 markets. In 2013 an average of $652 per capita was spent on insurance, with an average of $129 in emerging markets and $3,621 in advanced markets. Among the 10 largest insurance markets, premiums per capita ranged from a high of $6,012 in the Netherlands to a low of $201 in China. In the United States, the world's largest insurance market, premiums per capita totaled $3,979, including $1,684 for life insurance and $2,296 for nonlife insurance. By region, total premiums per capita were $3,938 in North America; $2,429 in Oceania (Australia and New Zealand); $1,833 in Europe; $303 in Asia; and $66 in Africa.

WORLD LIFE AND NONLIFE INSURANCE DIRECT PREMIUMS WRITTEN, 2013

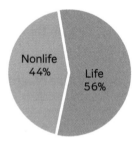

Source: Swiss Re, *sigma*, No. 3/2014.

WORLD LIFE AND NONLIFE INSURANCE DIRECT PREMIUMS WRITTEN, 2011-2013[1]

(U.S. $ millions)

Year	Life	Nonlife[2]	Total
2011	$2,611,718	$1,954,445	$4,566,163
2012	2,630,274	1,968,677	4,598,951
2013	2,608,091	2,032,850	4,640,941

[1]Before reinsurance transactions.
[2]Includes accident and health insurance.

Source: Swiss Re, *sigma*, No. 3/2014.

Reinsurance

Each year the Reinsurance Association of America (RAA) provides an overview of the countries from which U.S. insurance companies obtain reinsurance, i.e., the countries to which they have ceded, or transferred, some of their risk. The analysis includes premiums that a U.S. insurance company cedes to "offshore" i.e., foreign, reinsurance companies that are not part of the insurer's own corporate group ("unaffiliated offshore insurers" in the chart below), as well as business ceded to overseas reinsurers that are part of the insurer's corporate family ("affiliated offshore reinsurers" in the chart below).

The RAA report compares U.S. insurance premiums ceded to U.S. professional reinsurance companies to the U.S. premiums ceded to offshore, i.e., foreign, companies. U.S. professional reinsurance companies accounted for 38.2 percent of the U.S. premium written that was ceded in 2013, while offshore companies accounted for 61.8 percent. However, a number of U.S.-based reinsurers are owned by foreign companies. Taking this into consideration, foreign reinsurers accounted for 91.9 percent while U.S. professional reinsurers accounted for 8.1 percent.

U.S. REINSURANCE PREMIUMS CEDED TO UNAFFILIATED AND AFFILIATED OFFSHORE REINSURERS BY COUNTRY, 2011-2013[1]

($ millions)

Rank	Country	Unaffiliated offshore reinsurers			Affiliated offshore reinsurers			2013 total
		2011	2012	2013	2011	2012	2013	
1	Bermuda	$9,798	$9,387	$9,676	$21,802	$23,918	$22,597	$32,273
2	Switzerland	1,316	1,151	1,388	7,496	9,013	10,434	11,822
3	United Kingdom	4,680	4,719	4,781	792	544	1,654	6,435
4	Germany	2,697	2,883	3,655	972	1,318	1,579	5,234
5	Cayman Islands	2,548	2,963	3,308	377	591	1,321	4,629
6	Turks and Caicos	733	873	1,047	79	234	270	1,317
7	Channel Islands	1,518	2,883	1,261	NA	NA	NA	1,261
8	Ireland	485	454	490	323	194	174	664
9	Barbados	607	652	659	NA	NA	NA	659
10	France	NA	NA	NA	436	256	630	630
11	British Virgin Islands	355	434	464	NA	NA	NA	464
12	Spain	NA	NA	NA	164	278	266	266
13	Canada	NA	NA	NA	92	96	100	100
	Total, countries shown	**$24,737**	**$26,399**	**$26,729**	**$32,533**	**$36,442**	**$39,025**	**$65,754**
	Total, all countries	**$26,374**	**$26,790**	**$28,386**	**$33,051**	**$36,929**	**$37,357[2]**	**$65,743[2]**

[1]Ranked by 2013 total reinsurance premiums. [2]Includes ($1.91) billion in affiliated premiums ceded to Japan. NA=Data not available.

Source: Reinsurance Association of America.

TOP TEN GLOBAL INSURANCE COMPANIES BY REVENUES, 2013[1]
($ millions)

Rank	Company	Revenues	Country	Industry
1	Berkshire Hathaway	$182,150.0	U.S.	Property/casualty
2	AXA	165,893.5	France	Life/health
3	Japan Post Holdings	152,125.8	Japan	Life/health
4	Allianz	134,636.1	Germany	Property/casualty
5	UnitedHealth Group	122,489.0	U.S.	Health
6	Assicurazioni Generali	115,224.4	Italy	Life/health
7	Munich Re Group	83,844.8	Germany	Property/casualty
8	Prudential	81,867.7	U.K.	Life/health
9	China Life Insurance	80,909.4	China	Life/health
10	Zurich Insurance Group	72,045.0	Switzerland	Property/casualty

[1]Based on an analysis of companies in the Global Fortune 500. Includes stock and mutual companies.
Source: Fortune.

TOP TEN GLOBAL PROPERTY/CASUALTY REINSURERS BY NET REINSURANCE PREMIUMS WRITTEN, 2013
($ millions)

Rank	Company	Net reinsurance premiums written	Country
1	Munich Reinsurance Co.	$22,545.9	Germany
2	Swiss Re Ltd.	14,542.0	Switzerland
3	Hannover Re S.E.	12,905.8	Germany
4	Berkshire Hathaway Reinsurance Group	11,440.0	U.S.
5	Lloyd's of London	11,363.7	U.K.
6	Scor S.E.	5,931.9	France
7	Everest Re Group Ltd.	5,004.8	Bermuda
8	PartnerRe Ltd.	4,479.1	Bermuda
9	Korean Reinsurance Co.	3,499.0[1]	South Korea
10	Transatlantic Holdings Inc.	3,248.0	U.S.

[1]Fiscal year ending March 31.
Source: Business Insurance, September 1, 2014.

TOP TEN GLOBAL INSURANCE BROKERS BY REVENUES, 2013[1]

($ millions)

Rank	Company	Brokerage revenues	Country
1	Marsh & McLennan Cos. Inc.	$12,270	U.S.
2	Aon P.L.C.	11,787	U.K.
3	Willis Group Holdings P.L.C.	3,633	U.K.
4	Arthur J. Gallagher & Co.	2,742	U.S.
5	Jardine Lloyd Thompson Group P.L.C.	1,746	U.K.
6	BB&T Insurance Holdings Inc.	1,582	U.S.
7	Brown & Brown Inc.	1,356	U.S.
8	Wells Fargo Insurance Services USA Inc.	1,350	U.S.
9	Hub International Ltd.	1,148	U.S.
10	Lockton Cos. L.L.C.[2]	1,117	U.S.

■ Revenue generated by the world's 10 largest brokers increased to $38.7 billion in 2013 from $25.2 billion in 2004.

[1]Revenue generated by insurance brokerage and related services.
[2]Fiscal year ending April 30.

Source: Business Insurance, July 21, 2014.

TOP TEN GLOBAL REINSURANCE BROKERS BY GROSS REINSURANCE REVENUES, 2013[1]

($000)

Rank	Company	Gross reinsurance revenues	Country
1	Aon Benfield	$1,505,000	U.K.
2	Guy Carpenter & Co. L.L.C.[2]	1,131,267	U.S.
3	Willis Re	860,000	U.K.
4	JLT Reinsurance Brokers Ltd.	375,869	U.K.
5	Cooper Gay Swett & Crawford Ltd.	158,466	U.K.
6	Miller Insurance Services L.L.P.[3]	93,528	U.K.
7	UIB Holdings Ltd.[2]	67,463	U.K.
8	THB Group Ltd.	58,094	U.K.
9	BMS Group Ltd.	54,300	U.K.
10	Lockton Re[3]	46,029	U.K.

[1]Includes all reinsurance revenue reported through holding and/or subsidiary companies.
[2]Includes aviation reinsurance business placed by Marsh L.L.C.
[3]Fiscal year ending April 30.

Source: Business Insurance, October 27, 2014

The U.S. Department of Commerce provides estimates on two methods of international delivery of insurance services: cross-border trade, in which a domestic company transacts directly with a foreign company (for example, a European firm purchasing insurance from a U.S. firm through a broker), and sales by subsidiaries of multinational corporations (for example, sales to the European market through a European-based subsidiary of a U.S. insurer). The combination of these methods of delivery creates a broad measure of insurance services provided and received from abroad.

U.S. INSURANCE SALES ABROAD, 2006-2012

($ millions)

Year	Sold directly[1]	Sold through majority-owned foreign affiliates of U.S. multinational corporations[2]
2006	$9,445	$47,614
2007	10,841	55,290
2008	13,403	61,794
2009	14,586	61,609
2010	14,397	58,379
2011	14,958	61,177
2012	16,067	NA

[1]Largely based on premiums. Includes adjustments for "normal" i.e., expected losses and premium supplements (income due to policy holders). BEA refers to this category as "cross border sales." Includes property/casualty, life insurance and reinsurance.
[2]Based on sales by primary industry of the affiliate; there could be other services, such as financial services, included in the data.
NA=Data not available.

Source: U.S. Department of Commerce, Bureau of Economic Analysis, International Division.

INSURANCE BUSINESS IN THE U.S. WRITTEN BY SUBSIDIARIES OF FOREIGN CONTROLLED COMPANIES, 2012

($ billions)

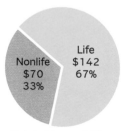

Total: $211.2 billion

Source: Organization for Economic Cooperation and Development.

INSURANCE BUSINESS IN THE U.S. WRITTEN BY SUBSIDIARIES OF FOREIGN CONTROLLED COMPANIES, 2008-2012

($ millions)

	Gross premiums written				
	2008	2009	2010	2011	2012
Life	$149,256	$172,464	$132,870	$139,311	$141,524
Nonlife	109,542	103,296	78,504	82,199	69,688
Total	**$258,798**	**$275,760**	**$211,374**	**$221,510**	**$211,212**

Source: Organization for Economic Cooperation and Development.

Captives and Other Risk-Financing Options

Over the years, a number of alternatives to traditional commercial insurance have emerged to respond to fluctuations in the marketplace. Captives—a special type of insurance company set up by a parent company, trade association or group of companies to insure the risks of its owner or owners—emerged during the 1980s, when businesses had trouble obtaining some types of commercial insurance coverage. Today alternative risk transfer (ART) arrangements include self insurance, risk retention groups and risk purchasing groups, as well as more recent innovations such as catastrophe bonds and microinsurance.

LEADING CAPTIVE DOMICILES, 2012-2013

| Rank | Domicile | Number of captives | |
		2012	2013
1	Bermuda	856	831
2	Cayman Islands	740[1]	759
3	Vermont	586	588
4	Guernsey	333	344
5	Utah	287	342
6	Delaware	212[1]	298
7	Anguilla	291	295
8	Nevis	203	276
9	Barbados	261	264
10	Luxembourg	238	225
11	Hawaii	178[1]	184
12	D.C.	167[1]	172
13	Montana	114	150
14	Nevada	133	148
15	British Virgin Islands	157	147
16	South Carolina	149	145
17	Dublin/Ireland	141[2]	142[2]
18	Kentucky	139	128
19	Isle of Man	125	125
20	Arizona	101	106
	Total, top 20	**5,411**	**5,669**
	Total, all captives	**6,125**	**6,342**

[1]Restated.
[2]Combined Dublin and Ireland.

Source: Business Insurance, March 17, 2014.

The Securitization of Insurance Risk: Catastrophe Bonds

Catastrophe (cat) bonds are one of a number of innovative risk transfer products that have emerged as an alternative to traditional insurance and reinsurance products. Insurers and reinsurers typically issue cat bonds through a special purpose vehicle, a company set up specifically for this purpose. Cat bonds pay high interest rates and diversify an investor's portfolio because natural disasters occur randomly and are not associated with economic factors. Depending on how the cat bond is structured, if losses reach the threshold specified in the bond offering, the investor may lose all or part of the principal or interest.

Catastrophe bond issuance reached a record high of $7.1 billion in 2013, up from $5.9 billion in 2012, according to the GC Securities division of MMC Securities Corporation. Catastrophe bond risk capital outstanding rose to $18.6 billion during the same period, also a record high. GC Securities reported that catastrophe bond issuance was extremely strong in the first-half of 2014, with a record issuance of $5.7 billion. Total risk capital outstanding was at an all-time high of $20.8 billion. The firm noted that even with no further activity for the remainder of 2014, the year would still place as the fourth largest year in terms of new issuance.

TOP TEN CATASTROPHE BOND TRANSACTIONS, 2013
($ millions)

Rank	Special purpose vehicle	Sponsor name	Risk amount	Peril	Risk location
1	Tar Heel Re 2013-1	NCJUA / NCIUA	$500.0	Hurricane	North Carolina
2	Bosphorus 1 Re 2013-1	TCIP (Turkey)	400.0	Earthquake	Turkey
3	Green Fields II 2013-1	Groupama S.A.	365.7	Windstorm	France
4	Caelus Re 2013-2	Nationwide	320.0	Hurricane/ earthquake	U.S.
5	Galileo Re 2013-1	Catlin	300.0	Hurricane/ earthquake/ windstorm	U.S. and Europe
6	Long Point Re III 2013-1	Travelers	300.0	Hurricane	Northeast U.S.
7	Merna Re IV	State Farm	300.0	Earthquake	U.S., New Madrid
8	Nakama Re 2013-1	Zenkyoren	300.0	Earthquake	Japan
9	Caelus Re 2013-1	Nationwide	270.0	Hurricane/ earthquake	U.S.
10	Everglades Re 2013-1	Florida Citizens	250.0	Hurricane	Florida

Source: GC Securities, a division of MMC Securities Corp., a U.S. registered broker-dealer, member FINRA/SIPC, and Guy Carpenter.

CATASTROPHE BONDS, ANNUAL RISK CAPITAL ISSUED, 2004-2013
($ billions)

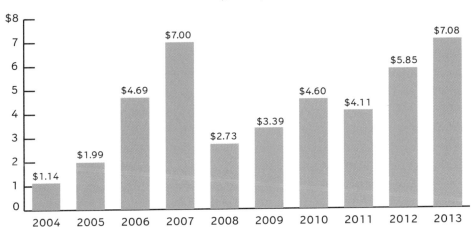

Source: GC Securities, a division of MMC Securities Corp., a U.S. registered broker-dealer, member FINRA/SIPC, and Guy Carpenter.

CATASTROPHE BONDS, RISK CAPITAL OUTSTANDING, 2004-2013
($ billions)

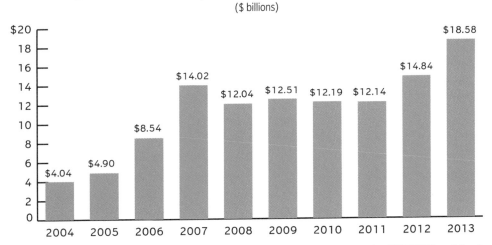

Source: GC Securities, a division of MMC Securities Corp., a U.S. registered broker-dealer, member FINRA/SIPC, and Guy Carpenter.

Microinsurance and Emerging Markets

A growing number of insurers are tapping into markets in developing countries through microinsurance projects, which provide low-cost insurance to individuals generally not covered by traditional insurance or government programs. Microinsurance products tend to be much less costly than traditional products and thus extend protection to a much wider market. Microinsurance products vary in type and structure but are generally distinguished by high volumes, low cost and efficient administration. Microinsurance policies may be offered along with a small loan, with premiums a small percentage of the loan amount. The approach is an outgrowth of the microfinancing projects developed by Bangladeshi Nobel Prize-winning banker and economist Muhammad Yunus, which helped millions of low-income individuals in Asia and Africa to set up businesses and buy houses. Today a number of innovative microinsurance products have been developed to protect the working poor against the financial impact of losses.

The 9th International Microinsurance Conference, held in November 2013 in Indonesia, brought together some 400 participants from nearly 60 countries to discuss the challenges and opportunities in microinsurance. "The Landscape of Microinsurance in Asia and Oceania," a new study released at the conference by Munich Re Foundation and Deutsche Gesellschaft für International Zusammenarbeit (GIZ) revealed that the number of insured low-income people in the region has increased by over 30 percent from 2010 to 2012. The study estimates that more than 170 million people now benefit from microinsurance.

A 2014 A.M. Best report states that about 500 million people globally have microinsurance and that there is increasing evidence from numerous academic studies that its impact has been beneficial for the poor in many ways. The report also cites a 2011 survey by the Microinsurance Network that found that 33 of the world's largest insurance companies were involved in microinsurance projects, up from seven in 2005. The report sums up 95 microinsurance projects that cover over one million people in Asia or Latin America or at least 500,000 in Africa. Findings include: About 50 percent of microinsurance projects provide different types of life insurance such as term life, credit life and funeral. Also about 50 percent of the projects receive subsidies that mainly target agricultural and health insurance. The report also notes a 2014 Economist Intelligence Unit survey of insurers that found that 45 percent of respondents believe that the work of international organizations to inform policymakers in the developing world of the value of insurance is a top priority.

Insurance in Emerging Markets

With limited growth prospects in the insurance markets of developed countries, insurers see emerging economies as presenting significant potential for growth and profitability. Premium growth in developing countries has been outpacing growth in industrialized countries. Swiss Re's 2014 *sigma* report on world insurance markets found that premiums in emerging countries rose 7.4 percent in 2013, after adjusting for inflation, following a 7.1 percent rise in 2012. Growth in developing markets outpaced growth in advanced markets, which increased by 0.3 percent in 2013 and 1.7 percent in 2012. Emerging markets accounted for 17 percent of total global premium volume in 2013, up from 16 percent in 2012.

Swiss Re identifies emerging markets as countries in South and East Asia, Latin America and the Caribbean, Central and Eastern Europe, Africa, the Middle East (excluding Israel), Central Asia and Turkey. Emerging market premiums rose from $728 billion in 2012 to $788 billion in 2013, driven by strong growth in the nonlife sector. Nonlife premiums have been rising by more than the annual average emerging market economic growth rate since 2006. Life sector premiums had 6.4 percent growth in 2013, compared with 5.2 percent in 2012, when growth in the sector was constrained by declines in two key markets, China and India.

INSURANCE IN EMERGING MARKETS, 2013
($ millions)

	Direct premiums written, 2013	Percent change from 2012[1]	Share of world market	Premiums as a percent of GDP	Premiums per capita
Total industry					
Advanced markets	$3,853,267	0.3%	83.0%	8.3%	$3,621
Emerging markets	787,674	7.4	17.0	2.7	129
World	**$4,640,941**	**1.4%**	**100.0%**	**6.3%**	**$652**
Life					
Advanced markets	$2,200,249	-0.2	84.4	4.7	$2,074
Emerging markets	407,842	6.4	15.6	1.4	67
World	**$2,608,091**	**0.7%**	**100.0%**	**3.5%**	**$366**
Nonlife					
Advanced markets	$1,653,018	1.1	81.3	3.5	$1,547
Emerging markets	379,832	8.3	18.7	1.3	62
World	**$2,032,850**	**2.3%**	**100.0%**	**2.8%**	**$286**

[1] Inflation-adjusted.

Source: Swiss Re, *sigma*, No. 3/2014.

World Insurance Markets

Microinsurance and Emerging Markets

China is the largest emerging market country, based on insurance premiums written (including life and nonlife business), with $278 billion in premiums written in 2013, followed by Brazil, with $89 billion, and India, with $66 billion, according to Swiss Re. When measured by insurance density, however, the Bahamas ranked first, with $1,839 in premiums per capita (including life and nonlife business).

TOP TEN EMERGING MARKETS BY INSURANCE DENSITY, 2013[1]

Rank	Country	Total premiums[2]	
		Per capita (U.S. dollars)	As a percent of GDP
1	Bahamas	$1,839	8.4%
2	Slovenia	1,309	5.6
3	South Africa	1,025	15.4
4	United Arab Emirates	872	2.0
5	Czech Republic	760	3.8
6	Qatar	697	0.7
7	Trinidad and Tobago	688	4.0
8	Chile	664	4.2
9	Bahrain	557	2.1
10	Mauritius	552	5.8

[1]Based on insurance premiums per capita. Excludes cross-border business.
[2]Life and nonlife premiums. Data are estimated except for Chile.
Source: Swiss Re, *sigma*, No. 3/2014.

Net Premiums Written, Property/Casualty and Life/Health

There are three main insurance sectors. Property/casualty (P/C) consists mainly of auto, home and commercial insurance. Life/health (L/H) consists mainly of life insurance and annuity products. Most private health insurance is written by insurers whose main business is health insurance. However, life/health and property/casualty insurers also write this coverage. P/C net premiums written rose by 4.5 percent and L/H net premiums written fell by 10.1 percent in 2013.

PROPERTY/CASUALTY AND LIFE/HEALTH INSURANCE NET PREMIUMS WRITTEN, 2004-2013
($000)

Year	Property/casualty[1]	Life/health[2]	Total
2004	$425,465,344	$507,250,884	$932,716,228
2005	422,448,786	520,220,499	942,669,285
2006	447,803,479	574,660,770	1,022,464,249
2007	446,179,922	608,878,377	1,055,058,299
2008	440,318,983	607,469,969	1,047,788,952
2009	423,528,077	491,845,993	915,374,070
2010	425,878,773	560,737,868	986,616,641
2011	441,562,154	602,522,189	1,044,084,343
2012	460,486,285	623,563,597	1,084,049,882
2013	481,237,455	560,279,427	1,041,516,882
Percent change, 2004-2013	**13.1%**	**10.5%**	**11.7%**

[1]Net premiums written after reinsurance transactions, excludes state funds.
[2]Premiums, annuity considerations (fees for annuity contracts) and deposit-type funds for life/health insurance companies.

Source: SNL Financial LC.

U.S. PROPERTY/CASUALTY AND LIFE/HEALTH INSURANCE PREMIUMS, 2013[1]

$481.2 billion — Property/casualty 46%

Life/health 54% — $560.3 billion

**Total:
$1,041.5 billion**

[1]Property/casualty: net premiums written after reinsurance transactions, excludes state funds; life/health: premiums, annuity considerations (fees for annuity contracts) and deposit-type funds.

Source: SNL Financial LC.

GROWTH IN U.S. PREMIUMS, PROPERTY/CASUALTY AND LIFE/HEALTH INSURANCE, 2004-2013
(Percent change from prior year)

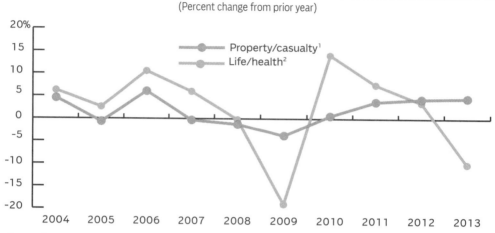

[1]Net premiums written after reinsurance transactions, excludes state funds.
[2]Premiums and annuity considerations (fees for annuity contracts) and deposit-type funds for life/health insurance companies.
Source: SNL Financial LC.

Direct Premiums Written, Property/Casualty and Life/Health

PROPERTY/CASUALTY AND LIFE/HEALTH INSURANCE DIRECT PREMIUMS WRITTEN, 2004-2013
($000)

Year	Property/casualty[1]	Life/health[2]	Total
2004	$483,463,200	$544,478,105	$1,027,941,306
2005	494,700,641	559,584,322	1,054,284,963
2006	508,324,604	610,243,523	1,118,568,128
2007	510,979,916	658,181,098	1,169,161,014
2008	498,690,753	662,168,809	1,160,859,562
2009	483,081,379	608,511,809	1,091,593,188
2010	484,404,467	613,203,020	1,097,607,488
2011	502,005,179	657,210,448	1,159,215,626
2012	523,879,204	685,192,219	1,209,071,423
2013	546,135,543	646,937,321	1,193,072,864
Percent change, 2004-2013	**13.0%**	**18.8%**	**16.1%**

[1]Direct premiums written before reinsurance transactions, excludes some state funds.
[2]Premiums, annuity considerations (fees for annuity contracts) and deposit-type funds for life/health insurance companies.
Source: SNL Financial LC.

Leading Companies

TOP TEN WRITERS OF PROPERTY/CASUALTY INSURANCE
BY DIRECT PREMIUMS WRITTEN, 2013
($000)

Rank	Group/company	Direct premiums written[1]	Market share[2]
1	State Farm Mutual Automobile Insurance	$55,994,246	10.3%
2	Liberty Mutual	28,906,283	5.3
3	Allstate Corp.	27,583,581	5.1
4	American International Group	23,169,106	4.2
5	Travelers Companies Inc.	22,842,941	4.2
6	Berkshire Hathaway Inc.	18,284,148	3.4
7	Farmers Insurance Group of Companies[3]	18,079,537	3.3
8	Nationwide Mutual Group	17,802,678	3.3
9	Progressive Corp.	17,562,610	3.2
10	USAA Insurance Group	14,562,012	2.7

[1]Before reinsurance transactions, includes state funds.
[2]Based on U.S. total, includes territories.
[3]Data for Farmers Insurance Group of Companies and Zurich Financial Group (which owns Farmers' management company) are reported separately by SNL Financial.

Source: SNL Financial LC.

TOP TEN WRITERS OF LIFE INSURANCE/ANNUITIES BY DIRECT PREMIUMS WRITTEN, 2013
($000)

Rank	Group/company	Direct premiums written[1]	Market share[2]
1	MetLife Inc.	$85,001,696	14.9%
2	Prudential Financial Inc.	41,407,447	7.3
3	Jackson National Life Group	25,728,116	4.5
4	AEGON	24,499,916	4.3
5	Lincoln National Corp.	24,274,104	4.3
6	New York Life Insurance Group	24,223,396	4.3
7	American International Group	21,698,620	3.8
8	Voya Financial Inc.	20,228,599	3.6
9	Manulife Financial Corp.	19,263,216	3.4
10	Principal Financial Group Inc.	18,909,416	3.3

[1]Includes life insurance, annuity considerations, deposit-type contract funds and other considerations; excludes accident and health insurance. Before reinsurance transactions.
[2]Based on U.S. total, includes territories.

Source: SNL Financial LC.

Healthcare Expenditures

Nearly half of the nation's healthcare costs are covered under Medicaid, Medicare and other public programs.

THE NATION'S HEALTHCARE DOLLAR: WHERE IT CAME FROM, 2012[1]

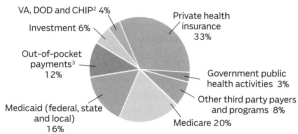

VA, DOD and CHIP[2] 4%
Investment 6%
Out-of-pocket payments[3] 12%
Medicaid (federal, state and local) 16%
Private health insurance 33%
Government public health activities 3%
Other third party payers and programs 8%
Medicare 20%

[1]Sum of components does not add to 100 percent due to rounding.
[2]Department of Veterans Affairs, Department of Defense and Children's Health Insurance Program.
[3]Includes co-payments, deductibles, and any amounts not covered by health insurance.

Source: Centers for Medicare and Medicaid Services, Office of the Actuary, National Health Statistics Group.

National healthcare expenditures rose by 3.7 percent to $2.8 trillion in 2012, the fourth consecutive year of slow growth, according to the U.S. Department of Health and Human Services' Centers for Medicare and Medicaid Services (CMS). Between 1970 and 1993, the beginning of the shift to managed care, healthcare expenditures rose 11.5 percent on an average annual basis. In 2012 the health spending share of GDP was 17.2 percent, down slightly from 17.3 percent in 2011. Healthcare spending rose to $8,915 per capita in 2012 from $8,658 in 2011, a 3.0 percent increase. CMS projects that annual health expenditures grew 3.6 percent in 2013, dampened by the modest economic recovery. Health spending is expected to rise to 5.6 percent in 2014 and average 6.0 percent a year through 2023 as the economy improves and coverage expands under the Affordable Care Act.

NATIONAL HEALTH EXPENDITURES, AVERAGE ANNUAL PERCENT GROWTH FROM PRIOR YEAR, 1993-2017

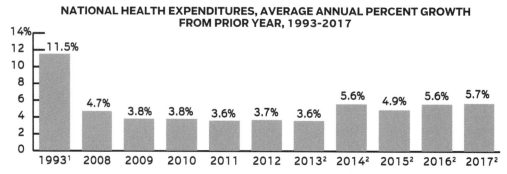

1993[1]	2008	2009	2010	2011	2012	2013[2]	2014[2]	2015[2]	2016[2]	2017[2]
11.5%	4.7%	3.8%	3.8%	3.6%	3.7%	3.6%	5.6%	4.9%	5.6%	5.7%

[1]Average annual growth from 1970 through 1993; marks the beginning of the shift to managed care.
[2]Projected.

Source: Centers for Medicare and Medicaid Services, Office of the Actuary.

Employment and Other Economic Contributions

Property/casualty and life/health insurance companies contribute to our economy far beyond their core function of helping to manage risk. Insurers contributed $413 billion, or 2.5 percent, to the nation's gross domestic product in 2012. The taxes they pay include special levies on insurance premiums, which amounted to $17.4 billion in 2013, or 2.0 percent of all taxes collected by the states. Insurance companies invested $740.6 billion in state and local municipal bonds and loans in 2013, helping to fund the building of roads, schools and other public projects. They provide businesses with capital for research, expansions and other ventures through their holdings in stocks and bonds, a figure which totaled $3.9 trillion in 2013. The industry is also a major contributor to charitable causes. The Insurance Industry Charitable Foundation, established by the property/casualty insurance industry in 1994, has contributed more than $21 million in local community grants and 179,000 volunteer hours to hundreds of community nonprofit organizations. The sector is also a very large employer, providing some 2.4 million jobs, or 2.1 percent of U.S. employment in 2013.

EMPLOYMENT IN INSURANCE, 2004-2013
(Annual averages, 000)

| Year | Insurance carriers | | | | Insurance agencies, brokerages and related services | | | Total industry |
| | Direct insurers[1] | | | | | | | |
	Life, health and medical	Property/ casualty	Reinsurers	Total	Insurance agencies and brokers	Other insurance-related activities[2]	Total	
2004	767.3	691.2	29.8	1,488.3	645.6	233.6	879.2	2,367.5
2005	764.9	652.1	28.8	1,445.7	652.5	240.7	893.2	2,338.9
2006	790.6	649.1	28.0	1,467.7	662.4	249.0	911.4	2,379.1
2007	787.1	647.0	27.0	1,461.1	677.8	252.7	930.5	2,391.6
2008	800.8	646.7	27.9	1,475.4	671.6	258.1	929.6	2,405.1
2009	802.8	632.9	27.5	1,463.2	653.3	254.2	907.4	2,370.6
2010	804.1	614.3	26.8	1,445.2	642.3	253.1	895.5	2,340.6
2011	788.9	611.6	25.6	1,426.1	649.2	261.1	910.3	2,336.4
2012	811.3	599.5	25.7	1,436.4	659.6	272.3	931.8	2,368.3
2013	812.1	597.1	27.0	1,436.2	664.4	278.8	943.2	2,379.4

[1]Establishments primarily engaged in initially underwriting insurance policies.
[2]Includes claims adjusters, third-party administrators of insurance funds and other service personnel such as advisory and insurance ratemaking services.

Source: U.S. Department of Labor, Bureau of Labor Statistics.

U.S. Insurance Industry, All Sectors

Employment and Other Economic Contributions

INSURANCE CARRIERS AND RELATED ACTIVITIES EMPLOYMENT BY STATE, 2013[1]

State	Number of employees	State	Number of employees
Alabama	36,355	Montana	8,583
Alaska	2,667	Nebraska	33,511
Arizona	54,371	Nevada	17,456
Arkansas	21,094	New Hampshire	17,096
California	289,304	New Jersey	98,284
Colorado	52,387	New Mexico	11,470
Connecticut	69,303	New York	191,930
Delaware	8,889	North Carolina	73,274
D.C.	4,433	North Dakota	10,543
Florida	194,299	Ohio	130,068
Georgia	96,693	Oklahoma	30,588
Hawaii	10,270	Oregon	32,261
Idaho	12,407	Pennsylvania	151,898
Illinois	142,865	Rhode Island	11,576
Indiana	59,043	South Carolina	41,430
Iowa	54,463	South Dakota	11,959
Kansas	38,289	Tennessee	59,147
Kentucky	39,981	Texas	247,032
Louisiana	34,555	Utah	24,801
Maine	13,221	Vermont	5,022
Maryland	47,930	Virginia	63,850
Massachusetts	79,380	Washington	52,121
Michigan	77,336	West Virginia	11,535
Minnesota	81,966	Wisconsin	81,086
Mississippi	18,593	Wyoming	3,455
Missouri	65,130	**United States**	**3,025,200**

[1]Total full-time and part-time employment.

Note: Does not match data shown shown elsewhere due to the use of different surveys. Data as of September 2014.

Source: U.S. Department of Commerce, Bureau of Economic Analysis, Regional Economic Information System.

Gross Domestic Product

INSURANCE SECTOR'S SHARE OF GROSS DOMESTIC PRODUCT (GDP), 2008-2012
($ billions)

| Year | Total GDP | Insurance carriers and related activities | |
		GDP	Percent of total GDP
2008	$14,720.3	$339.7	2.3%
2009	14,417.9	357.5	2.5
2010	14,958.3	364.8	2.4
2011	15,533.8	378.5	2.4
2012	16,244.6	413.1	2.5

Source: U.S. Department of Commerce, Bureau of Economic Analysis.

- Gross domestic product (GDP) is the total value of all final goods and services produced in the economy. The GDP growth rate is the primary indicator of the state of the economy.

- The insurance industry contributed $413.1 billion to the $16.2 trillion GDP in 2012.

Ownership of Municipal Bonds

Insurance companies help fund the construction of schools, roads and healthcare facilities as well as a variety of other public sector projects through their investments in municipal bonds. The property/casualty insurance industry invested $326 billion in such bonds in 2013, and the life insurance industry invested $141 billion, according to the Federal Reserve. (See pages 33 and 50 for further information on insurance industry investments.)

INSURANCE COMPANY HOLDINGS OF U.S. MUNICIPAL SECURITIES AND LOANS, 2009-2013
($ billions, end of year)

	2009	2010	2011	2012	2013
Property/casualty insurance companies	$369.4	$348.4	$331.0	$328.1	$325.8
Life insurance companies	73.1	112.3	121.8	131.5	141.2
Total	**$442.5**	**$460.7**	**$452.8**	**$459.6**	**$467.0**

Source: Board of Governors of the Federal Reserve System, June 5, 2014.

The number of global insurance-related mergers and acquisitions (M&A) dropped to 695 transactions in 2013 from 741 in 2012, due to an improving economy, regulatory initiatives such as the Affordable Care Act, higher valuations, buyer interest in small specialists and companies in financial distress seeking healthier parents, according to an analysis by Conning Research. The value of M&A transactions dropped to $42.6 billion from $62.4 billion during the same period.

In 2013 the number of insurance-related deals in which a U.S. firm was either a buyer or a target dropped by 6.7 percent, and the value of properties acquired in such deals fell 55.3 percent, according to Conning data. There were 446 U.S. insurance M&A transactions in 2013, down from 478 in 2012. The overall value of U.S. deals dropped to $19.3 billion from $43.2 billion during the same period. The number of non-U.S. insurance M&A transactions (i.e., where a non-U.S. company was both buyer and seller) dropped by 5.3 percent to 249 in 2013 from 263 in 2012. However, the overall reported value of non-U.S. deals rose by 21.0 percent to $23.3 billion from $19.3 billion during the same period.

REPORTED GLOBAL INSURANCE-RELATED MERGERS AND ACQUISITIONS BY SECTOR, U.S. AND NON-U.S. ACQUIRERS, 2013

Sector	Number of transactions			Transaction values ($ millions)		
	U.S.[1]	Non-U.S.[2]	Total	U.S.[1]	Non-U.S.[2]	Total
Property/casualty	39	68	107	$4,397	$11,009	$15,406
Life/annuity	18	46	64	3,299	11,321	14,620
Health/managed care	15	5	20	33	319	352
Distribution	317	112	429	8,246	697	8,943
Services	57	18	75	3,349	NA	3,349
Total	**446**	**249**	**695**	**$19,300**	**$23,300**	**$42,600**

[1]Includes transactions where a U.S. company was the acquirer and/or the target.
[2]Includes transactions where a non-U.S. company was the acquirer and the target.
NA=Data not available.
Source: Conning Research & Consulting, Inc. analysis.

While M&A activity fell in both the U.S. and overseas, non-U.S. M&A represented a higher proportion of the global total, according to Conning Research. Acquisitions of Central and Eastern European insurance companies by non-U.S. buyers were due to the higher economic growth rates in Eastern European countries. The second largest transaction of the year, as shown below, reflected this type of transaction.

TOP TEN GLOBAL INSURANCE-RELATED MERGERS AND ACQUISITIONS ANNOUNCED, 2013

($ millions)

Rank	Buyer (country)	Target (country)	Sector	Transaction value
1	Hellman & Friedman LLC (U.S.)	Hub International Ltd. (U.S.)	Distribution	$4,400
2	Assicurazioni Generali SpA. (Italy)	Generali PPF Holding B.V. (Czech Republic)	Property/casualty	3,300
3	Hellman & Friedman LLC and JMI Equity (U.S.)	Applied Systems, Inc. (U.S.)	Services	1,800
4	Great-West Lifeco, Inc. (Canada)	Irish Life Group Ltd. (Ireland)	Life/annuity	1,736
5	Insurance Australia Group Ltd. (Australia)	Insurance underwriting operations in Australia and New Zealand from Wesfarmers Ltd. (Australia)	Property/casualty	1,660
6	MBK Partners Ltd. (South Korea)	ING Life Insurance Korea Ltd. (South Korea)	Life/annuity	1,611
7	Madison Dearborn Partners LLC (U.S.)	National Financial Partners Corp. (U.S.)	Distribution	1,300
8	CVC Capital Partners Ltd. (Luxembourg)	Domestic & General Group Ltd. (U.K.)	Property/casualty	1,200
9	Goldman Sachs Group, Inc. (U.S.)	Hastings Insurance Services Ltd. (U.K.)	Property/casualty	1,125
10	The Travelers Cos., Inc. (U.S.)	Dominion of Canada General Insurance Co. (Canada)	Property/casualty	1,100

Source: Conning Research & Consulting, Inc. analysis.

U.S. INSURANCE-RELATED MERGERS AND ACQUISITIONS, 2004-2013[1]
($ millions)

Year	Property/casualty		Life/annuity		Health/managed care	
	Number of transactions	Transaction values	Number of transactions	Transaction values	Number of transactions	Transaction values
2004	22	$425	17	$3,817	26	$8,342
2005	49	9,264	21	21,865	22	15,886
2006	48	35,221	23	5,055	20	646
2007	67	13,615	19	5,849	52	9,661
2008	59	16,294	14	382	19	1,691
2009	63	3,507	22	840	18	640
2010	60	6,419	20	23,848	15	692
2011	77	12,458	34	3,063	25	4,703
2012	46	4,651	21	6,083	26	18,520
2013	39	4,397	18	3,299	15	33

Year	Distribution		Insurance services		Total U.S. mergers and acquisitions	
	Number of transactions	Transaction values	Number of transactions	Transaction values	Number of transactions	Transaction values
2004	190	$60	37	$2,234	292	$14,878
2005	180	212	63	3,566	335	50,793
2006	246	944	69	1,156	406	43,022
2007	312	15,205	72	6,087	478	50,417
2008	284	5,812	94	7,256	470	31,435
2009	176	615	41	8,771	320	14,373
2010	243	1,727	98	13,823	436	46,509
2011	351	2,608	105	31,892	592	54,724
2012	323	4,225	62	9,673	478	43,152
2013	317	8,246	57	3,349	446	19,324

[1]Includes transactions where a U.S. company was the acquirer and/or the target.

Source: Conning proprietary database.

Insurance Companies by State

An insurance company is said to be "domiciled" in the state that issued its primary license; it is "domestic" in that state. Once it receives its primary license, it may seek licenses in other states as an out-of-state insurer. These out-of-state insurers are called "foreign" insurers. An insurer incorporated in a foreign country is called an "alien" insurer in states where it is licensed.

DOMESTIC INSURANCE COMPANIES BY STATE, PROPERTY/CASUALTY AND LIFE/ANNUITIES, 2013

State	Property/ casualty	Life/ annuities	State	Property/ casualty	Life/ annuities
Alabama	19	7	Montana	3	1
Alaska	5	0	Nebraska	33	28
Arizona	40	30	Nevada	11	3
Arkansas	12	29	New Hampshire	51	2
California	109	16	New Jersey	70	2
Colorado	12	9	New Mexico	13	2
Connecticut	71	29	New York	205	81
Delaware	98	29	North Carolina	68	5
D.C.	6	1	North Dakota	13	4
Florida	120	11	Ohio	133	37
Georgia	34	15	Oklahoma	31	27
Hawaii	17	3	Oregon	15	4
Idaho	7	1	Pennsylvania	179	27
Illinois	193	58	Rhode Island	22	2
Indiana	75	27	South Carolina	24	9
Iowa	69	33	South Dakota	16	3
Kansas	26	12	Tennessee	16	14
Kentucky	9	7	Texas	208	125
Louisiana	32	38	Utah	10	16
Maine	11	3	Vermont	13	2
Maryland	35	5	Virginia	18	5
Massachusetts	54	17	Washington	12	9
Michigan	72	25	West Virginia	19	0
Minnesota	39	12	Wisconsin	173	20
Mississippi	14	15	Wyoming	1	1
Missouri	47	27	**United States**[1]	**2,583**	**888**

[1]Excludes territories, health insurers, risk retention groups, fraternals, title and other insurers. Source: Insurance Department Resources Report, 2014, published by the National Association of Insurance Commissioners (NAIC). Reprinted with permission. Further reprint or redistribution strictly prohibited without written permission of NAIC.

- According to the National Association of Insurance Commissioners, in the U.S. (including territories) there were 6,086 insurance companies in 2013, including property/casualty (2,623), life/annuities (904), health (835), fraternal (87), title (58), risk retention groups (256) and other companies (1,323).

- Many insurance companies are part of larger organizations. According to A.M. Best, in 2012 the P/C insurance industry contained about 1,300 organizations or groups (as opposed to 2,800 companies), including 804 stock (or public) organizations, 406 mutual organizations (firms owned by their policyholders) and 70 reciprocals (a type of self-insurance). The remainder consisted of Lloyd's organizations and state funds.

U.S. Insurance Industry, All Sectors

Premium Taxes by State

All insurance companies pay a state tax based on their premiums. Other payments are made to states for licenses and fees, income and property taxes, sales and use taxes, unemployment compensation taxes and franchise taxes.

- Insurance companies, including life/health and property/casualty companies, paid $17.4 billion in premium taxes to the 50 states in 2013. On a per capita basis, this works out to $55 for every person living in the United States.

- Premium taxes accounted for 2.0 percent of all taxes collected by the states in 2013.

- The Bureau of the Census does not collect data on premium taxes for the District of Columbia.

- According to the Government of the District of Columbia, the District collected $77.5 million in gross revenues for insurance premiums in 2013.

PREMIUM TAXES BY STATE, PROPERTY/CASUALTY AND LIFE/HEALTH INSURANCE, 2013
($000)

State	Amount	State	Amount
Alabama	$297,958	Montana	$74,667
Alaska	60,236	Nebraska	69,248
Arizona	424,369	Nevada	249,390
Arkansas	162,962	New Hampshire	83,547
California	2,242,379	New Jersey	568,484
Colorado	211,320	New Mexico	125,836
Connecticut	242,448	New York	1,435,166
Delaware	87,512	North Carolina	542,551
Florida	657,710	North Dakota	47,867
Georgia	329,237	Ohio	504,075
Hawaii	136,542	Oklahoma	268,121
Idaho	72,251	Oregon	101,569
Ilinois	359,578	Pennsylvania	790,975
Indiana	207,800	Rhode Island	94,915
Iowa	104,885	South Carolina	150,213
Kansas	174,531	South Dakota	71,989
Kentucky	139,471	Tennessee	686,280
Louisiana	399,551	Texas	1,788,471
Maine	99,693	Utah	108,872
Maryland	429,410	Vermont	57,517
Massachusetts	403,757	Virginia	392,397
Michigan	294,313	Washington	436,118
Minnesota	400,974	West Virginia	151,136
Mississippi	212,493	Wisconsin	176,710
Missouri	274,089	Wyoming	18,419
		United States	**$17,420,002**

Source: U.S. Department of Commerce, Bureau of the Census.

Overview

Many insurance companies use a number of different channels to distribute their products. In the early days of the U.S. insurance industry, insurers hired agents, often on a part-time basis, to sign up applicants for insurance. Some agents, known nowadays as "captive" or "exclusive" agents, represented a single company. Others, the equivalent of today's independent agent, worked for a number of companies. At the same time that the two agency systems were expanding, commercial insurance brokers, who were often underwriters, began to set up shop in cities. While agents usually represented insurers, brokers represented clients who were buying insurance. These three distribution channels (captive agents, independent agents and brokers) exist in much the same form today. But with the development of information technology, which provided faster access to company representatives and made the exchange of information for underwriting purposes much easier, alternative distribution channels sprang up, including direct sales by telephone, mail and the Internet. In addition, insurers are using other types of outlets, such as banks, workplaces, associations and car dealers, to access potential policyholders.

Online Property/Casualty Insurance Sales

Insurance distribution systems have evolved to encompass many of the new ways of transacting business online. Recent studies have shown the Internet playing an increasingly important role in the sales and distribution of auto insurance. J.D. Power's 2012 Insurance Shopping study found that the majority of consumers (65 percent) visited the website of at least one insurer or quote aggregator in the shopping process, about the same percentage as in 2009. However, the percentage that relied exclusively on the Internet to obtain quotes increased significantly, rising from 15 percent of shoppers in 2009 to 23 percent in 2012. A 2013 study by comScore estimates that 3.1 million auto insurance policies were sold online in 2012, about the same as in 2011 but up 6 percent from 2010. Sixty-seven percent of shoppers reported getting an online quote in 2012, according to comScore.

Distribution

Property/Casualty

- There were 38,500 independent agencies in the U.S. in 2012, up 3 percent from 2010, according to the Independent Insurance Agents and Brokers of America's 2012 Agency Universe survey.

- 18 percent of the agencies have been founded since 2008.

- 44 percent of these new agencies are located in the South, compared with 36 percent of older independent agencies. 11 percent of new agencies are located in the Northeast, compared with 15 percent of older independent agencies. 55 percent of new agencies are located in large metropolitan areas.

- 14 percent of agencies report that they had operated as exclusive agencies at some point in the past.

Property/Casualty Insurance Distribution

Agency writers, whose products are sold by independent agents or brokers representing several companies; and direct writers, which sell their own products through captive agents by mail, telephone, the Internet and other means, each account for about half of the property/casualty market. There is a degree of overlap as many insurers use multiple channels.

A.M. Best organizes insurance into two main distribution channels: agency writers and direct writers. Its "agency writers" category includes insurers that distribute through independent agencies, brokers, general agents and managing general agents. Its "direct writers" category includes insurers that distribute through the Internet, exclusive/captive agents, direct response and affinity groups.

- In 2013 direct writers accounted for 51.6 percent of P/C insurance net premiums written and agency writers accounted for 46.8 percent, according to A.M. Best.*

- In the personal lines market, direct writers accounted for 71.4 percent of net premiums written in 2013 and agency writers accounted for 27.5 percent. Direct writers accounted for 68.8 percent of the homeowners market and agency writers accounted for 28.8 percent. Direct writers accounted for 72.5 percent of the personal auto market and agency writers accounted for 27.0 percent.*

- Agency writers accounted for 67.2 percent of commercial P/C net premiums written and direct writers accounted for 30.7 percent.*

*Unspecified distribution channels accounted for the remainder.

Life Insurance Distribution

In 2013 independent agents held 49 percent of the new individual life insurance sales market, followed by affiliated (i.e., captive) agents with 41 percent, direct marketers with 4 percent and others accounting for the remaining 6 percent, according to LIMRA, a life insurance trade association.

LIFE INDIVIDUAL MARKET SHARE BY DISTRIBUTION CHANNEL, 2004-2013
(Based on first year collected premium)

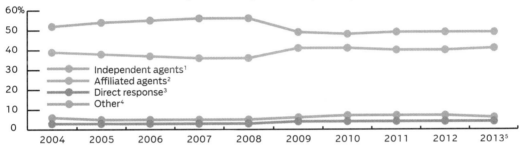

[1]Includes brokers, stockbrokers and personal producing general agents.
[2]Includes career, multiline exclusive and home service agents.
[3]No producers are involved. Excludes direct marketing efforts involving agents.
[4]Includes financial institutions, worksite and other channels.
[5]Estimate.

Source: LIMRA's *U.S. Individual Life Insurance Sales Survey* and LIMRA estimates.

Online Life Insurance Sales

Eighty-three percent of consumers say they would use the Internet to research life insurance before purchasing coverage, according to the 2014 Insurance Barometer Study by the Life and Health Insurance Foundation for Education (LIFE) and LIMRA. Face-to-face with a financial advisor or agent was the most favored life insurance sales channel, with 53 percent preferring that method, but one in four respondents under the age of 45 said their preference is to apply online. Overall, online was a strong second by all age groups (favored by 22 percent of respondents), followed by workplace sales (11 percent), mail (7 percent), phone (4 percent) and email (3 percent). When asked about the concept of retail sales, 12 percent of respondents said they would be willing to purchase life insurance through a retail outlet such as a drugstore or warehouse store, down from 17 percent a year ago.

Distribution

Annuities Distribution

Insurance agents, including career agents, who sell the products of a single life insurance company, and independent agents, who represent several insurers, accounted for 37 percent of annuity sales in 2013. State and federal regulators require sellers of variable annuities to register with the Financial Industry Regulatory Authority (FINRA) and the Securities and Exchange Commission.

SALES OF INDIVIDUAL ANNUITIES BY DISTRIBUTION CHANNELS, 2009 AND 2013

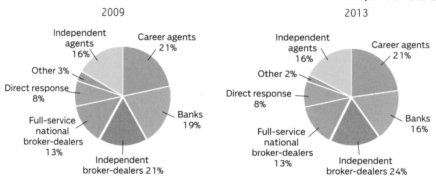

2009

- Independent agents 16%
- Career agents 21%
- Other 3%
- Direct response 8%
- Full-service national broker-dealers 13%
- Banks 19%
- Independent broker-dealers 21%

2013

- Independent agents 16%
- Career agents 21%
- Other 2%
- Direct response 8%
- Full-service national broker-dealers 13%
- Banks 16%
- Independent broker-dealers 24%

Source: *U.S. Individual Annuity Yearbook - 2013*, LIMRA Retirement Institute.

Bank Insurance Sales

The Gramm-Leach-Bliley Financial Services Modernization Act of 1999 (GLB) removed many of the Depression-era barriers that restricted affiliations between banks, securities firms and insurance companies. The arrangement that provided the major impetus for the passage of GLB, Citigroup's merger with Travelers Insurance Group, was short lived, with Citigroup selling off its Travelers property/casualty insurance and life insurance units in 2002 and 2005, respectively. The "financial supermarkets" envisioned by GLB have not transpired. Instead, banks have tended to concentrate on distributing insurance products by buying existing agencies and brokers rather than by setting up their own agencies or purchasing insurers. For their part, insurance companies have set up thrift or banking divisions rather than buying existing banks. The 2007 to 2009 recession and resulting regulatory changes prompted some structural changes in the financial services industry, with some insurers selling their banking units.

BANK HOLDING COMPANY INSURANCE BROKERAGE, UNDERWRITING AND TOTAL INSURANCE FEE INCOME, 2009-2013[1]

	Insurance brokerage fee income[2]				
	Reporting insurance brokerage fee income		Insurance brokerage fee income ($ billions)	Average insurance brokerage fee income	Median insurance brokerage fee income[4]
Year	Number	Percent[3]			
2009	605	66.1%	$6.66	$11,005,294	$139,000
2010	592	65.1	7.05	11,916,748	131,500
2011	606	65.2	7.70	12,702,413	119,000
2012	665	63.2	6.20	9,318,084	123,000
2013	664	62.5	6.22	9,360,139	117,500

	Insurance underwriting fee income				
	Reporting insurance underwriting fee income		Insurance underwriting fee income ($ billions)	Average insurance underwriting fee income	Median insurance underwriting fee income[4]
Year	Number	Percent[3]			
2009	68	7.4%	$8.42	$123,788,103	$500,500
2010	67	7.4	7.16	106,825,388	452,000
2011	63	6.8	5.09	80,756,651	360,000
2012	66	6.3	4.41	66,769,970	503,000
2013	60	5.7	4.00	66,645,533	581,000

	Total insurance fee income				
	Reporting total insurance fee income		Total insurance fee income ($ billions)	Average total insurance fee income	Median total insurance fee income[4]
Year	Number	Percent[3]			
2009	608	66.5%	$15.08	$24,795,714	$154,500
2010	594	65.3	14.21	23,925,953	156,000
2011	608	65.5	12.79	21,028,595	133,000
2012	670	63.6	10.60	15,825,887	141,000
2013	669	63.0	10.21	15,267,360	141,000

[1]Bank holding companies (BHCs) own one or more banks. Excludes MetLife, Inc., which during some of these years was a financial holding company subject to reporting and supervision to the Federal Reserve Board. Other traditional insurers were similarly excluded from these findings.
[2]Income from nonunderwriting activities, mostly from insurance product sales and referrals, service charges and commissions, and fees earned from insurance and annuity sales.
[3]Percent of top-tier BHCs defined by the Federal Reserve with consolidated assets in excess of $500 million.
[4]Represents the midpoint. Half are above the median and half are below.

Source: Michael White Bank Insurance Fee Income Report - 2014.

Distribution

Bank Insurance Sales

TOP TEN BANK HOLDING COMPANIES IN INSURANCE BROKERAGE FEE INCOME, 2012-2013[1]
($000)

Rank	Bank holding company	State	Insurance brokerage fee income				2013 Assets
			2012	2013	Percent change, 2012-2013	Percent of noninterest income, 2013	
1	Wells Fargo & Co.	California	$1,556,000	$1,463,000	-5.98%	3.60%	$1,527,008,000
2	BB&T Corporation	North Carolina	1,246,403	1,377,772	10.54	35.69	183,005,909
3	Citigroup Inc.	New York	1,171,000	733,000	-37.40	2.46	1,880,081,000
4	Bank of America Corporation	North Carolina	-195,764	289,000	NA	0.65	2,098,613,000
5	American Express Company	New York	179,000	184,000	2.79	0.66	152,988,000
6	Regions Financial Corporation	Alabama	108,563	114,412	5.39	5.60	117,661,732
7	Morgan Stanley	New York	99,000	99,000	[2]	0.32	832,702,000
8	Bancorpsouth, Inc.	Mississippi	90,592	98,141	8.33	37.05	13,045,442
9	Discover Financial Services	Illinois	90,047	78,906	-12.37	3.90	79,031,613
10	First Command Financial Services, Inc.	Texas	77,409	76,736	-0.87	35.46	891,759

[1]Bank holding companies own one or more banks. Includes income from nonunderwriting activities, mostly insurance product sales and referrals, service charges and commissions, and fees earned from insurance and annuity sales. [2]Less than 0.01 percent. NA=Not applicable. Source: Michael White Bank Insurance Fee Income Report - 2014.

TOP TEN BANK HOLDING COMPANIES IN INSURANCE UNDERWRITING NET INCOME, 2013[1]

Rank	Bank holding company	State	Total insurance underwriting net income	Total net income/loss	Insurance net income as a percent of total net income	2013 Assets
1	Wells Fargo & Co.	California	$552,000	$21,878,000	2.52%	$1,527,008,000
2	Ally Financial Inc.	Michigan	475,000	361,000	131.58	151,167,000
3	Citigroup Inc.	New York	413,000	13,673,000	3.02	1,880,081,000
4	Goldman Sachs Group, Inc.	New York	141,000	8,040,000	1.75	909,404,000
5	HSBC North America Holdings Inc.	New York	121,912	40,753	299.15	290,013,509
6	American Express Company	New York	96,000	5,359,000	1.79	152,988,000
7	Bank of America Corporation	North Carolina	85,000	11,431,000	0.74	2,098,613,000
8	BB&T Corporation	North Carolina	51,326	1,679,097	3.06	183,005,909
9	JPMorgan Chase & Co.	New York	33,000	17,923,000	0.18	2,408,874,000
10	Old National Bancorp	Indiana	29,727	100,920	29.46	9,581,797

[1]Bank holding companies own one or more banks. Source: Michael White Bank Insurance Fee Income Report - 2014.

Life/Health Sector

Whether measured by premium income or by assets, traditional life insurance is no longer the primary business of many companies in the life/health insurance industry. Today, the emphasis has shifted to the underwriting of annuities. Annuities are contracts that accumulate funds and/ or pay out a fixed or variable income stream. An income stream can be for a set period of time or over the lifetimes of the contract holder and his or her beneficiaries.

Nevertheless, traditional life insurance products such as universal life and term life for individuals as well as group life remain an important part of the business, as do disability income and health insurance.

Life insurers invest primarily in corporate bonds but also significantly in corporate equities. Besides annuities and life insurance products, life insurers may offer other types of financial services such as asset management.

Life Insurance Ownership

Sixty-two percent of all people in the United States were covered by some type of life insurance in 2013, according to LIMRA's *2014 Insurance Barometer Study*. One in four Americans said they need more life insurance in 2014, as reported in the LIMRA Study. Other findings from the 2014 report include:

- Only 1 person in 10 is very likely to purchase a life insurance policy within the next year. Sixty-three percent said that they have not purchased more life insurance because they think it is too expensive.
- The most common financial worry among consumers is being able to afford a comfortable retirement.
- Only 13 percent of Americans have long-term care insurance.
- Twenty-nine percent of Americans have disability insurance.

2013 Financial Results

While the life insurance industry continued to face challenges from a sluggish economy and low interest rates in 2013 for the second year in a row, operating results and capitalization improved as conditions in the stock market eased, according to a May 2014 report by A.M. Best. Capital, as measured by policyholders' surplus, rose to $331.9 billion in 2013 from $329.0 billion in 2012, according to SNL Financial. The industry's net gain from operations before federal income taxes rose slightly to $63.7 billion in 2013, or 5.4 percent, from $60.5 billion in 2012. Net income rose from $40.9 billion to $43.2 billion during the same period, the highest level in at least a dozen years according to SNL. See the income statement on page 32 for details.

Investments

The life/health insurance industry's cash and invested assets totaled $3.5 trillion in 2013, according to SNL Financial.

LIFE/HEALTH INSURANCE INDUSTRY INCOME STATEMENT, 2009-2013
(\$ billions, end of year)

	2009	2010	2011	2012	2013	Percent change, 2012-2013[1]
Revenue						
Life insurance premiums	$120.6	$100.3	$122.8	$130.5	$126.1	-3.4%
Annuity premiums and deposits	225.5	286.3	327.0	339.9	279.4	-17.8
Accident and health premiums	145.2	150.9	151.3	151.7	153.4	1.1
Credit life and credit accident and health premiums	1.6	1.6	1.6	1.6	1.4	-7.2
Other premiums and considerations	0.5	23.1	2.1	2.2	2.3	4.4
Total premiums, consideration and deposits	**$493.4**	**$562.2**	**$604.8**	**$626.0**	**$562.8**	**-10.1%**
Net investment income	156.6	164.1	167.3	166.9	167.9	0.6
Reinsurance allowance	61.5	-29.3	-16.3	-30.8	-21.2	-31.0
Separate accounts revenue	20.4	23.4	26.1	29.5	31.4	6.5
Other income	44.9	52.9	53.1	60.3	43.1	-28.6
Total revenue	**$776.7**	**$773.3**	**$835.0**	**$851.9**	**$783.9**	**-8.0%**
Expense						
Benefits	230.1	231.7	239.1	242.0	250.9	3.7
Surrenders	228.7	216.8	237.3	245.7	248.8	1.2
Increase in reserves	99.2	96.2	141.2	83.8	86.2	2.9
Transfers to separate accounts	11.1	29.3	32.4	61.6	-0.8	-101.3
Commissions	48.5	48.9	51.4	52.6	53.0	0.8
General and administrative expenses	52.1	54.7	56.5	57.3	58.5	2.2
Insurance taxes, licenses and fees	7.1	7.5	7.8	8.0	8.2	1.9
Other expenses	7.4	2.2	8.1	6.7	-0.4	-105.6
Total expenses	**$684.2**	**$687.3**	**$773.8**	**$757.7**	**$704.5**	**-7.0%**
Net income						
Policyholder dividends	15.0	15.0	15.1	15.2	15.7	3.2
Net gain from operations before Federal income tax	61.0	53.1	28.0	60.5	63.7	5.4
Federal income tax	10.5	8.6	4.7	9.9	8.6	-13.2
Net income before capital gains	**$50.3**	**$44.1**	**$22.9**	**$50.3**	**$55.2**	**9.6%**
Net realized capital gains (losses)	-28.7	-16.0	-8.5	-9.4	-12.0	27.3
Net income	**$21.5**	**$28.0**	**$14.4**	**$40.9**	**$43.2**	**5.5%**
Pre-tax operating income	61.0	53.1	28.0	60.5	63.7	5.4

[1]Calculated from unrounded data.

Source: SNL Financial LC.

INVESTMENTS, LIFE/HEALTH INSURERS, 2011-2013[1]
($ billions, end of year)

Investment type	Amount			Percent of total investments		
	2011	2012	2013	2011	2012	2013
Bonds	$2,531.8	$2,543.3	$2,601.3	75.34%	74.65%	74.70%
Stocks	78.4	78.0	80.3	2.33	2.29	2.31
Preferred stock	8.1	7.8	8.3	0.24	0.23	0.24
Common stock	70.3	70.2	72.1	2.09	2.06	2.07
Mortgage loans on real estate	323.1	335.6	353.1	9.61	9.85	10.14
First lien real estate mortgage loans	321.1	333.1	350.1	9.56	9.78	10.05
Real estate loans less first liens	2.0	2.5	3.1	0.06	0.07	0.09
Real estate	20.6	21.4	22.4	0.61	0.63	0.64
Occupied properties	5.7	5.5	5.4	0.17	0.16	0.16
Income generating properties	14.6	15.4	16.0	0.43	0.45	0.46
Properties for sale	0.3	0.5	0.9	0.01	0.02	0.03
Cash, cash equivalent and short term investments	96.5	106.6	94.8	2.87	3.13	2.72
Contract loans including premium notes	126.0	127.5	128.4	3.75	3.74	3.69
Derivatives	44.4	41.6	37.8	1.32	1.22	1.09
Other invested assets	124.0	136.6	145.5	3.69	4.01	4.18
Receivables for securities	2.1	2.1	3.2	0.06	0.06	0.09
Securities lending reinvested collateral assets	10.1	10.8	13.8	0.30	0.32	0.40
Write-ins for invested assets	0.2	-0.3	1.6	0.01	-0.01	0.05
Total cash and invested assets	**$3,360.5**	**$3,407.1**	**$3,482.2**	**100.00%**	**100.00%**	**100.00%**

[1]Includes cash and net admitted assets of life/health insurers.

Source: SNL Financial LC.

INVESTMENTS, LIFE/HEALTH INSURERS, BOND PORTFOLIO, 2013[1]

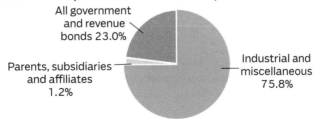

All government and revenue bonds 23.0%

Parents, subsidiaries and affiliates 1.2%

Industrial and miscellaneous 75.8%

[1]Long-term bonds with maturity dates over one year, as of December 31, 2013.

Source: SNL Financial LC.

Life/Health Financial Data

Payouts

Life insurance benefits and claims totaled $586 billion in 2013, including life insurance death benefits, annuity benefits, disability benefits and other payouts. The largest payout, $249 billion, was for surrender benefits and withdrawals from life insurance contracts made to policyholders who terminated their policies early or withdrew cash from their policies.

LIFE INSURANCE INDUSTRY BENEFITS AND CLAIMS, 2009-2013
($000)

	2009	2010	2011	2012	2013
Death benefits	$57,595,091	$56,507,462	$60,611,373	$61,701,439	$62,577,038
Matured endowments, excluding annual pure endowments	649,867	679,242	767,092	415,088	369,299
Annuity benefits	64,061,288	66,781,512	70,873,226	70,296,382	74,882,585
Disability, accident and health benefits[1]	106,246,906	106,119,469	105,151,994	107,765,827	111,016,901
Coupons, pure endowment and similar benefits	17,027	16,264	16,075	17,179	17,234
Surrender benefits, withdrawals for life contracts	228,688,291	216,846,768	237,281,879	245,728,482	248,768,774
Group conversions	26,516	29,136	27,884	27,891	52,893
Interest and adjustments on deposit-type contracts	10,404,385	9,541,403	9,829,729	7,321,437	8,197,554
Payments on supplementary contracts with life contingencies	1,527,354	1,578,300	1,690,841	1,809,677	1,985,919
Increase in aggregate reserve	88,782,277	86,623,252	131,335,226	76,437,745	78,012,695
Total benefits and claims	**$558,001,763**	**$544,723,271**	**$617,585,318**	**$571,521,145**	**$585,880,892**

[1]Excludes benefits paid by health insurance companies and property/casualty insurance companies.

Source: SNL Financial LC.

Measured by premiums written, annuities are the largest life/health product line, followed by life insurance and health insurance (also referred to in the industry as accident and health). Life insurance policies can be sold on an individual, or "ordinary," basis or to groups such as employees and associations. Accident and health insurance includes medical expense, disability income and long-term care. Other lines include credit life, which pays the balance of a loan if the borrower dies or becomes disabled, and industrial life, small policies whose premiums are generally collected by an agent on a weekly basis.

DIRECT PREMIUMS WRITTEN BY LINE, LIFE/HEALTH INSURANCE INDUSTRY, 2011-2013
($000)

Lines of insurance	2011 Direct premiums written[1]	2011 Percent of total	2012 Direct premiums written[1]	2012 Percent of total	2013 Direct premiums written[1]	2013 Percent of total
Annuities						
Ordinary individual annuities	$212,365,662	32.3%	$192,291,621	28.1%	$198,862,072	30.7%
Group annuities	122,453,628	18.6	164,069,697	23.9	120,091,136	18.6
Total	**$334,819,290**	**50.9%**	**$356,361,318**	**52.0%**	**$318,953,208**	**49.3%**
Life						
Ordinary life	130,935,596	19.9	132,640,130	19.4	129,963,644	20.1
Group life	31,478,628	4.8	34,420,250	5.0	33,532,415	5.2
Credit life (group and individual)	1,224,617	0.2	1,129,433	0.2	990,170	15.3
Industrial life	173,147	[2]	165,688	[2]	146,248	[2]
Total	**$163,811,988**	**24.9%**	**$168,355,500**	**24.6%**	**$164,632,477**	**25.4%**
Accident and health[3]						
Group	87,795,765	13.4	90,647,379	13.2	94,705,454	14.6
Other	69,851,576	10.6	68,870,879	10.1	67,677,104	10.5
Credit	929,424	0.1	954,569	0.1	966,052	0.1
Total	**$158,576,766**	**24.1%**	**$160,472,827**	**23.4%**	**$163,348,610**	**25.2%**
All other lines	2,404	[2]	2,574	[2]	3,027	[2]
Total, all lines[4]	**$657,210,448**	**100.0%**	**$685,192,219**	**100.0%**	**$646,937,321**	**100.0%**

[1]Before reinsurance transactions.
[2]Less than 0.1 percent.
[3]Excludes accident and health premiums reported on the property/casualty and health annual statements.
[4]Excludes deposit-type funds.

Source: SNL Financial LC.

Private Health Insurance

Most private health insurance is written by insurers whose main business is health insurance. However, life/health and property/casualty insurers also write this coverage, referred to as accident and health insurance on their Annual Statements. Total private health insurance direct written premiums were $628.3 billion in 2013, including $459.2 billion from the health insurance segment, $163.3 billion from the life/health segment and $5.8 billion from the property/casualty annual statement.

In 2013, 42 million Americans did not have health insurance, according to a redesigned U.S. Census report, which makes prior year estimates not directly comparable. The percentage of uninsured Americans in 2013 stood at 13.4 percent. The Census Bureau said that according to another report, the percentage of people without health insurance declined 0.2 percent between 2012 and 2013. There is other evidence, not directly comparable to the Census Bureau data, of falling uninsured rates in 2014: according to the Gallup Health-Ways Well-Being Index, the percentage of Americans without health insurance fell to 15.9 percent in the first two months of 2014, compared with 17.1 percent in the fourth quarter of 2013.

Other Census Bureau findings include:

- 64.2 percent of Americans were covered by private health insurance in 2013.
- The percentage covered by employment-based health insurance in 2013 was 53.9 percent. The percentage of people covered by government health insurance was 34.3 percent during the same period.
- The percentage of children under the age of 19 without health insurance was 7.6 percent (5.9 million) in 2013. Children under 19 are eligible for Medicaid and the Children's Health Insurance Program. Only 1.6 percent of people age 65 and older, eligible for Medicare, did not have health insurance.
- In 2013 the uninsured rate was 21.6 percent for those in households with annual income less than $25,000. This contrasts with uninsured rates of 13.1 percent for those in households with income between $50,000 and $75,000 and 5.3 percent with income of $150,000 or more.

HEALTH INSURANCE COVERAGE STATUS AND TYPE OF COVERAGE, 2013
(000)

Total U.S. population	Uninsured		Insured		
	Number of people	Percent of total population	Private health insurance	Government health insurance	Individuals with some form of insurance[1]
313,395	41,953	13.4%	201,064	107,581	271,442

[1]Includes individuals with some form of insurance (government, private or a combination of both).

Source: U.S. Department of Commerce, Census Bureau.

TOP TEN HEALTH INSURANCE GROUPS BY DIRECT PREMIUMS WRITTEN, 2013[1]

($000)

Rank	Group/company	Direct premiums written	Market share
1	WellPoint Inc.	$51,356,097	11.2%
2	UnitedHealth Group Inc.	51,269,926	11.2
3	Health Care Service Corporation	23,682,045	5.2
4	Aetna Inc.	20,628,578	4.5
5	Humana Inc.	17,836,173	3.9
6	Highmark Insurance Group	11,600,299	2.5
7	Kaiser Foundation Health Plan Inc.	10,597,597	2.3
8	Independence Blue Cross	10,370,198	2.3
9	EmblemHealth Inc.	9,953,798	2.2
10	Centene Corp.	9,928,499	2.2

[1]Based on health insurer annual statement data. Excludes health insurance data from the property/casualty and life/health Annual Statements. Excludes territories.

Source: SNL Financial LC.

Disability Insurance

Disability insurance pays an insured person an income when he or she is unable to work because of an accident or illness.

INDIVIDUAL DISABILITY INSURANCE, NEW ISSUES SALES, 2012[1]

	Number of policies	Percent change, 2011– 2012	Annualized premiums	Percent change, 2011– 2012
Noncancellable	152,827	2%	$314,944,244	5%
Guaranteed renewable	327,944	-6	211,957,298	-3
Total	**480,771**	**-3%**	**$526,901,544**	**2%**

■ Annualized premiums for new disability income policies rose by 2 percent in 2012, following a 6 percent increase the previous year.

[1]Short-term and long-term individual disability income insurance. Based on a LIMRA survey of 21 disability insurance companies. Excludes commercial disability income.

Source: LIMRA International.

INDIVIDUAL DISABILITY INSURANCE IN FORCE, 2012[1]

	Number of policies	Percent change, 2011-2012	Annualized premiums	Percent change, 2011-2012
Noncancellable	2,434,921	-1%	$4,054,384,941	2%
Guaranteed renewable	1,637,803	1	1,138,954,027	3
Total	**4,072,724**	2	**$5,193,338,968**	**2%**

[1]Short-term and long-term individual disability income insurance. Based on a LIMRA survey of 21 disability insurance companies. Excludes commercial disability income.
[2]Less than -0.5 percent.

Source: LIMRA International.

Long-Term Care Insurance

Long-term care (LTC) insurance pays for services to help individuals who are unable to perform certain activities of daily living without assistance or who require supervision due to a cognitive impairment such as Alzheimer's disease. According to the U.S. Department of Health and Human Services, about 70 percent of individuals over age 65 will require at least some type of long-term care services. There were 45 million people age 65 and older in 2013, accounting for 14.1 percent of the U.S. population, or about one in every seven Americans, according to the U.S. Census Bureau. By 2030 the Census Bureau projects there will be about 73 million older people and about 83.7 million in 2050.

Nearly 5 million people were covered by long-term care insurance in 2013, according to a study by LIMRA International. The average first-year premium for individual LTC coverage purchased in 2013 was $2,359, down 5 percent from 2012. In 2012, 28.7 percent of new long-term care insurance policies were purchased by individuals under the age of 55, and 82.7 percent of buyers were under the age of 65, according to a study by the American Association for Long-Term Care Insurance. The average age when people applied for coverage was 56 years. The age of new buyers has been slowly dropping, according to the association. A decade or so ago the age of the average buyer was between 66 and 67.

- The number of Americans purchasing LTC insurance in 2013 fell 26 percent from 2012, and premiums declined by 30 percent, based on new business.

INDIVIDUAL LONG-TERM CARE (LTC) INSURANCE, 2013[1]

	Lives	Percent change, 2012-2013	Premium ($ millions)	Percent change, 2012-2013
New business	172,178	-26%	$406	-30%
In-force[3]	4,850,000	2	9,800	3

[1]Based on LIMRA International's Individual LTC Sales survey, representing over 95% of the individual LTC market.
[2]Less than 1 percent.
[3]Includes estimates for non-participants.

Source: LIMRA International.

Premiums by Line by State

LIFE/HEALTH INSURERS DIRECT PREMIUMS WRITTEN AND
ANNUITY CONSIDERATIONS BY STATE, 2013[1]
($ millions)

State	Life insurance	Annuities	Accident and health insurance[2]	Deposit-type contract funds	Other considerations	Total
Alabama	$2,049	$2,694	$1,342	$263	$394	$6,742
Alaska	336	398	333	24	156	1,246
Arizona	2,070	4,129	3,352	325	1,264	11,141
Arkansas	1,035	1,404	1,021	99	234	3,793
California	14,550	22,103	13,855	2,333	7,023	59,865
Colorado	2,263	4,724	3,169	759	713	11,627
Connecticut	2,444	4,350	2,622	8,937	1,577	19,930
Delaware	1,263	2,347	500	36,799	1,482	42,391
D.C.	393	586	676	196	380	2,230
Florida	8,106	17,266	11,401	1,160	3,899	41,832
Georgia	4,428	4,832	5,786	589	2,455	18,090
Hawaii	779	1,264	886	81	344	3,355
Idaho	505	922	531	66	185	2,209
Illinois	6,640	9,964	5,247	1,728	3,167	26,746
Indiana	2,606	4,900	3,614	899	814	12,834
Iowa	1,682	2,795	1,270	8,142	2,554	16,442
Kansas	1,275	2,278	3,089	1,148	369	8,160
Kentucky	1,504	2,458	1,574	208	814	6,558
Louisiana	2,161	3,442	1,867	233	635	8,339
Maine	430	998	927	94	213	2,662
Maryland	2,840	5,199	3,057	682	1,771	13,548
Massachusetts	3,719	6,924	2,820	1,285	4,653	19,400
Michigan	3,930	9,531	3,269	1,194	1,544	19,468
Minnesota	4,078	4,528	1,522	543	1,906	12,576
Mississippi	1,223	1,425	1,547	90	169	4,453
Missouri	2,623	7,010	3,372	876	1,101	14,983
Montana	323	497	379	33	133	1,365
Nebraska	939	1,575	1,134	374	298	4,320

(table continues)

**LIFE/HEALTH INSURERS DIRECT PREMIUMS WRITTEN AND
ANNUITY CONSIDERATIONS BY STATE, 2013[1] (Cont'd)**

($ millions)

State	Life insurance	Annuities	Accident and health insurance[2]	Deposit-type contract funds	Other considerations	Total
Nevada	$871	$1,381	$1,018	$220	$331	$3,822
New Hampshire	566	1,582	635	449	347	3,578
New Jersey	5,711	11,060	5,607	2,302	2,685	27,365
New Mexico	634	941	833	71	320	2,798
New York	11,076	16,797	7,944	16,687	9,459	61,962
North Carolina	4,244	7,109	4,472	1,580	2,149	19,554
North Dakota	362	606	272	49	123	1,411
Ohio	4,889	9,443	6,126	4,108	2,088	26,654
Oklahoma	1,343	1,835	1,607	179	366	5,331
Oregon	1,106	2,303	1,829	238	1,145	6,621
Pennsylvania	6,121	12,247	5,556	3,498	8,378	35,799
Rhode Island	462	1,090	673	72	198	2,495
South Carolina	1,930	3,431	1,895	164	387	7,807
South Dakota	558	537	362	55	82	1,594
Tennessee	2,715	4,478	2,596	495	962	11,247
Texas	10,254	15,269	13,554	1,586	2,866	43,528
Utah	1,227	1,974	909	168	406	4,685
Vermont	257	514	321	49	111	1,252
Virginia	3,952	6,016	3,875	740	1,294	15,878
Washington	2,245	4,153	2,692	292	1,382	10,763
West Virginia	625	1,098	631	109	150	2,613
Wisconsin	2,511	4,893	3,557	508	1,066	12,536
Wyoming	275	390	340	26	50	1,080
United States[3]	**$140,130**	**$239,688**	**$147,462**	**$102,809**	**$76,591**	**$706,679**

[1]Direct premiums written before reinsurance transactions, excludes state funds.
[2]Excludes accident and health premiums reported on property/casualty and health annual statements.
[3]Excludes territories, dividends and other nonstate specific data.

Source: SNL Financial LC.

TOP TWENTY WRITERS OF LIFE INSURANCE BY DIRECT PREMIUMS WRITTEN, 2013

($000)

Rank	Group/company	Direct premiums written[1]	Market share
1	MetLife Inc.	$12,178,426	8.2%
2	Northwestern Mutual Life Insurance Co.	9,469,028	6.4
3	Prudential Financial Inc.	8,372,368	5.7
4	New York Life Insurance Group	7,896,125	5.3
5	Lincoln National Corp.	6,167,075	4.2
6	Aflac Inc.	5,765,822	3.9
7	Massachusetts Mutual Life Insurance Company	5,096,774	3.4
8	Manulife Financial Corp.	4,865,768	3.3
9	AEGON	4,111,101	2.8
10	State Farm Mutual Automobile Insurance	4,016,444	2.7
11	American International Group	3,491,931	2.4
12	Guardian Life Insurance Co. of America	3,382,895	2.3
13	Securian Financial Group	3,171,539	2.1
14	Hartford Financial Services	3,085,566	2.1
15	AXA	3,004,940	2.0
16	Pacific MHC	2,837,866	1.9
17	Voya Financial Inc.	2,658,916	1.8
18	Protective Life Corp.	2,608,633	1.8
19	Nationwide Mutual Group	2,090,416	1.4
20	Sammons Enterprises Inc.	2,078,505	1.4

[1]Before reinsurance transactions. Based on U.S. total, includes territories. Excludes annuities, accident and health, deposit-type contract funds and other considerations.

Source: SNL Financial LC.

TOP TEN WRITERS OF INDIVIDUAL LIFE INSURANCE
BY DIRECT PREMIUMS WRITTEN, 2013
($000)

Rank	Group/company	Direct premiums written[1]	Market share
1	Northwestern Mutual Life Insurance Co.	$9,469,028	8.1%
2	MetLife Inc.	6,743,722	5.7
3	New York Life Insurance Group	6,234,927	5.3
4	Aflac Inc.	5,750,188	4.9
5	Lincoln National Corp.	5,436,152	4.6
6	Manulife Financial Corp.	4,859,644	4.1
7	Prudential Financial Inc.	4,822,805	4.1
8	Massachusetts Mutual Life Insurance Co.	3,988,732	3.4
9	State Farm Mutual Automobile Insurance	3,976,209	3.4
10	AEGON	3,766,265	3.2

[1]Before reinsurance transactions. Based on U.S. total, includes territories. Excludes annuities, accident and health, deposit-type contract funds and other considerations.
Source: SNL Financial LC.

TOP TEN WRITERS OF GROUP LIFE INSURANCE
BY DIRECT PREMIUMS WRITTEN, 2013
($000)

Rank	Group/company	Direct premiums written[1]	Market share
1	MetLife Inc.	$5,399,652	18.4%
2	Prudential Financial Inc.	3,549,561	12.1
3	Securian Financial Group	1,880,118	6.4
4	New York Life Insurance Group	1,661,198	5.6
5	Cigna Corp.	1,594,059	5.4
6	Unum Group	1,257,255	4.3
7	Hartford Financial Services	1,253,243	4.3
8	Massachusetts Mutual Life Insurance Co.	1,108,042	3.8
9	Aetna Inc.	992,859	3.4
10	StanCorp Financial Group Inc.	780,390	2.7

[1]Before reinsurance transactions. Based on U.S. total, includes territories. Excludes annuities, accident and health, deposit-type contract funds and other considerations.
Source: SNL Financial LC.

2013 Financial Results

Profitability in the property/casualty insurance industry surged to its highest level in the post-crisis era in 2013. Sharply lower catastrophe losses, modestly higher premium growth, improved realized investment gains and favorable prior-year reserve loss development pushed the industry's return on average surplus to 10.3 percent, up from 6.1 percent in 2012 and just 3.5 percent in 2011, according to data compiled by ISO, a Verisk Analytics company, and the Property Casualty Insurers Association of America (PCI). The industry combined ratio in 2013 fell to 96.1 from 102.9 in 2012, leading to an underwriting profit of $15.5 billion. Overall net income after taxes climbed more than 80 percent, to $63.8 billion. Net written premiums rose 4.6 percent, the strongest annual growth recorded since the financial crisis. Policyholders' surplus rose to a record $653.3 billion as of December 31, 2013—up $66.3 billion, or 11.3 percent, from $587.1 billion as of year-end 2012, according to data from ISO and PCI.

PROPERTY/CASUALTY INSURANCE INDUSTRY INCOME ANALYSIS, 2009-2013[1]
($ billions)

	2009	2010	2011	2012	2013
Net written premiums	$418.4	$423.8	$438.0	$456.7	$477.7
Percent change	-3.8%	1.3%	3.4%	4.3%	4.6%
Earned premiums	$422.3	$422.2	$434.4	$448.9	$467.9
Losses incurred	253.8	257.7	290.8	277.7	259.3
Loss adjustment expenses incurred	52.5	52.9	53.8	55.5	55.7
Other underwriting expenses	117.0	119.8	124.2	128.9	134.8
Policyholder dividends	2.0	2.3	1.9	2.1	2.5
Underwriting gain/loss	-3.0	-10.5	-36.2	-15.4	15.5
Net investment income	47.1	47.6	49.2	48.0	47.4
Miscellaneous income/loss	0.9	1.1	2.5	2.4	1.5
Operating income/loss	45.0	38.2	15.4	35.0	64.3
Realized capital gain/loss	-7.9	5.9	7.0	6.2	11.4
Federal and foreign income tax	8.4	8.8	3.0	6.1	12.0
Net income after taxes	28.7	35.2	19.5	35.1	63.8

[1]Data in this chart exclude state funds and other residual market insurers and may not agree with similar data shown elsewhere from different sources.

Source: ISO®, a Verisk Analytics® company.

- The property/casualty insurance industry had an underwriting gain of $15.5 billion in 2013, the first such gain since 2007, as catastrophe losses fell to $12.9 billion in 2013 from $35.5 billion in 2012.

Property/Casualty Financial Data

Premiums, Expenses and Combined Ratio

Insurers use various measures to gauge financial performance. The combined ratio after dividends is a measure of underwriting profitability. It reflects the percentage of each premium dollar an insurer spends on claims and expenses. The combined ratio does not take investment income into account. A combined ratio above 100 indicates an underwriting loss.

NET PREMIUMS WRITTEN AND COMBINED RATIO, PROPERTY/CASUALTY INSURANCE, 2004-2013
($ billions)

Year	Net premiums written[1]	Annual percent change	Combined ratio after dividends[2]	Annual point change[3]	Year	Net premiums written[1]	Annual percent change	Combined ratio after dividends[2]	Annual point change[3]
2004	$425.5	4.5%	98.5	-1.7 pts.	2009	$423.5	-3.8%	100.4	-4.8 pts.
2005	422.4	-0.7	100.7	2.2	2010	425.9	0.6	102.5	2.1
2006	447.8	6.0	92.4	-8.2	2011	441.6	3.7	108.3	5.8
2007	446.2	-0.4	95.6	3.2	2012	460.5	4.3	103.1	5.2
2008	440.3	-1.3	105.2	9.5	2013	481.2	4.5	96.3	-6.8

[1]After reinsurance transactions, excludes state funds. [2]After dividends to policyholders. A drop in the combined ratio represents an improvement; an increase represents a deterioration. [3]Calculated from unrounded numbers.

Source: SNL Financial LC.

PROPERTY/CASUALTY INSURANCE INDUSTRY UNDERWRITING EXPENSES, 2013[1]

Expense	Percent of premiums
LOSSES AND RELATED EXPENSES[2]	
Loss and loss adjustment expense (LAE) ratio	**67.4%**
Incurred losses	55.5
Defense and cost containment expenses incurred	4.6
Adjusting and other expenses incurred	7.3
UNDERWRITING EXPENSES[3]	
Expense ratio	**28.3%**
Net commissions and brokerage expenses incurred	10.5
Taxes, licenses and fees	2.6
Other acquisition and field supervision expenses incurred	8.0
General expenses incurred	7.2
DIVIDENDS TO POLICYHOLDERS[2]	**0.6%**
COMBINED RATIO AFTER DIVIDENDS[4]	**96.3%**

[1]After reinsurance transactions.
[2]As a percent of net premiums earned ($471.6 billion in 2013).
[3]As of percent of net premiums written ($481.2 billion in 2013).
[4]Sum of loss and LAE, expense and dividends ratios.

Source: SNL Financial LC.

Profitability: Insurance and Other Selected Industries

According to an analysis conducted by ISO, profitability of property/casualty (P/C) insurance companies measured on a generally accepted accounting principles (GAAP) basis lags other industries. The return on net worth for Fortune 500 combined companies for the years 2004 to 2013 exceeded that of the P/C industry in every year. Insurers are required to use statutory accounting principles (SAP), which are more conservative than GAAP, when filing annual financial reports with state regulators and the Internal Revenue Service. Insurers outside the United States use standards that differ from SAP and GAAP. Some insurers support a move toward uniform global standards. The P/C industry's GAAP rate of return in 2013 was 9.0 percent, up from 5.3 percent in 2012.

ANNUAL RATE OF RETURN:
NET INCOME AFTER TAXES AS A PERCENT OF EQUITY, 2004-2013

Year	Property/casualty[1]		Life/health		Selected other industries[2]			Fortune 500 combined industrials and service[8]
	Statutory accounting[3]	GAAP accounting[4]	Life/health insurance[5]	Healthcare insurance[6]	Diversified financial[7]	Commercial banks	Electric and gas utilities	
2004	10.4%	9.4%	11.0%	NA	15.0%	15.5%	10.5%	13.9%
2005	10.8	9.6	13.0	16.2%	15.0	16.0	10.0	14.9
2006	14.4	12.7	12.0	19.0	15.0	15.0	11.0	15.4
2007	12.4	10.9	11.0	19.0	-1.0	11.0	11.0	15.2
2008	0.6	0.1	1.0	11.0	8.0	3.0	13.0	13.1
2009	5.9	5.0	4.0	14.0	9.0	4.0	9.0	10.5
2010	6.6	5.6	7.0	12.0	10.0	8.0	10.0	12.7
2011	3.5	3.0	8.0	15.0	12.0	8.0	10.0	14.5
2012	6.1	5.3	7.0	12.0	18.0	9.0	8.0	15.0
2013	10.3	9.0	7.0	13.0	18.0	9.0	9.0	13.7

[1]Excludes state funds for workers compensation and other residual market carriers.
[2]Return on equity on a GAAP accounting basis, Fortune.
[3]Statutory net income after taxes, divided by the average of current and prior year-end policyholders' surplus. Calculated by ISO. Statutory accounting is used by insurers when preparing the Annual Statements they submit to regulators.
[4]Estimated from statutory data. Equals GAAP net income divided by the average of current and prior year-end GAAP net worth. Calculated by ISO.
[5]Return on equity on a GAAP accounting basis, Fortune. Combined stock and mutual companies, calculated by the Insurance Information Institute.
[6]Healthcare insurance and managed care.
[7]Companies whose major source of revenue comes from providing diversified financial services. These companies are not specifically chartered as insurance companies, banks or savings institutions, or brokerage or securities companies, but they may earn revenue from these sources.
[8]Fortune 500 Combined Industrial and Service Businesses median return on shareholders' equity.
NA=Data not available.

Source: ISO®, a Verisk Analytics® company; Fortune.

Property/Casualty Insurance Cycle

Most industries are cyclical to some extent. The property/casualty (P/C) insurance industry cycle is characterized by periods of soft market conditions, in which premium rates are stable or falling and insurance is readily available, and by periods of hard market conditions, where rates rise, coverage may be more difficult to find and insurers' profits increase.

A dominant factor in the P/C insurance cycle is intense competition within the industry. Premium rates drop as insurance companies compete vigorously to increase market share. As the market softens to the point that profits diminish or vanish completely, the capital needed to underwrite new business is depleted. In the up phase of the cycle, competition is less intense, underwriting standards become more stringent, the supply of insurance is limited due to the depletion of capital and, as a result, premiums rise. The prospect of higher profits draws more capital into the marketplace, leading to more competition and the inevitable down phase of the cycle.

The chart below shows the real, or inflation-adjusted, growth of P/C net premiums written over more than three decades and three hard markets. Premiums can be accounted for in several ways. This chart uses net premiums written, which reflect premium amounts after deductions for reinsurance transactions.

During the last three hard markets, inflation-adjusted net premiums written grew 7.7 percent (1975 to 1978), 10.0 percent (1984 to 1987) and 6.3 percent (2001 to 2004).

PERCENT CHANGE FROM PRIOR YEAR, NET PREMIUMS WRITTEN, P/C INSURANCE, 1975-2013[1]

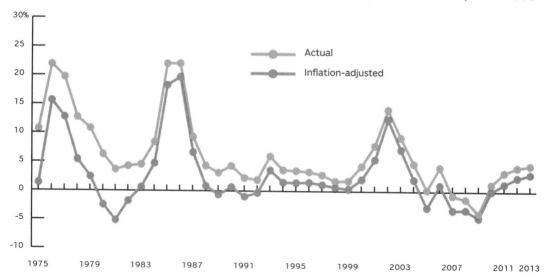

[1]Excludes state funds.

Source: ISO®, a Verisk Analytics® company.

Operating Results

In many years the insurance industry does not generate profits from its underwriting operations. Investment income from a number of sources—including capital and surplus accounts, money set aside as loss reserves and unearned premium reserves—generally offsets these losses. Underwriting results were favorable in 2004, 2006, 2007 and 2009, according to SNL Financial. The industry posted underwriting losses in 2010 through 2012, including 2011's $35.3 billion loss, the largest since 2001's $50.3 billion loss. Results for 2013 show an underwriting gain of $17.5 billion, the most favorable since 2007's $21.6 billion gain.

OPERATING RESULTS, PROPERTY/CASUALTY INSURANCE, 2004-2013[1]
($ millions)

Year	Net underwriting gain/loss	Net investment income earned	Net realized capital gain/loss	Policyholder dividends	Taxes[2]	Net income after taxes[3]
2004	$5,558	$40,383	$9,070	$1,818	$14,575	$38,342
2005	-3,152	49,960	11,933	1,974	10,642	47,198
2006	34,753	55,719	3,670	3,611	22,651	67,479
2007	21,637	56,320	8,817	2,814	19,857	63,138
2008	-19,810	53,430	-19,609	2,211	7,730	4,446
2009	1,579	48,640	-7,895	2,141	8,481	32,492
2010	-8,422	48,833	8,003	2,709	8,951	37,716
2011	-35,305	51,000	6,891	2,315	3,026	19,532
2012	-13,827	49,605	8,525	2,656	6,267	37,565
2013	17,537	48,781	17,194	3,017	11,949	70,047

[1]Excludes state funds. [2]Includes federal and foreign taxes. [3]Does not equal the sum of the columns shown due to the omission of miscellaneous income.
Source: SNL Financial LC.

OPERATING RESULTS, PROPERTY/CASUALTY INSURANCE, 2004-2013[1]
($ billions)

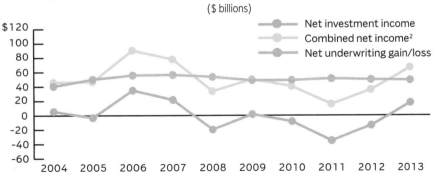

[1]Excludes state funds. [2]Net underwriting gain/loss plus net investment income.
Source: SNL Financial LC.

Policyholders' Surplus

A property/casualty insurer must maintain a certain level of surplus to underwrite risks. This financial cushion is known as "capacity". When the industry is hit by high losses, such as a major hurricane, capacity is diminished. It can be restored by increases in net income, favorable investment returns, reinsuring more risk and/or raising additional capital.

CONSOLIDATED ASSETS AND POLICYHOLDERS' SURPLUS, P/C INSURANCE, 2004-2013
($ millions)

Year	Net admitted assets	Annual percent change	Statutory liabilities	Annual percent change	Policyholders' surplus	Annual percent change	Total net premiums written[1]	Annual percent change
2004	$1,300,814	9.0%	$897,083	7.5%	$403,733	12.4%	$427,197	4.4%
2005	1,386,853	6.6	951,719	6.1	435,135	7.8	426,671	-0.1
2006	1,549,509	11.7	1,045,931	9.9	503,578	15.7	448,967	5.2
2007	1,468,776	-5.2	940,758	-10.1	528,016	4.9	446,378	-0.6
2008	1,405,742	-4.3	943,732	0.3	462,006	-12.5	440,681	-1.3
2009	1,456,852	3.6	936,261	-0.8	520,591	12.7	423,545	-3.9
2010	1,514,190	3.9	947,390	1.2	566,800	8.9	426,380	0.7
2011	1,537,222	1.5	974,699	2.9	562,522	-0.8	441,925	3.6
2012	1,594,419	3.7	996,473	2.2	597,946	6.3	460,930	4.3
2013	1,682,073	5.5	1,014,652	1.8	667,420	11.6	481,506	4.5

[1]After reinsurance transactions, excludes state funds. May not match total premiums written shown elsewhere in this book because of the use of different exhibits from SNL Financial.

Source: SNL Financial LC.

- Policyholders' surplus dropped substantially in 2008, reflecting the deterioration in global financial markets.

- Policyholders' surplus reached a record $667.4 billion in 2013, rising 11.6 percent from 2012.

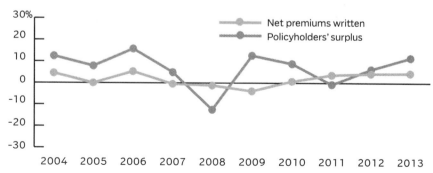

PERCENT CHANGE FROM PRIOR YEAR, NET PREMIUMS WRITTEN AND POLICYHOLDERS' SURPLUS, P/C INSURANCE, 2004-2013[1]

[1]After reinsurance transactions, excludes state funds.

Source: SNL Financial LC.

The Combined Ratio

The combined ratio represents the percentage of each premium dollar an insurer spends on claims and expenses. The following chart shows the components of the combined ratio, a measure of the industry's underwriting performance.

The combined ratio is the sum of the loss ratio and the expense ratio. The loss ratio expresses the relationship between losses and premiums in percentage terms. The expense ratio expresses the relationship between underwriting expenses and premiums.

COMPONENTS OF THE COMBINED RATIO, PROPERTY/CASUALTY INSURANCE, 2004-2013[1]

Year	Loss ratio[2]	Expense ratio[3]	Combined ratio	Dividends to policyholders[4]	Combined ratio after dividends
2004	72.7	25.2	97.9	0.4	98.3
2005	74.6	25.8	100.4	0.4	100.9
2006	65.2	26.4	91.6	0.8	92.4
2007	67.7	27.3	94.9	0.6	95.5
2008	77.1	27.5	104.6	0.4	105.0
2009	72.5	28.0	100.5	0.5	101.0
2010	73.6	28.3	101.8	0.5	102.4
2011	79.3	28.4	107.7	0.4	108.1
2012	74.2	28.2	102.5	0.5	102.9
2013	67.3	28.2	95.6	0.5	96.1

[1]Excludes state funds and other residual insurers.
[2]Incurred loss and loss adjustment expenses as a percent of earned premiums.
[3]Other underwriting expenses as a percent of written premiums.
[4]Dividends to policyholders as a percent of earned premiums.

Source: ISO®, a Verisk Analytics® company.

PROPERTY/CASUALTY INSURANCE COMBINED RATIO, 1975-2013[1]

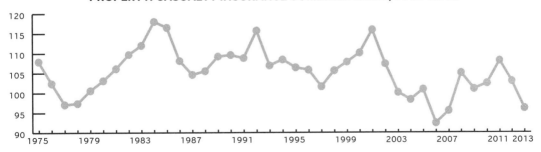

[1]Excludes state funds and other residual insurers.

Source: ISO®, a Verisk Analytics® company.

Property/Casualty Financial Data

Cash and invested assets of property/casualty insurance companies totaled $1.48 trillion in 2013. This represents 84 percent of total assets, which were $1.74 trillion. Most of these assets were invested in highly liquid securities (high-quality stocks and bonds, for example, rather than real estate), which can be sold quickly to pay claims in the event of a major catastrophe.

INVESTMENTS, PROPERTY/CASUALTY INSURERS, 2011-2013[1]

($ millions, end of year)

Investment type	Amount			Percent of total investments		
	2011	2012	2013	2011	2012	2013
Bonds	$902,533	$907,509	$926,335	67.26%	65.34%	62.55%
Stocks	238,873	266,063	327,849	17.80	19.16	22.14
Preferred	11,619	11,930	11,537	0.87	0.86	0.78
Common	227,254	254,133	316,312	16.94	18.30	21.36
Mortgage loans on real estate	4,969	5,682	7,985	0.37	0.41	0.54
First liens	4,767	5,428	7,778	0.36	0.39	0.53
Other than first liens	202	254	207	0.02	0.02	0.01
Real estate	10,374	10,387	9,953	0.77	0.75	0.67
Properties occupied by company	8,905	8,961	8,462	0.66	0.65	0.57
Properties held for income production	1,216	1,228	1,249	0.09	0.09	0.08
Properties held for sale	252	198	243	0.02	0.01	0.02
Cash, cash equivalent and short-term investments	72,608	82,612	83,612	5.41	5.95	5.65
Derivatives	649	592	578	0.05	0.04	0.04
Other invested assets	104,204	108,584	117,588	7.77	7.82	7.94
Receivable for securities	1,529	960	1,485	0.11	0.07	0.10
Securities lending reinvested collateral assets	2,628	2,640	2,637	0.20	0.19	0.18
Aggregate write-in for invested assets	3,568	4,006	2,934	0.27	0.29	0.20
Total cash and invested assets	**$1,341,904**	**$1,388,998**	**$1,480,955**	**100.00%**	**100.00%**	**100.00%**

[1]Includes cash and net admitted assets of property/casualty insurers.

Source: SNL Financial LC.

Bonds

Property/casualty insurers invest primarily in safe, liquid securities, mainly bonds. These provide stability against underwriting results, which can vary considerably from year to year. The vast majority of bonds are government-issued or are high-grade corporates. Bonds in or near default accounted for less than 1 percent (0.16 percent) of all short- and long-term bonds owned by insurers at the end of 2013, according to SNL Financial.

INVESTMENTS, PROPERTY/CASUALTY INSURERS, 2013

INVESTMENTS BY TYPE[1]

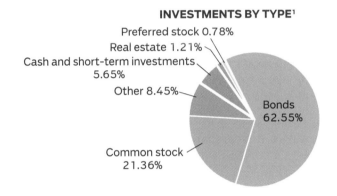

Preferred stock 0.78%
Real estate 1.21%
Cash and short-term investments 5.65%
Other 8.45%
Bonds 62.55%
Common stock 21.36%

BOND PORTFOLIO
(Represents 62.6% of total investments)

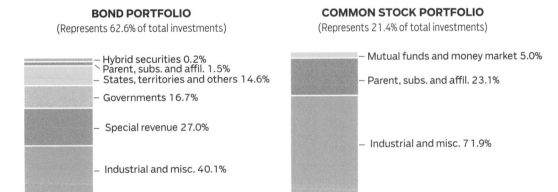

- Hybrid securities 0.2%
- Parent, subs. and affil. 1.5%
- States, territories and others 14.6%
- Governments 16.7%
- Special revenue 27.0%
- Industrial and misc. 40.1%

COMMON STOCK PORTFOLIO
(Represents 21.4% of total investments)

- Mutual funds and money market 5.0%
- Parent, subs. and affil. 23.1%
- Industrial and misc. 71.9%

[1]Cash and invested net admitted assets, as of December 31, 2013.
Source: SNL Financial LC.

Surplus Lines

The surplus lines market exists to assume risks that licensed companies decline to insure or will only insure at a very high price, with many exclusions or with a very high deductible. To be eligible to seek coverage in the surplus lines market, a diligent effort must have been made to place insurance with an admitted company, usually defined by a certain number of "declinations," or rejections, by licensed insurers, typically three to five. Many states provide an "export list" of risks that can be insured in the surplus lines market. This obviates the diligent search requirement.

The terms applied to the surplus lines market—nonadmitted, unlicensed and unauthorized—do not mean that surplus lines companies are barred from selling insurance in a state or are unregulated. They are just less regulated. Each state has surplus lines regulations and each surplus lines company is overseen for solvency by its home state. More than half of the states maintain a list of eligible surplus lines companies and some a list of those that are not eligible to do business in that state.

In a number of states, surplus lines companies are also monitored by surplus lines organizations, known as "Stamping Offices," which assist their state's department of insurance in the regulation and oversight of surplus lines insurers. They also evaluate insurers for eligibility to do business in the state and review insurance policies obtained by surplus lines agents or brokers for their clients. Surplus lines companies thrive in hard markets, when certain kinds of coverages may be more difficult to obtain.

The 2010 Dodd-Frank Wall Street and Consumer Protection Act streamlines the regulation of surplus lines insurance through state-based reforms, including a requirement that multistate transactions be subject to regulatory oversight by a single state, the home state of the insured.

GROSS SURPLUS LINES PREMIUMS WRITTEN, 2009-2013
($ billions)

- Surplus lines gross premiums rose 18.6 percent in 2013, after falling 2.9 percent the previous year.

- At $10.36 billion in 2013, nonadmitted direct premiums written for the top ten surplus lines insurers rose 12.2 percent from 2012.

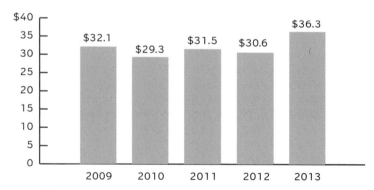

Year	2009	2010	2011	2012	2013
$ billions	$32.1	$29.3	$31.5	$30.6	$36.3

Source: 2011 to 2013 premiums from Business Insurance, September 15, 2014; earlier premiums from other issues.

TOP TEN U.S.-BASED SURPLUS LINES INSURANCE COMPANIES BY NONADMITTED DIRECT PREMIUMS WRITTEN, 2013

Rank	Company	Parent	Nonadmitted direct premiums
1	Lexington Insurance Co.	American International Group Inc.	$4,024,535,033
2	Scottsdale Insurance Co.	Nationwide Mutual Insurance Co.	3,430,759,927
3	Steadfast Insurance Co.	Zurich Insurance Group Ltd.	1,088,634,478
4	AIG Specialty Insurance Co.	American International Group Inc.	834,809,707
5	Columbia Casualty Co.	CNA Financial Corp.	809,356,487
6	Landmark American Insurance Co.	Alleghany Corp.	573,553,537
7	Westchester Surplus Lines Insurance Co.	Ace Ltd.	532,172,687
8	Arch Specialty Insurance Co.	Arch Capital Group Ltd.	515,913,985
9	Nautilus Insurance Co.	W.R. Berkley Corp.	488,329,279
10	Illinois Union Insurance Co.	Ace Ltd.	454,670,860

Source: Business Insurance, September 15, 2014.

Concentration

According to ISO, concentration in the property/casualty insurance sector as measured by the Herfindahl-Hirschman Index increased from 229 in 1980 to 357 in 2008, and then fell, albeit irregularly, to 343 in 2013. The U.S. Department of Justice classifies any market with an HHI under 1,500 as unconcentrated and any market with an HHI over 2,500 as highly concentrated.

MARKET SHARE TRENDS BY SIZE OF INSURER, 1993-2013[1]

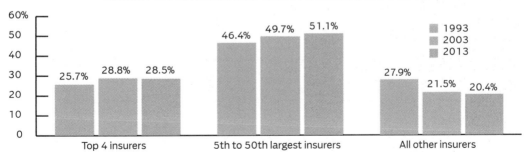

¹Based on net premiums written. Excludes state funds and other residual market carriers.

Source: ISO®, a Verisk Analytics® company.

Property/Casualty Financial Data

Reinsurance

Reinsurance protects primary insurers against unforeseen losses.

NET PREMIUMS WRITTEN, MAJOR U.S. PROPERTY/CASUALTY REINSURERS, 2004-2013[1]
($000)

Year	Net premiums written	Annual percent change	Combined ratio[2]	Annual point change
2004	$28,759,085	-6.1%	106.2	5.0 pts.
2005	25,330,697	-11.9	129.4	23.2
2006	25,834,026	2.0	94.9	-34.5
2007	22,711,994	-12.1	94.7	-0.2
2008	23,920,333	5.3	101.8	7.1
2009	23,906,150	-0.1	93.5	-8.3
2010	23,305,291	-2.5	95.4	1.9
2011	26,390,657	13.2	107.2	11.8
2012	29,481,444	11.7	96.2	-11.0
2013	26,843,064	-8.9	86.8	-9.4

[1]Based on reinsurance companies responding to quarterly surveys conducted by the Reinsurance Association of America.
[2]After dividends to policyholders.

Source: Reinsurance Association of America.

TOP TEN U.S. PROPERTY/CASUALTY REINSURERS OF U.S. BUSINESS BY GROSS PREMIUMS WRITTEN, 2013
($000)

Rank	Company[1]	Country of parent company	Gross premiums written
1	QBE North America	Australia	$5,896,257
2	National Indemnity Company (Berkshire Hathaway)[2]	U.S.	5,494,058
3	Swiss Reinsurance America Corporation	Switzerland	4,941,108
4	Everest Reinsurance Company	Bermuda	4,348,736
5	Munich Re America, Corp.	Germany	4,267,168
6	XL Reinsurance America	Ireland	3,380,109
7	Transatlantic Reinsurance	U.S.	3,138,346
8	Odyssey Reinsurance Group	Canada	2,539,263
9	Partner Reinsurance Company of the U.S.	Bermuda	1,623,083
10	General Re Group	U.S.	1,206,713

[1]See Reinsurance Underwriting Report footnotes posted at www.reinsurance.org for list of affiliated companies included.
[2]Underwriting results exclude assumptions from affiliated General Re Group.

Source: Reinsurance Association of America.

Direct Premiums Written by State

Direct premiums written represent premium amounts before reinsurance transactions. This contrasts with charts based on net premiums written, i.e., premium amounts after reinsurance transactions.

DIRECT PREMIUMS WRITTEN, P/C INSURANCE BY STATE, 2013[1]
($000)

State	Total, all lines	State	Total, all lines
Alabama	$7,308,160	Montana	$2,098,309
Alaska	1,733,447	Nebraska	4,237,103
Arizona	8,639,181	Nevada	4,050,432
Arkansas	4,488,889	New Hampshire	2,131,824
California	61,708,000	New Jersey	18,982,651
Colorado	9,260,041	New Mexico	2,865,535
Connecticut	7,697,195	New York	40,175,905
Delaware	2,139,027	North Dakota	2,568,181
D.C.	1,668,117	North Carolina	13,229,797
Florida	41,400,669	Ohio	14,486,203
Georgia	15,039,745	Oklahoma	7,439,138
Hawaii	2,183,003	Oregon	5,668,210
Idaho	2,201,377	Pennsylvania	21,586,269
Illinois	22,218,661	Rhode Island	2,024,660
Indiana	9,782,372	South Carolina	7,516,298
Iowa	6,019,009	South Dakota	2,319,233
Kansas	5,988,291	Tennessee	9,955,458
Kentucky	6,476,885	Texas	44,525,832
Louisiana	10,400,932	Utah	3,648,017
Maine	1,969,640	Vermont	1,382,455
Maryland	9,952,664	Virginia	11,768,965
Massachusetts	12,629,616	Washington	9,697,873
Michigan	16,563,175	West Virginia	2,832,651
Minnesota	10,237,095	Wisconsin	9,141,331
Mississippi	4,586,377	Wyoming	1,038,812
Missouri	9,842,171	**United States**	**$537,504,881**

[1]Before reinsurance transactions, includes some state funds, excludes territories.

Source: SNL Financial LC.

- In 2013 California accounted for the largest amount of direct premiums written, followed by Texas, Florida, New York and Illinois.

- Among the states with the most premiums, Florida experienced the highest increase in 2013 (15.6 percent), followed by New York, with a 14.1 percent increase. Premiums rose 10.8 percent in Texas, 9.8 percent in California and 4.7 percent in Illinois.

- Nationally, direct premiums written rose 9.2 percent in 2013.

Property/Casualty Financial Data

Incurred Losses by State

Property/casualty insurers pay out billions of dollars each year to settle claims. Many of the payments go to businesses, such as auto repair companies, that help claimants get their lives back together after an accident, fire, windstorm or other incident that caused the injury or property damage. Insurance claim payments support local businesses, enabling them to provide jobs and pay taxes that support the local economy. When property/casualty insurance claims are paid, funds flow to the industries that supply claimants with the goods and services necessary for their recovery. The chart below shows incurred losses, i.e., losses occurring during a fixed period, whether or not adjusted or paid during the same period.

INCURRED LOSSES BY STATE, PROPERTY/CASUALTY INSURANCE, 2013[1]

($000)

State	Incurred losses	State	Incurred losses	State	Incurred losses
Alabama	$3,685,353	Louisiana	$5,380,059	Oklahoma	$6,191,936
Alaska	641,849	Maine	982,581	Oregon	2,890,355
Arizona	4,590,840	Maryland	5,612,042	Pennsylvania	11,309,632
Arkansas	2,441,582	Massachusetts	6,070,072	Rhode Island	1,080,667
California	33,523,386	Michigan	13,549,259	South Carolina	3,627,063
Colorado	6,302,530	Minnesota	6,683,611	South Dakota	1,418,869
Connecticut	4,145,000	Mississippi	3,368,013	Tennessee	5,004,379
Delaware	862,153	Missouri	5,302,132	Texas	23,707,903
D.C.	781,702	Montana	1,119,300	Utah	1,983,285
Florida	17,340,381	Nebraska	3,069,914	Vermont	569,684
Georgia	9,051,085	Nevada	2,513,240	Virginia	5,654,725
Hawaii	867,650	New Hampshire	1,064,743	Washington	4,953,601
Idaho	1,175,380	New Jersey	11,433,517	West Virginia	1,283,262
Illinois	13,768,320	New Mexico	1,814,606	Wisconsin	5,387,638
Indiana	5,637,923	New York	18,993,882	Wyoming	533,975
Iowa	4,300,199	North Carolina	6,561,521		
Kansas	3,869,263	North Dakota	1,827,533		
Kentucky	3,239,711	Ohio	7,100,686	**United States**	**$294,267,995**

[1]Losses occurring within a fixed period whether or not adjusted or paid during the same period, on a direct basis before reinsurance.

Source: SNL Financial LC.

Guaranty Funds

All 50 states; Washington, D.C.; Puerto Rico; and the Virgin Islands have procedures under which solvent property/casualty insurance companies cover claims against insolvent insurers. New York has a pre-assessment system, under which estimates are made annually of how much will be needed in the coming year to fulfill the system's obligations to pay the claims of insolvent insurers. Some states—including New Jersey, New York and Pennsylvania—have separate pre-assessment funds for workers compensation. Florida has a post-assessment fund, which covers the claims of insolvent workers compensation insurers and self-insurers.

The property/casualty lines of insurance covered by guaranty funds and the maximum amount paid on any claim vary from state to state. Assessments are used to pay claims against companies that became insolvent in the past as well as for current insolvencies. A similar system for life and health insurers is coordinated by the National Organization of Life and Health Insurance Guaranty Associations.

PROPERTY/CASUALTY GUARANTY FUND NET ASSESSMENTS, 2004-2013

Year	Net assessments[1]
2004	$952,695,278
2005	836,130,812
2006[2]	1,344,487,899
2007	943,164,094
2008	368,451,899
2009	523,609,705
2010	171,159,059
2011	281,991,694
2012[3]	311,694,359
2013	455,103,717
Total, inception-2013[4]	**$15,670,865,205**

[1]Assessments less refunds and abatements (cancellations of uncalled portions of assessments when funds on hand are sufficient to pay claims).
[2]Includes New York and New York Workers Compensation after 2005.
[3]Includes Arizona Workers Compensation after 2011.
[4]Includes pre-1978 net assessments.

Source: National Conference of Insurance Guaranty Funds.

- At $455 million, guaranty fund net assessments in 2013 were up 46 percent from $312 million in 2012.

- Net assessments in 2013 were at their highest level since 2009, when they totaled $524 million.

PROPERTY/CASUALTY GUARANTY FUND NET ASSESSMENTS BY STATE, 2013

State	Net assessments[1]	State	Net assessments[1]
Alabama	$6,707,409	Montana	0
Alaska	2,913,577	Nebraska	0
Arizona	0	Nevada	0
Arkansas	0	New Hampshire	0
California	175,326,075	New Jersey	$143,489,979
Colorado	0	New Mexico	0
Connecticut	10,869,353	New York	0
Delaware	0	North Carolina	2,650,000
D.C.	1,500,000	North Dakota	0
Florida	0	Ohio	0
Georgia	0	Oklahoma	13,100,000
Hawaii	35,817,559	Oregon	0
Idaho	0	Pennsylvania	-75,000
Illinois	41,300,000	Rhode Island	-1,827,139
Indiana	0	South Carolina	0
Iowa	0	South Dakota	798,830
Kansas	0	Tennessee	0
Kentucky	1,580,000	Texas	0
Louisiana	0	Utah	0
Maine	-605,268	Vermont	1,000,000
Maryland	0	Virginia	0
Massachusetts	20,000,000	Washington	558,342
Michigan	0	West Virginia	0
Minnesota	0	Wisconsin	0
Mississippi	0	Wyoming	0
Missouri	0	**United States**	**$455,103,717**

[1]Assessments less refunds and abatements (cancellations of uncalled portions of assessments when funds on hand are sufficient to pay claims). Negative numbers represent net refunds.

Source: National Conference of Insurance Guaranty Funds.

Premiums by Line

Premiums can be accounted for in two major ways: net premiums written, which reflect premium amounts after deductions for reinsurance, and direct premiums written, which are calculated before reinsurance transactions.

PREMIUMS WRITTEN BY LINE, PROPERTY/CASUALTY INSURANCE, 2013

($ billions)

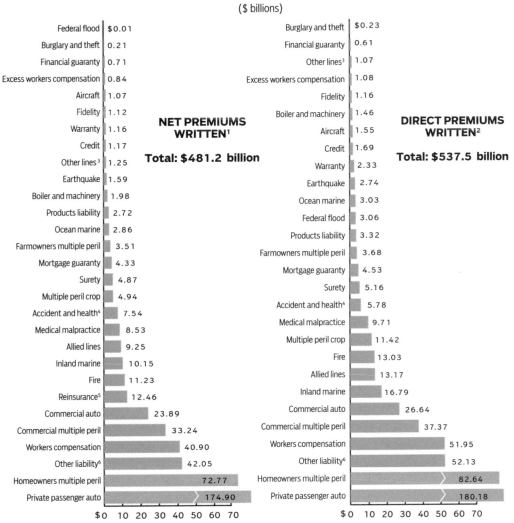

NET PREMIUMS WRITTEN[1]

Total: $481.2 billion

Line	$ billions
Federal flood	$0.01
Burglary and theft	0.21
Financial guaranty	0.71
Excess workers compensation	0.84
Aircraft	1.07
Fidelity	1.12
Warranty	1.16
Credit	1.17
Other lines[3]	1.25
Earthquake	1.59
Boiler and machinery	1.98
Products liability	2.72
Ocean marine	2.86
Farmowners multiple peril	3.51
Mortgage guaranty	4.33
Surety	4.87
Multiple peril crop	4.94
Accident and health[4]	7.54
Medical malpractice	8.53
Allied lines	9.25
Inland marine	10.15
Fire	11.23
Reinsurance[5]	12.46
Commercial auto	23.89
Commercial multiple peril	33.24
Workers compensation	40.90
Other liability[6]	42.05
Homeowners multiple peril	72.77
Private passenger auto	174.90

DIRECT PREMIUMS WRITTEN[2]

Total: $537.5 billion

Line	$ billions
Burglary and theft	$0.23
Financial guaranty	0.61
Other lines[3]	1.07
Excess workers compensation	1.08
Fidelity	1.16
Boiler and machinery	1.46
Aircraft	1.55
Credit	1.69
Warranty	2.33
Earthquake	2.74
Ocean marine	3.03
Federal flood	3.06
Products liability	3.32
Farmowners multiple peril	3.68
Mortgage guaranty	4.53
Surety	5.16
Accident and health[4]	5.78
Medical malpractice	9.71
Multiple peril crop	11.42
Fire	13.03
Allied lines	13.17
Inland marine	16.79
Commercial auto	26.64
Commercial multiple peril	37.37
Workers compensation	51.95
Other liability[6]	52.13
Homeowners multiple peril	82.64
Private passenger auto	180.18

[1]After reinsurance transactions, excludes state funds. [2]Before reinsurance transactions, includes some state funds. [3]Includes international and miscellaneous coverages. [4]Premiums from certain insurers that write health insurance but file financial statements with state regulators on a property/casualty rather than life/health basis. [5]Only includes nonproportional reinsurance, an arrangement in which a reinsurer makes payments to an insurer whose losses exceed a predetermined amount. [6]Coverages protecting against legal liability resulting from negligence, carelessness or failure to act.

Source: SNL Financial LC.

Property/Casualty Insurance by Line

Premiums

Personal vs. Commercial

The property/casualty (P/C) insurance industry is divided into two main segments: personal lines and commercial lines. Personal lines include coverage for individuals, mainly auto and homeowners. Commercial lines includes the many kinds of insurance products designed for businesses. In 2013 private passenger auto insurance was the largest line of insurance, based on net premiums written, making up 36 percent of all P/C insurance (commercial and personal combined) and 71 percent of personal insurance. Homeowners multiple peril insurance is the second largest line. Other liability is the largest commercial line and third-largest P/C line. It accounted for 9 percent of all P/C net premiums and 18 percent of all commercial premiums.

NET PREMIUMS WRITTEN, PERSONAL AND COMMERCIAL LINES, 2013

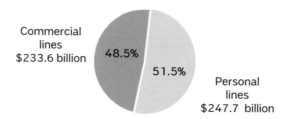

Commercial lines $233.6 billion — 48.5%

51.5% — Personal lines $247.7 billion

Source: SNL Financial LC.

NET PREMIUMS WRITTEN BY LINE, PROPERTY/CASUALTY INSURANCE, 2011-2013[1]
($ millions)

Lines of insurance	2011	2012	2013	Percentage change from prior year			Percent of total, 2013
				2011	2012	2013	
Private passenger auto	$163,317.7	$168,049.3	$174,898.0	1.9%	2.9%	4.1%	36.3%
Liability	100,369.4	103,429.7	107,446.4	2.8	3.0	3.9	22.3
Collision and comprehensive	62,948.3	64,619.7	67,451.6	0.6	2.7	4.4	14.0
Commercial auto	21,029.5	22,084.0	23,889.5	-0.4	5.0	8.2	5.0
Liability	16,382.1	16,984.6	18,353.3	0.8	3.7	8.1	3.8
Collision and comprehensive	4,647.4	5,099.4	5,536.2	-4.6	9.7	8.6	1.2
Fire	10,318.0	10,795.6	11,229.4	1.2	4.6	4.0	2.3
Allied lines	7,800.2	8,161.3	9,250.5	4.1	4.6	13.3	1.9
Multiple peril crop	5,457.0	5,321.8	4,942.5	55.8	-2.5	-7.1	1.0
Federal flood[2]	23.9	0.4	5.1	288.9	-98.2	1,110.4	[3]
Farmowners multiple peril	2,932.6	3,277.4	3,511.7	6.4	11.8	7.1	0.7
Homeowners multiple peril	64,131.1	67,847.0	72,773.2	4.0	5.8	7.3	15.1

(table continues)

NET PREMIUMS WRITTEN BY LINE, PROPERTY/CASUALTY INSURANCE, 2011-2013[1] (Cont'd)
($ millions)

Lines of insurance	2011	2012	2013	Percentage change from prior year			Percent of total, 2013
				2011	2012	2013	
Commercial multiple peril	$29,995.2	$31,502.7	$33,244.7	3.7%	5.0%	5.5%	6.9%
Mortgage guaranty	4,242.3	3,965.9	4,329.9	-0.2	-6.5	9.2	0.9
Ocean marine	2,760.9	2,704.7	2,863.5	0.7	-2.0	5.9	0.6
Inland marine	8,768.8	9,603.7	10,147.0	2.8	9.5	5.7	2.1
Financial guaranty	968.9	692.5	710.5	-29.4	-28.5	2.6	0.1
Medical malpractice	8,833.4	8,713.6	8,530.8	-2.9	-1.4	-2.1	1.8
Earthquake	1,467.4	1,593.5	1,587.0	1.6	8.6	-0.4	0.3
Accident and health[4]	7,685.8	7,941.1	7,538.6	2.4	3.3	-5.1	1.6
Workers compensation	35,664.2	38,747.6	40,897.0	12.7	8.6	5.5	8.5
Excess workers compensation	816.4	815.8	844.1	2.1	-0.1	3.5	0.2
Products liability	2,320.5	2,575.2	2,718.9	13.2	11.0	5.6	0.6
Other liability[5]	36,511.6	38,307.7	42,053.1	2.0	4.9	9.8	8.7
Aircraft	1,121.9	1,160.5	1,067.7	1.7	3.4	-8.0	0.2
Fidelity	1,098.2	1,096.4	1,124.2	1.4	-0.2	2.5	0.2
Surety	4,849.5	4,695.8	4,868.8	[3]	-3.2	3.7	1.0
Burglary and theft	194.7	220.8	205.2	16.5	13.4	-7.1	[3]
Boiler and machinery	1,810.9	1,887.6	1,979.5	5.2	4.2	4.9	0.4
Credit	1,490.1	1,457.8	1,167.3	10.8	-2.2	-19.9	0.2
Warranty	1,695.8	1,386.4	1,155.3	-9.0	-18.2	-16.7	0.2
International	92.8	105.8	113.2	-28.6	14.0	6.9	[3]
Reinsurance[6]	13,192.7	14,673.9	12,458.6	15.5	11.2	-15.1	2.6
Other lines[7]	970.2	1,100.2	1,132.4	-7.1	13.4	2.9	0.2
Total, all lines[8]	**$441,562.2**	**$460,486.3**	**$481,237.5**	**3.7%**	**4.3%**	**4.5%**	**100.0%**

[1]After reinsurance transactions, excludes state funds.
[2]Provided by FEMA through participating private insurers.
[3]Less than 0.1 percent.
[4]Premiums from certain insurers that write health insurance but file financial statements with state regulators on a property/casualty basis.
[5]Coverages protecting against legal liability resulting from negligence, carelessness or failure to act.
[6]Only includes nonproportional reinsurance, an arrangement in which a reinsurer makes payments to an insurer whose losses exceed a predetermined amount.
[7]Includes miscellaneous coverages.
[8]May not match total premiums shown elsewhere in this book because of the use of different exhibits from SNL Financial LC.

Source: SNL Financial LC.

DIRECT PREMIUMS WRITTEN, PROPERTY/CASUALTY INSURANCE BY STATE BY LINE, 2013[1]

($000)

State	Private passenger auto		Commercial auto		Homeowners multiple peril
	Liability	Coll./comp.	Liability	Coll./comp.	
Alabama	$1,382,538	$1,144,386	$286,498	$99,067	$1,562,262
Alaska	271,175	169,103	50,172	12,871	151,242
Arizona	2,130,707	1,430,971	302,538	80,408	1,358,032
Arkansas	843,981	704,744	212,257	86,748	802,904
California	11,717,827	8,727,151	2,032,561	572,838	7,063,964
Colorado	1,850,982	1,225,919	292,894	106,290	1,718,348
Connecticut	1,580,982	942,561	287,042	66,319	1,308,798
Delaware	498,698	206,026	80,624	15,292	218,163
D.C.	151,678	131,379	35,420	5,855	141,236
Florida	10,724,756	3,403,537	1,410,956	277,185	8,767,373
Georgia	3,476,892	2,346,569	602,370	160,843	2,523,811
Hawaii	395,378	247,146	76,500	18,909	343,324
Idaho	419,316	282,105	92,896	40,649	285,492
Illinois	3,433,135	2,593,897	813,958	249,183	3,178,473
Indiana	1,722,694	1,246,999	406,962	160,669	1,689,748
Iowa	718,888	708,415	209,596	123,925	668,441
Kansas	784,728	744,036	162,534	102,163	983,897
Kentucky	1,657,100	808,690	261,558	87,329	1,019,402
Louisiana	2,199,650	1,301,722	490,763	101,410	1,751,444
Maine	342,775	270,854	84,395	34,008	367,093
Maryland	2,423,554	1,571,987	368,574	95,369	1,483,926
Massachusetts	2,516,123	1,800,633	523,198	163,764	1,982,175
Michigan	4,744,678	2,565,328	530,679	231,458	2,462,970
Minnesota	1,734,652	1,229,567	318,338	148,545	1,833,837
Mississippi	839,234	666,430	221,317	72,785	890,363
Missouri	1,709,708	1,341,933	366,171	144,928	1,744,794
Montana	323,292	260,683	89,939	47,915	255,709
Nebraska	533,398	454,502	127,653	85,041	552,724
Nevada	1,196,984	541,089	174,168	29,577	478,455
New Hampshire	373,156	329,993	81,148	28,547	362,358
New Jersey	4,780,764	2,043,503	935,364	164,129	2,391,724
New Mexico	709,084	411,493	125,056	41,185	450,539
New York	7,399,166	3,712,963	1,710,488	279,942	4,925,004
North Carolina	2,658,587	2,062,315	490,652	149,030	2,180,304
North Dakota	188,433	222,063	82,640	67,623	174,569
Ohio	3,070,782	2,377,986	581,724	200,150	2,561,189
Oklahoma	1,246,528	948,145	276,622	117,263	1,417,307
Oregon	1,538,872	640,880	214,949	60,068	690,006
Pennsylvania	4,330,058	3,039,025	877,267	317,521	3,054,206
Rhode Island	488,647	236,731	71,615	18,408	341,460
South Carolina	1,768,002	1,079,329	248,141	71,592	1,467,760
South Dakota	210,554	222,496	60,534	42,862	187,668
Tennessee	1,810,240	1,401,494	349,402	149,647	1,743,832
Texas	8,534,212	6,671,322	1,879,218	572,035	7,252,301
Utah	871,931	517,888	160,354	61,501	441,508
Vermont	168,415	153,347	45,711	18,971	177,849
Virginia	2,611,477	1,926,022	428,347	125,889	1,984,298
Washington	2,692,381	1,304,935	375,844	99,971	1,469,817
West Virginia	674,563	481,258	115,561	39,413	397,519
Wisconsin	1,444,072	1,095,042	339,511	141,539	1,226,127
Wyoming	165,175	172,260	54,028	29,989	159,002
United States	**$110,060,603**	**$70,118,853**	**$20,416,706**	**$6,218,618**	**$82,644,747**

[1]Includes some state funds.

Source: SNL Financial LC.

DIRECT PREMIUMS WRITTEN, PROPERTY/CASUALTY INSURANCE BY STATE BY LINE, 2013[1]
($000)

Farmowners multiple peril	Commercial multiple peril	Workers compensation	Excess workers compensation	Medical malpractice	Products liability
$71,113	$569,562	$312,513	$22,235	$132,340	$34,638
537	119,596	294,005	4,059	22,443	6,498
14,769	582,717	760,808	12,401	228,783	36,516
26,018	307,511	265,336	7,004	66,128	19,552
203,008	4,360,717	10,292,655	201,597	742,749	419,862
71,760	683,164	813,919	10,455	159,268	67,930
5,051	612,146	818,171	20,433	151,718	56,341
4,614	313,441	177,789	1,389	37,718	9,791
0	153,550	162,973	1,632	31,720	6,645
22,487	2,101,642	2,326,340	52,341	594,239	175,713
110,852	912,461	1,235,063	36,389	259,893	78,991
409	147,835	216,788	4,377	27,779	7,790
54,733	181,532	324,115	1,490	30,599	10,201
156,701	1,622,166	2,685,243	52,511	542,535	151,249
185,542	774,371	829,907	13,864	117,348	58,663
166,336	349,934	724,799	10,021	67,735	39,058
204,634	368,610	476,799	9,751	64,597	37,141
150,966	485,044	490,834	20,948	122,733	28,779
12,543	519,431	811,745	46,851	103,261	49,201
3,695	208,619	203,522	3,026	43,115	7,276
25,376	605,197	889,650	12,037	248,733	47,478
2,861	1,049,909	1,028,734	25,258	306,806	95,107
132,314	1,010,575	1,140,914	35,642	192,885	87,802
130,259	661,419	880,076	-389	82,142	86,427
21,113	329,909	325,884	13,450	54,935	18,038
151,785	723,492	826,257	25,093	151,904	54,402
60,516	157,334	275,743	8,001	40,562	10,058
183,630	242,392	369,816	5,675	36,602	22,975
7,393	289,085	309,258	17,529	80,841	16,230
2,684	218,398	265,464	3,047	38,482	13,676
2,375	1,379,336	2,210,214	35,985	461,163	205,380
23,888	214,341	272,760	6,863	51,897	11,418
38,249	3,562,364	5,191,492	52,245	1,660,113	220,851
55,560	954,629	1,355,527	24,227	198,713	88,618
101,167	134,713	6,262	1	11,398	16,537
145,519	1,204,466	24,664	71,757	316,925	114,552
134,193	496,846	972,300	22,828	112,385	48,793
61,378	432,844	644,899	12,937	92,246	36,529
95,998	1,644,723	2,578,575	41,183	692,420	156,211
175	149,991	184,406	2,133	42,528	10,643
10,626	453,118	664,830	9,304	64,378	37,496
100,010	123,524	172,361	1,308	16,845	10,343
138,153	649,453	894,711	18,374	239,653	54,229
229,206	2,490,154	2,673,606	34,604	314,394	310,220
11,615	238,953	376,654	4,466	62,187	29,722
13,638	173,215	195,859	1,271	19,165	7,579
68,676	736,801	886,873	21,929	208,218	55,406
66,720	745,197	19,714	26,998	188,761	50,931
12,603	194,871	337,453	4,922	71,868	12,377
155,639	633,497	1,746,795	7,779	84,115	77,386
31,319	93,204	6,143	186	24,303	7,217
$3,680,409	**$37,367,999**	**$51,951,219**	**$1,079,416**	**$9,714,268**	**$3,316,467**

[1]Includes some state funds.
Source: SNL Financial LC.

(table continues)

DIRECT PREMIUMS WRITTEN, PROPERTY/CASUALTY INSURANCE BY STATE BY LINE, 2013[1] (Cont'd)

($000)

State	Other liability	Fire	Allied lines	Inland marine	Ocean marine	Surety
Alabama	$533,850	$229,631	$191,458	$233,401	$37,582	$59,481
Alaska	149,031	57,537	31,315	215,621	37,634	29,970
Arizona	697,382	141,352	114,707	259,132	16,436	88,526
Arkansas	295,121	154,232	125,665	179,756	17,185	35,853
California	6,402,389	1,247,217	767,901	2,229,274	267,605	675,513
Colorado	979,556	135,885	159,846	271,091	14,279	100,576
Connecticut	913,456	139,986	120,763	249,951	51,652	67,660
Delaware	256,134	27,051	21,646	55,307	7,059	16,702
D.C.	364,954	38,062	30,507	95,805	2,473	124,833
Florida	2,937,721	1,610,781	3,096,866	1,005,883	292,818	269,882
Georgia	1,292,968	347,019	248,558	460,651	45,786	127,249
Hawaii	267,306	82,397	104,185	66,601	14,111	35,048
Idaho	164,647	31,059	43,797	62,924	4,930	18,816
Illinois	2,972,621	407,852	397,295	630,574	88,999	213,283
Indiana	775,729	271,481	189,619	268,951	25,619	66,238
Iowa	494,190	105,179	225,956	192,956	6,991	45,326
Kansas	414,636	112,480	195,742	152,830	9,505	46,219
Kentucky	395,714	137,902	110,568	217,607	21,634	65,624
Louisiana	790,966	366,554	461,438	366,281	226,976	117,278
Maine	145,005	46,141	38,576	56,151	24,548	13,532
Maryland	948,954	166,148	124,226	290,604	89,658	151,036
Massachusetts	1,546,633	317,094	215,099	392,151	88,385	129,018
Michigan	1,140,919	331,128	170,245	394,832	52,039	77,426
Minnesota	959,306	188,784	335,228	272,321	29,677	75,003
Mississippi	288,465	142,481	128,724	149,909	19,524	42,956
Missouri	896,279	205,520	192,520	274,188	31,532	73,752
Montana	139,285	29,295	32,163	62,234	3,520	26,488
Nebraska	293,860	55,283	233,327	121,843	4,187	31,234
Nevada	368,598	95,747	79,422	126,860	6,989	61,681
New Hampshire	168,717	37,678	28,560	64,790	11,843	15,213
New Jersey	2,120,054	407,562	304,375	471,649	138,011	146,678
New Mexico	201,382	48,000	39,934	88,827	1,896	37,303
New York	6,125,465	812,122	567,790	1,288,601	446,304	345,046
North Carolina	1,001,537	290,754	271,132	448,473	37,135	114,441
North Dakota	157,162	30,656	126,548	65,602	1,337	22,156
Ohio	1,454,763	415,373	257,608	484,722	51,020	127,394
Oklahoma	547,526	179,327	182,280	217,486	25,671	62,485
Oregon	445,798	94,349	69,671	187,159	28,899	66,831
Pennsylvania	2,259,840	444,269	284,300	579,191	53,790	193,810
Rhode Island	184,163	49,085	40,186	65,706	27,655	13,032
South Carolina	410,967	208,668	201,060	254,313	25,531	60,971
South Dakota	102,047	24,374	76,621	48,464	822	39,197
Tennessee	1,040,931	270,138	173,304	311,204	59,399	81,311
Texas	4,422,961	1,674,988	1,767,471	1,658,686	338,917	493,643
Utah	328,357	79,492	45,032	113,053	8,051	42,000
Vermont	104,268	24,327	14,605	29,976	10,156	9,272
Virginia	1,113,235	234,854	179,416	361,912	59,338	159,714
Washington	941,460	224,884	151,447	372,668	125,273	126,221
West Virginia	194,561	64,803	36,202	65,727	3,835	35,445
Wisconsin	881,281	166,821	146,756	218,148	33,515	53,941
Wyoming	98,212	26,704	23,064	41,093	865	29,071
United States	**$52,130,362**	**$13,030,505**	**$13,174,727**	**$16,793,138**	**$3,028,596**	**$5,161,373**

[1]Includes some state funds.

Source: SNL Financial LC.

DIRECT PREMIUMS WRITTEN, PROPERTY/CASUALTY INSURANCE BY STATE BY LINE, 2013[1]

($000)

Fidelity	Burglary and theft	Boiler and machinery	Financial guaranty	Aircraft	Earthquake	Federal flood
$13,252	$2,326	$27,260	$39,176	$19,771	$10,593	$28,556
2,178	346	10,268	246	29,647	24,973	2,086
12,055	2,522	22,344	307	61,871	10,150	17,420
12,411	1,770	15,135	1,034	21,480	28,330	11,106
116,094	23,479	133,305	28,090	141,878	1,636,448	168,089
21,601	3,545	20,813	4,899	36,103	9,448	14,668
26,027	4,059	19,370	1,115	38,098	6,720	47,282
3,316	3,012	4,325	32,969	12,289	1,110	15,607
13,938	1,910	4,330	166	2,103	2,513	1,121
59,875	12,989	61,201	4,994	93,940	29,244	912,976
32,852	6,373	35,757	680	63,742	15,964	56,353
4,860	566	6,238	4,362	12,020	11,602	33,527
3,011	494	7,983	0	13,362	3,441	3,701
62,287	13,459	68,150	8,311	83,648	63,616	30,625
16,872	3,235	48,269	472	22,546	36,269	17,759
11,893	2,040	21,677	3,058	11,923	5,076	11,267
11,778	1,890	18,070	1,148	19,689	7,602	7,284
10,263	1,559	22,297	1,622	6,692	41,366	16,398
12,302	3,368	28,200	4,242	62,934	8,398	262,307
3,788	585	8,085	436	3,692	1,879	8,328
26,200	3,975	21,180	6,441	16,185	11,728	38,144
39,757	6,241	34,526	6,828	14,103	19,809	62,536
34,182	5,651	50,127	1,911	27,523	7,390	16,420
27,102	4,102	33,506	11,134	26,249	5,972	7,471
8,477	1,709	13,168	1,421	10,351	18,174	33,945
22,932	4,335	26,202	3,109	22,611	90,310	17,763
3,538	538	4,949	121	9,314	3,993	2,969
7,752	1,307	12,233	361	11,515	2,670	7,875
7,204	1,721	11,728	1,006	21,259	19,898	7,396
3,169	783	5,863	414	6,453	2,563	7,655
43,641	7,737	45,331	14,160	18,269	16,687	207,556
4,027	681	8,551	482	6,600	2,376	9,560
141,879	25,204	103,017	375,034	62,927	44,211	165,650
32,485	4,658	34,305	1,773	28,686	12,261	91,758
2,713	309	9,216	610	7,402	1,176	6,795
39,769	10,638	56,809	1,861	55,712	28,777	27,135
10,450	2,081	20,055	578	16,741	13,107	9,341
9,195	2,182	15,693	264	31,610	63,239	20,251
50,148	9,499	64,655	19,064	34,072	14,892	57,767
4,993	595	4,904	603	15,645	2,215	19,861
10,451	2,126	19,492	1,119	10,458	36,702	113,893
3,218	443	5,467	21	6,475	662	3,503
18,230	6,385	27,904	459	25,614	77,636	19,239
74,053	20,054	118,365	17,848	169,507	33,743	305,626
6,772	1,343	9,174	239	24,982	38,977	2,365
4,012	377	3,739	1,267	2,318	28,337	4,712
31,421	6,690	28,429	658	44,511	17,147	66,221
17,560	3,947	33,331	749	32,732	157,949	29,884
4,668	511	7,032	44	2,963	1,688	13,747
22,262	3,934	37,783	138	20,665	5,546	10,464
1,375	227	8,965	0	5,110	2,944	1,630
$1,164,284	**$229,511**	**$1,458,776**	**$607,046**	**$1,545,987**	**$2,737,523**	**$3,055,589**

[1]Includes some state funds.
Source: SNL Financial LC.

(table continues)

DIRECT PREMIUMS WRITTEN, PROPERTY/CASUALTY INSURANCE BY STATE BY LINE, 2013[1] (Cont'd)
($000)

State	Credit	Warranty	Accident and health	Multiple peril crop	Mortgage guaranty	Misc.
Alabama	$16,169	$7,695	$75,090	$71,449	$68,287	$25,980
Alaska	8,245	4,730	10,948	100	15,699	1,172
Arizona	19,508	19,741	88,751	19,263	92,097	16,967
Arkansas	16,012	4,341	40,687	146,583	32,342	7,665
California	116,964	123,342	516,198	313,119	390,128	76,035
Colorado	14,659	17,047	97,196	222,021	121,177	14,703
Connecticut	28,878	13,578	51,408	4,903	58,537	4,189
Delaware	15,591	4,697	63,770	12,932	20,398	1,566
D.C.	12,962	109	115,378	0	33,622	1,242
Florida	109,286	357,324	251,206	100,633	233,896	102,586
Georgia	41,559	22,700	150,735	131,765	170,507	44,394
Hawaii	5,436	3,258	19,647	2,118	20,736	2,752
Idaho	3,462	3,158	17,859	67,827	25,747	2,032
Illinois	70,228	300,596	271,567	811,227	210,531	34,739
Indiana	24,931	39,738	214,053	440,347	101,770	11,708
Iowa	9,928	3,017	78,602	948,188	49,357	5,236
Kansas	14,982	117,682	76,434	790,648	45,210	5,574
Kentucky	18,972	10,458	58,921	163,373	37,660	4,870
Louisiana	26,966	12,887	64,751	96,782	59,939	40,338
Maine	5,224	3,701	12,484	10,583	16,991	1,535
Maryland	19,852	16,112	76,241	39,259	124,380	10,461
Massachusetts	32,938	9,589	88,820	2,126	119,133	10,263
Michigan	87,838	507,940	184,928	186,322	126,216	24,894
Minnesota	21,189	19,874	136,398	837,228	124,627	17,052
Mississippi	18,102	4,574	61,598	147,110	27,222	15,008
Missouri	31,522	27,081	173,415	410,114	89,641	8,877
Montana	5,353	1,393	24,295	203,188	13,302	2,619
Nebraska	4,662	3,473	64,786	731,700	28,618	6,007
Nevada	16,761	5,587	33,743	6,082	35,122	3,020
New Hampshire	6,304	6,185	18,411	414	26,824	3,034
New Jersey	81,463	27,210	131,557	7,441	156,019	27,316
New Mexico	6,770	4,666	23,245	29,005	25,824	7,883
New York	147,426	87,341	422,778	35,308	183,818	43,107
North Carolina	57,237	37,336	164,870	210,336	147,278	25,178
North Dakota	1,431	840	13,690	1,105,660	8,192	1,279
Ohio	54,895	37,903	198,445	309,423	164,779	39,465
Oklahoma	26,182	10,949	51,625	211,774	44,683	13,586
Oregon	23,569	9,612	63,209	32,702	64,560	13,811
Pennsylvania	59,382	56,973	309,236	65,791	178,175	24,228
Rhode Island	4,573	1,347	27,305	-418	16,281	191
South Carolina	43,335	6,007	74,392	72,110	78,086	12,040
South Dakota	1,821	1,467	30,162	814,697	10,098	1,169
Tennessee	33,871	44,031	110,532	108,726	83,221	14,132
Texas	212,212	218,593	528,384	1,001,202	360,650	147,658
Utah	13,266	22,359	59,387	4,148	68,981	3,258
Vermont	7,289	2,176	7,359	3,735	9,259	140,249
Virginia	32,081	20,157	114,379	71,845	155,385	17,637
Washington	29,225	43,004	97,838	112,201	138,099	18,133
West Virginia	7,452	3,507	29,007	2,972	13,027	3,052
Wisconsin	19,557	23,448	164,505	280,567	91,134	9,363
Wyoming	1,679	803	20,673	20,441	12,350	781
United States	**$1,689,198**	**$2,331,336**	**$5,780,902**	**$11,417,073**	**$4,529,617**	**$1,070,030**

[1]Includes some state funds.
Source: SNL Financial LC.

TOTAL AUTO PREMIUMS BY SECTOR, 2013
($ billions, net premiums written)

Private passenger auto
$174.9

88.0%

12.0%

Commercial auto
$23.9

63.3%

Liability
$125.8

36.7%

Collision/
comprehensive
$73.0

AUTO SHARE OF P/C INDUSTRY, 2013
($ billions, net premiums written)

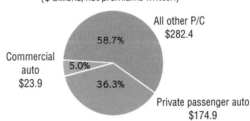

All other P/C
$282.4

58.7%

Commercial
auto
$23.9

5.0%

36.3%

Private passenger auto
$174.9

Source: SNL Financial LC.

PRIVATE PASSENGER AUTOMOBILE INSURANCE, 2004-2013
($000)

Year	Liability				Collision/comprehensive			
	Net premiums written[1]	Annual percent change	Combined ratio[2]	Annual point change[3]	Net premiums written[1]	Annual percent change	Combined ratio[2]	Annual point change[3]
2004	$92,936,566	4.1%	98.9	-4.2 pts.	$64,697,069	4.3%	87.0	-5.1 pts.
2005	94,384,329	1.6	98.4	-0.4	64,882,303	0.3	90.7	3.7
2006	95,325,685	1.0	98.6	0.2	65,125,977	0.4	91.4	0.7
2007	94,974,640	-0.4	101.8	3.1	64,700,792	-0.7	93.4	2.0
2008	94,545,647	-0.5	103.5	1.7	64,054,581	-1.0	95.8	2.4
2009	94,990,682	0.5	106.2	2.7	62,630,693	-2.2	93.0	-2.8
2010	97,672,826	2.8	105.9	-0.3	62,595,851	-0.1	93.4	0.4
2011	100,369,441	2.8	103.8	-2.1	62,948,280	0.6	99.6	6.3
2012	103,429,677	3.0	103.2	-0.6	64,619,667	2.7	100.2	0.6
2013	107,446,382	3.9	103.6	0.4	67,451,645	4.4	98.7	-1.5

[1]After reinsurance transactions, excludes state funds.
[2]After dividends to policyholders. A drop in the combined ratio represents an improvement; an increase represents a deterioration.
[3]Calculated from unrounded data.

Source: SNL Financial LC.

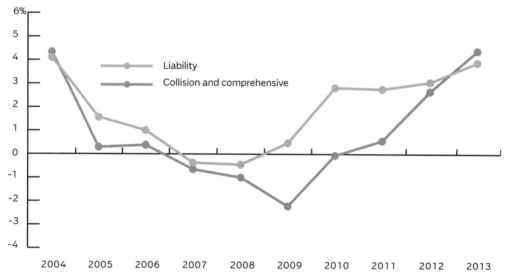

**PERCENT CHANGE FROM PRIOR YEAR,
NET PREMIUMS WRITTEN, PRIVATE PASSENGER AUTO INSURANCE, 2004-2013**

Liability

Collision and comprehensive

Source: SNL Financial LC.

TOP TEN WRITERS OF PRIVATE PASSENGER AUTO INSURANCE
BY DIRECT PREMIUMS WRITTEN, 2013
($000)

Rank	Group/company	Direct premiums written[1]	Market share[2]
1	State Farm Mutual Automobile Insurance	$33,610,201	18.5%
2	Berkshire Hathaway Inc.	18,622,591	10.2
3	Allstate Corp.	18,067,452	9.9
4	Progressive Corp.	15,373,142	8.5
5	Farmers Insurance Group of Companies[3]	9,880,905	5.4
6	USAA Insurance Group	9,167,242	5.0
7	Liberty Mutual	9,036,455	5.0
8	Nationwide Mutual Group	7,279,835	4.0
9	American Family Mutual	3,441,682	1.9
10	Travelers Companies Inc.	3,178,692	1.8

[1]Before reinsurance transactions, includes state funds.
[2]Based on U.S. total, includes territories.
[3]Data for Farmers Insurance Group of Companies and Zurich Financial Group (which owns Farmers' management company) are reported separately by SNL Financial.

Source: SNL Financial LC.

COMMERCIAL AUTOMOBILE INSURANCE, 2004-2013
($000)

Year	Liability				Collision/comprehensive			
	Net premiums written[1]	Annual percent change	Combined ratio[2]	Annual point change[3]	Net premiums written[1]	Annual percent change	Combined ratio[2]	Annual point change[3]
2004	$19,566,628	6.2%	96.9	-2.7 pts.	$7,148,629	1.9%	83.0	-0.7 pts.
2005	19,766,618	1.0	92.0	-4.9	6,929,335	-3.1	88.1	5.1
2006	19,704,282	-0.3	95.7	3.7	6,949,388	0.3	88.4	0.3
2007	18,803,425	-4.6	95.4	-0.3	6,630,652	-4.6	91.0	2.5
2008	17,833,085	-5.2	97.4	2.0	5,989,108	-9.7	94.7	3.7
2009	16,581,981	-7.0	100.6	3.1	5,347,981	-10.7	96.9	2.3
2010	16,249,433	-2.0	97.1	-3.5	4,870,380	-8.9	101.6	4.7
2011	16,382,082	0.8	101.1	4.0	4,647,376	-4.6	112.0	10.4
2012	16,984,612	3.7	106.6	5.5	5,099,427	9.7	109.2	-2.9
2013	18,353,335	8.1	107.2	0.6	5,536,173	8.6	105.2	-3.9

[1]Ater reinsurance transactions, excludes state funds.
[2]After dividends to policyholders. A drop in the combined ratio represents an improvement; an increase represents a deterioration.
[3]Calculated from unrounded data.

Source: SNL Financial LC.

TOP TEN WRITERS OF COMMERCIAL AUTO INSURANCE
BY DIRECT PREMIUMS WRITTEN, 2013
($000)

Rank	Group/company	Direct premiums written[1]	Market share[2]
1	Travelers Companies Inc.	$1,978,649	7.4%
2	Progressive Corp.	1,779,528	6.6
3	Nationwide Mutual Group	1,527,501	5.7
4	Liberty Mutual	1,524,882	5.7
5	Zurich Insurance Group[3]	1,238,757	4.6
6	American International Group	930,862	3.5
7	Old Republic International Corp.	875,705	3.3
8	Auto-Owners Insurance Co.	571,399	2.1
9	Hartford Financial Services	552,768	2.1
10	Cincinnati Financial Corp.	513,603	1.9

[1]Before reinsurance transactions, includes state funds.
[2]Based on U.S. total, includes territories.
[3]Data for Farmers Insurance Group of Companies and Zurich Financial Group (which owns Farmers' management company) are reported separately by SNL Financial.

Source: SNL Financial LC.

Property/Casualty Insurance by Line

Auto: Costs/Expenditures

AAA's 2014 Your Driving Costs study found that the average cost to own and operate a sedan was $8,876 in 2013, down 2.7 percent, or $246, from the previous year. The cost reflects a relatively large decrease in fuel costs and lower tire, depreciation and insurance costs. Average insurance costs for sedans dropped 0.6 percent, or $6, to $1,023, from $1,029 in 2012. AAA insurance cost estimates are based on typical coverage for a low-risk driver with a clean driving record for a policy with a $500 deductible for collision and a $100 deductible for comprehensive coverage. Figures are not comparable with the National Association of Insurance Commissioners' Auto Expenditures data below.

■ 76 percent of insured drivers purchase comprehensive coverage in addition to liability insurance, and 71 percent buy collision coverage, based on an I.I.I. analysis of 2011 NAIC data.

AVERAGE EXPENDITURES FOR AUTO INSURANCE, UNITED STATES, 2002-2011

Year	Average expenditure	Percent change
2002	$786	8.3%
2003	830	5.6
2004	843	1.6
2005	832	-1.3
2006	818	-1.7
2007	799	-2.3
2008	791	-1.0
2009	787	-0.5
2010	792	0.6
2011	797	0.6

Source: © 2013 National Association of Insurance Commissioners (NAIC).

Auto Insurance Expenditures, by State

The tables on the following pages show estimated average expenditures for private passenger automobile insurance by state from 2007 to 2011, providing approximate measures of the relative cost of automobile insurance to consumers in each state. To calculate average expenditures the National Association of Insurance Commissioners (NAIC) assumes that all insured vehicles carry liability coverage but not necessarily collision or comprehensive coverage. The average expenditure measures what consumers actually spend for insurance on each vehicle. It does not equal the sum of liability, collision and comprehensive expenditures because not all policyholders purchase all three coverages.

Expenditures are affected by the coverages purchased as well as other factors. In states where the economy is healthy, people are more likely to purchase new cars. Since new car owners are more likely to purchase physical damage coverages, these states will have a higher average expenditure. The NAIC notes that urban population, traffic density and per capita income have a significant impact on premiums. The latest report shows that high premium states tend also to be highly urban, with higher wage and price levels and greater traffic density. Tort liability and other auto laws, labor costs, liability coverage requirements, theft rates and other factors can also affect auto insurance prices.

TOP TEN MOST EXPENSIVE AND LEAST EXPENSIVE STATES FOR AUTOMOBILE INSURANCE, 2011[1]

Rank	Most expensive states	Average expenditure	Rank	Least expensive states	Average expenditure
1	New Jersey	$1,183.95	1	Idaho	$535.15
2	D.C.	1,138.03	2	South Dakota	540.04
3	Louisiana	1,110.68	3	North Dakota	549.81
4	New York	1,108.64	4	Iowa	552.54
5	Florida	1,090.65	5	Maine	577.38
6	Delaware	1,052.28	6	North Carolina	600.33
7	Rhode Island	1,004.14	7	Wisconsin	601.40
8	Michigan	983.60	8	Nebraska	602.57
9	Connecticut	970.22	9	Wyoming	619.88
10	Maryland	956.17	10	Ohio	619.96

[1]Based on average automobile insurance expenditures.

Source: © 2013 National Association of Insurance Commissioners (NAIC).

AVERAGE EXPENDITURES FOR AUTO INSURANCE BY STATE, 2007-2011

State	2011 Liability	Collision	Comprehensive	Average expenditure	Rank[1]
Alabama	$354.47	$293.88	$136.20	$653.64	37
Alaska	546.71	363.42	143.36	873.10	13
Arizona	462.95	249.10	187.41	776.83	18
Arkansas	367.28	290.96	169.10	665.86	35
California[2]	437.88	340.76	99.78	736.80	24
Colorado	441.41	251.14	142.95	723.67	27
Connecticut	614.26	334.69	119.78	970.22	9
Delaware	748.55	282.83	106.49	1,052.28	6
D.C.	622.58	426.32	225.00	1,138.03	2
Florida	813.60	236.69	109.83	1,090.65	5
Georgia	439.30	320.73	153.12	755.25	19
Hawaii	463.80	293.11	104.27	748.10	21
Idaho	327.96	206.32	107.69	535.15	51
Illinois	424.19	268.93	110.00	727.46	25
Indiana	368.72	231.61	110.13	621.76	41
Iowa	290.86	198.45	159.75	552.54	48
Kansas	327.21	244.67	208.57	625.93	40
Kentucky	503.53	245.49	123.50	744.58	22
Louisiana	687.56	386.31	207.68	1,110.68	3
Maine	328.25	242.80	90.83	577.38	47
Maryland	590.02	317.97	140.78	956.17	10
Massachusetts	565.87	324.13	121.13	942.12	11
Michigan	600.12	366.62	143.88	983.60	8
Minnesota	417.37	197.75	162.06	696.00	31
Mississippi	418.64	292.63	184.80	740.69	23
Missouri	385.46	249.75	155.11	675.02	34
Montana	387.71	240.85	187.65	654.56	36
Nebraska	339.58	211.63	181.07	602.57	44
Nevada	612.84	297.14	119.89	904.91	12
New Hampshire	387.51	262.52	96.51	705.84	30
New Jersey	831.45	352.03	118.04	1,183.95	1
New Mexico	432.78	268.32	168.75	691.74	32
New York	750.63	340.11	143.57	1,108.64	4
North Carolina	358.16	238.22	111.87	600.33	46
North Dakota	260.86	208.25	219.64	549.81	49
Ohio	357.34	236.15	104.24	619.96	42
Oklahoma	416.18	285.70	179.63	716.23	28
Oregon	507.32	207.18	90.21	723.90	26
Pennsylvania	488.19	296.35	121.45	815.45	16
Rhode Island	678.59	352.19	118.22	1,004.14	7
South Carolina	469.76	239.74	149.46	749.94	20
South Dakota	277.16	190.78	201.37	540.04	50
Tennessee	376.96	268.93	122.03	650.13	38
Texas	480.47	338.67	185.61	842.58	14
Utah	451.94	253.50	103.69	712.79	29
Vermont	335.79	269.66	110.75	633.54	39
Virginia	394.68	251.50	122.52	679.57	33
Washington	541.62	242.86	105.55	806.37	17
West Virginia	500.31	305.96	186.33	834.09	15
Wisconsin	356.54	198.60	115.18	601.40	45
Wyoming	320.47	272.66	198.01	619.88	43
United States	**$492.43**	**$286.37**	**$132.76**	**$797.44**	

[1]Ranked highest to lowest by average expenditure. [2]Preliminary. Note: Average expenditure=Total written premium/liability car years. A car year is equal to 365 days of insured coverage for a single vehicle. The NAIC does not rank state average expenditures and

AVERAGE EXPENDITURES FOR AUTO INSURANCE BY STATE, 2007-2011 (Cont'd)

2010 Average expenditure	Rank[1]	Average expenditure percent change, 2010-2011	2009	2008	2007	State
$651.22	37	0.4%	$652.07	$662.76	$683.74	Alabama
890.35	13	-1.9	896.74	904.12	923.33	Alaska
804.97	18	-3.5	842.21	863.81	883.40	Arizona
662.44	35	0.5	657.13	651.26	659.97	Arkansas
745.55	21	-1.2	758.81	779.49	810.22	California[2]
730.42	25	-0.9	741.28	728.67	738.36	Colorado
965.22	8	0.5	952.36	950.16	963.61	Connecticut
1,030.98	6	2.1	1,021.42	1,007.32	1,011.60	Delaware
1,133.87	2	0.4	1,127.72	1,126.56	1,139.82	D.C.
1,037.36	5	5.1	1,006.20	1,054.89	1,044.76	Florida
748.89	20	0.8	754.61	760.58	781.93	Georgia
765.83	19	-2.3	786.33	816.21	837.20	Hawaii
548.03	48	-2.4	554.80	562.76	564.00	Idaho
733.45	24	-0.8	727.82	713.97	723.96	Illinois
624.27	41	-0.4	620.31	611.21	618.20	Indiana
546.59	49	1.1	530.96	518.48	520.19	Iowa
625.12	40	0.1	622.16	622.14	610.13	Kansas
722.70	27	3.0	698.85	698.93	719.64	Kentucky
1,121.44	3	-1.0	1,100.09	1,104.62	1,095.98	Louisiana
582.29	47	-0.8	597.87	600.46	611.13	Maine
947.74	9	0.9	928.92	922.01	933.07	Maryland
890.83	12	5.8	860.49	903.27	981.39	Massachusetts
944.57	10	4.1	913.28	905.82	927.82	Michigan
693.08	32	0.4	692.08	697.09	719.66	Minnesota
745.17	22	-0.6	737.77	749.38	764.75	Mississippi
678.03	33	-0.4	668.29	656.33	658.11	Missouri
657.42	36	-0.4	655.61	666.69	666.08	Montana
592.56	46	1.7	575.26	561.46	571.33	Nebraska
930.51	11	-2.8	944.16	970.31	998.66	Nevada
706.24	29	-0.1	717.56	727.15	749.98	New Hampshire
1,157.30	1	2.3	1,100.66	1,081.28	1,103.53	New Jersey
703.64	30	-1.7	717.96	730.27	732.93	New Mexico
1,078.88	4	2.8	1,057.82	1,044.04	1,047.19	New York
599.90	45	0.1	609.80	595.48	591.11	North Carolina
528.81	50	4.0	509.72	503.18	511.79	North Dakota
619.45	43	0.1	616.33	616.51	628.37	Ohio
701.66	31	2.1	677.71	662.64	646.00	Oklahoma
724.47	26	-0.1	722.85	726.64	722.86	Oregon
812.15	17	0.4	811.15	816.65	820.00	Pennsylvania
984.95	7	1.9	969.02	985.89	1,017.12	Rhode Island
737.77	23	1.6	737.74	749.30	761.87	South Carolina
525.16	51	2.8	512.47	512.12	526.42	South Dakota
641.17	38	1.4	634.24	639.00	649.22	Tennessee
848.11	14	-0.7	860.42	853.55	807.70	Texas
716.97	28	-0.6	717.28	708.70	696.81	Utah
630.11	39	0.5	645.79	653.47	661.70	Vermont
673.72	34	0.9	667.51	662.72	661.82	Virginia
815.29	16	-1.1	826.59	839.23	840.97	Washington
830.10	15	0.5	815.00	807.49	818.75	West Virginia
613.41	44	-2.0	590.54	581.42	581.50	Wisconsin
621.15	42	-0.2	624.10	632.92	631.15	Wyoming
$791.52		**0.7%**	**$786.99**	**$790.57**	**$798.54**	**United States**

does not endorse any conclusion drawn from these data.

Source: © 2013 National Association of Insurance Commissioners (NAIC).

Auto Insurance Claims and Expenses

The combined ratio after dividends is a measure of underwriting profitability. It reflects the percentage of each premium dollar an insurer spends on claims (the claims ratio) and percent of each premium dollar that goes toward expenses (the expense ratio). The combined ratio does not take investment income into account. The private passenger auto combined ratio after dividends was 101.7 percent in 2013, reflecting a claims ratio of 76.1 percent and an expense ratio of 25.0 percent. A combined ratio above 100 indicates an underwriting loss.

PRIVATE PASSENGER AUTO INSURANCE INDUSTRY UNDERWRITING EXPENSES, 2013[1]

Expense	Percent of premiums
LOSSES AND RELATED EXPENSES[2]	
Loss and loss adjustment expense (LAE) ratio	**76.1%**
Incurred losses	63.5
Defense and cost containment expenses incurred	2.8
Adjusting and other expenses incurred	9.8
OPERATING EXPENSES[3]	
Expense ratio	**25.0%**
Net commissions and brokerage expenses incurred	8.2
Taxes, licenses and fees	2.3
Other acquisition and field supervision expenses incurred	8.8
General expenses incurred	5.8
DIVIDENDS TO POLICYHOLDERS[2]	**0.6%**
COMBINED RATIO AFTER DIVIDENDS[4]	**101.7%**

[1]After reinsurance transactions.
[2]As a percent of net premiums earned ($172.5 billion in 2013).
[3]As a percent of net premiums written ($174.9 billion in 2013).
[4]Sum of loss and LAE, expense and dividends ratios.

Source: SNL Financial LC.

Liability insurance pays for the policyholder's legal responsibility to others for bodily injury or property damage. Collision and comprehensive insurance cover property damage and theft to the policyholder's car.

PRIVATE PASSENGER AUTO INSURANCE LOSSES, 2004-2013[1]

Year	Liability					
---	---	---	---	---		
	Bodily injury[2]		Property damage[3]			
	Claim frequency[4]	Claim severity[5,6]	Claim frequency[4]	Claim severity[5,6]		
2004	1.11	$11,640	3.75	$2,596		
2005	1.04	12,282	3.55	2,717		
2006	0.98	12,907	3.40	2,796		
2007	0.90	13,361	3.46	2,847		
2008	0.91	14,067	3.42	2,903		
2009	0.89	13,891	3.49	2,869		
2010	0.91	14,406	3.53	2,881		
2011	0.92	14,848	3.56	2,958		
2012	0.95	14,690	3.50	3,073		
2013	0.94	15,443	3.55	3,231		

Year	Physical damage[7]			
	Collision		Comprehensive[8]	
	Claim frequency[4]	Claim severity[5]	Claim frequency[4]	Claim severity[5]
2004	4.85	$3,080	2.46	$1,417
2005	5.04	3,067	2.38	1,457
2006	4.87	3,194	2.40	1,528
2007	5.20	3,109	2.48	1,524
2008	5.35	3,005	2.57	1,551
2009	5.48	2,869	2.75	1,389
2010	5.69	2,778	2.62	1,476
2011	5.75	2,861	2.79	1,490
2012	5.57	2,950	2.62	1,585
2013	5.71	3,144	2.57	1,621

[1]For all limits combined. Data are for paid claims.
[2]Excludes Massachusetts and most states with no-fault automobile insurance laws.
[3]Excludes Massachusetts, Michigan and New Jersey.
[4]Claim frequency is claims per 100 earned car years. A car year is equal to 365 days of insured coverage for one vehicle.
[5]Claim severity is the size of the loss.
[6]Includes loss adjustment expenses.
[7]Excludes Massachusetts, Michigan and Puerto Rico. Based on coverage with a $500 deductible.
[8]Excludes wind and water losses.

Source: ISO®, a Verisk Analytics® company.

- In 2013 less than 1 percent of people with liability insurance had a bodily injury liability claim, while 3.6 percent of those with liability insurance had a property damage liability claim, according to ISO.

- In 2013, 5.7 percent of collision insurance policyholders had a claim, while 2.6 percent of people with comprehensive coverage had a claim.

- In 2013 the average auto liability claim for property damage was $3,231; the average auto liability claim for bodily injury was $15,443.

- In 2013 the average collision claim was $3,144; the average comprehensive claim was $1,621.

INCURRED LOSSES FOR AUTO INSURANCE, 2009-2013[1]
($000)

	2009	2010	2011	2012	2013
Private passenger auto					
Liability	$63,448,211	$64,110,267	$64,310,776	$65,135,976	$67,879,783
Physical damage	36,497,330	36,454,102	40,589,159	41,275,620	41,754,269
Commercial auto					
Liability	9,345,288	8,798,119	9,363,647	10,515,806	11,302,794
Physical damage	3,005,162	2,911,013	3,164,880	3,250,740	3,255,581
Total	**$112,295,991**	**$112,273,501**	**$117,428,462**	**$120,178,142**	**$124,192,427**

[1]Losses occurring within a fixed period, whether or not adjusted or paid during the same period, after reinsurance transactions.
Source: SNL Financial LC.

Auto: High-Risk Markets

The Shared/Residual Market

All states and the District of Columbia use special systems to guarantee that auto insurance is available to those who cannot obtain it in the private market. These systems are commonly known as assigned risk plans, although that term technically applies to only one type of plan. The assigned risk and other plans are known in the insurance industry as the shared, or residual, market. Policyholders in assigned risk plans are assigned to various insurance companies doing business in the state. In the voluntary, or regular, market, auto insurers are free to select policyholders.

The percentage of vehicles insured in the shared market is dropping, in part because of the evolution of the nonstandard sector of the voluntary market. The nonstandard market is a niche market for drivers who have a worse than average driving record or drive specialized cars such as high-powered sports cars or custom-built cars. It is made up of both small specialty companies, whose only business is the nonstandard market, and well-known auto insurance companies with nonstandard divisions.

Insured Vehicles

In 2012, 192 million private passenger vehicles were insured in the United States, up from 189 million in 2011, according to the Automobile Insurance Plans Service Office. The figures include cars insured by private auto insurers in the voluntary market as well as those insured in the so-called shared or residual markets set up by states to cover hard-to-insure risks. In 2012 California had the most insured private passenger cars (25 million), followed by Florida (11 million) and New York (9 million), including vehicles in the voluntary and residual markets.

**PRIVATE PASSENGER CARS INSURED
IN THE SHARED AND VOLUNTARY MARKETS, 2012**

State	Voluntary market	Shared market	Total	Shared market as a percent of total
Alabama	3,512,651	0	3,512,651	1
Alaska	488,440	78	488,518	0.016%
Arizona	4,260,695	0	4,260,695	1
Arkansas	2,131,327	2	2,131,329	1
California	25,391,859	587	25,392,446	0.002
Colorado	3,877,688	0	3,877,688	1
Connecticut	2,470,553	179	2,470,732	0.007
Delaware	631,210	1	631,211	1
D.C.	238,419	147	238,566	0.062
Florida	11,283,532	2,033	11,285,565	0.018
Georgia	7,010,414	0	7,010,414	1
Hawaii	834,816	3,950	838,766	0.471
Idaho	1,106,249	3	1,106,252	1
Illinois	7,980,752	572	7,981,324	0.007
Indiana	4,481,849	3	4,481,852	1
Iowa	2,437,335	13	2,437,348	0.001
Kansas	2,295,485	1,676	2,297,161	0.073
Kentucky	3,109,752	76	3,109,828	0.002
Louisiana	2,905,256	0	2,905,256	1
Maine	1,022,437	9	1,022,446	0.001
Maryland	3,920,154	43,289	3,963,443	1.092
Massachusetts	4,179,418	103,112	4,282,530	2.408
Michigan	6,202,697	1,563	6,204,260	0.025
Minnesota	3,891,523	23	3,891,546	0.001
Mississippi	1,873,730	16	1,873,746	0.001
Missouri	4,289,100	19	4,289,119	1
Montana	827,851	34	827,885	0.004
Nebraska	1,518,948	1	1,518,949	1
Nevada	1,812,804	2	1,812,806	1
New Hampshire	905,471	269	905,740	0.030
New Jersey	5,332,599	46,210	5,378,809	0.859

- From 2009 to 2012 about 1 percent of vehicles were insured in the shared market annually, compared with 3.6 percent in 1995 and 1.4 percent in 2000 (excluding Texas).

- The number of vehicles in the shared market nationwide fell by about 60,300 vehicles, or 3.1 percent in 2012, compared with the previous year.

- In 2012 North Carolina had the highest percentage of cars in the shared market, 22.0 percent, followed by Massachusetts, 2.4 percent, and Rhode Island, 1.5 percent.

(table continues)

The number of cars in shared market plans fell 0.9 percent in North Carolina and 6.7 percent in Massachusetts. The number rose 18.9 percent in Rhode Island.

PRIVATE PASSENGER CARS INSURED IN THE SHARED AND VOLUNTARY MARKETS, 2012 (Cont'd)

State	Voluntary market	Shared market	Total	Shared market as a percent of total
New Mexico	1,544,524	2	1,544,526	1
New York	9,299,087	61,638	9,360,725	0.658%
North Carolina	5,618,255	1,588,143	7,206,398	22.038
North Dakota	642,582	1	642,583	1
Ohio	8,174,369	0	8,174,369	1
Oklahoma	2,732,173	14	2,732,187	0.001
Oregon	2,743,083	1	2,743,084	1
Pennsylvania	8,643,621	7,252	8,650,873	0.084
Rhode Island	665,769	9,953	675,722	1.473
South Carolina	3,474,069	0	3,474,069	1
South Dakota	700,988	0	700,988	1
Tennessee	4,368,667	14	4,368,681	1
Texas[2]	NA	NA	NA	NA
Utah	1,879,547	1	1,879,548	1
Vermont	483,961	62	484,023	0.013
Virginia	6,232,027	601	6,232,628	0.010
Washington	4,698,148	0	4,698,148	1
West Virginia	1,329,442	16	1,329,458	0.001
Wisconsin	4,041,286	0	4,041,286	1
Wyoming	535,568	0	535,568	1
United States	**190,032,180**	**1,871,565**	**191,903,745**	**0.975%**

[1]Less than 0.001 percent.
[2]Texas information is longer available.
NA=Data not available.

Source: Automobile Insurance Plans Service Office.

Uninsured Motorists

Uninsured and underinsured motorist coverage reimburses policyholders in an accident involving an uninsured, underinsured or hit-and-run driver. Twenty states and the District of Columbia have mandatory requirements for uninsured or underinsured motorist coverage. A handful of states, including Nevada and Texas, have passed laws and begun to develop and implement online auto insurance verification systems to identify uninsured motorists.

In 2012, 12.6 percent of motorists, or about one in eight drivers, was uninsured, according to a 2014 study by the Insurance Research Council (IRC). The percentage has been declining in recent years. Oklahoma had the highest percentage of uninsured motorists, 26 percent, and Massachusetts had the lowest, 4 percent. IRC measures the number of uninsured motorists based on insurance claims, using a ratio of insurance claims made by people who were injured by uninsured drivers relative to the claims made by people who were injured by insured drivers.

ESTIMATED PERCENTAGE OF UNINSURED MOTORISTS, 1992-2012[1]

Year	Percent	Year	Percent	Year	Percent
1992	15.6%	1999	12.8%	2006	14.3%
1993	16.0	2000	13.4	2007	13.8
1994	15.1	2001	14.2	2008	14.3
1995	14.2	2002	14.5	2009	13.8
1996	13.8	2003	14.9	2010	12.3
1997	13.2	2004	14.6	2011	12.2
1998	13.0	2005	14.6	2012	12.6

[1]Percentage of uninsured drivers, as measured by the ratio of uninsured motorists (UM) claims to bodily injury (BI) claim frequencies.
Source: Insurance Research Council.

TOP TEN HIGHEST AND LOWEST STATES BASED ON ESTIMATED PERCENTAGE OF UNINSURED MOTORISTS, 2012[1]

Rank	Highest	Percent uninsured	Rank	Lowest	Percent uninsured
1	Oklahoma	25.9%	1	Massachusetts	3.9%
2	Florida	23.8	2	Maine	4.7
3	Mississippi	22.9	3	New York	5.3
4	New Mexico	21.6	4	Utah	5.8
5	Michigan	21.0	5	North Dakota	5.9
6	Tennessee	20.1	6	Pennsylvania	6.5
7	Alabama	19.6	7	Nebraska	6.7
8	Rhode Island	17.0	8	Idaho	6.7
9	Colorado	16.2	9	South Carolina	7.7
10	Washington	16.1	10	South Dakota	7.8

[1]Percentage of uninsured drivers, as measured by the ratio of uninsured motorists (UM) claims to bodily injury (BI) claim frequencies.
Source: Insurance Research Council.

ESTIMATED PERCENTAGE OF UNINSURED MOTORISTS BY STATE, 2012[1]

State	Uninsured	Rank[2]	State	Uninsured	Rank[2]	State	Uninsured	Rank[2]
Alabama	19.6%	7	Kentucky	15.8%	12	North Dakota	5.9%	47
Alaska	13.2	21	Louisiana	13.9	16	Ohio	13.5	17
Arizona	10.6	29	Maine	4.7	50	Oklahoma	25.9	1
Arkansas	15.9	11	Maryland	12.2	22	Oregon	9.0	36
California	14.7	13	Massachusetts	3.9	51	Pennsylvania	6.5	46
Colorado	16.2	9	Michigan	21.0	5	Rhode Island	17.0	8
Connecticut	8.0	41	Minnesota	10.8	28	South Carolina	7.7	43
Delaware	11.5	27	Mississippi	22.9	3	South Dakota	7.8	42
D.C.	11.9	24	Missouri	13.5	18	Tennessee	20.1	6
Florida[3]	23.8	2	Montana	14.1	15	Texas	13.3	19
Georgia	11.7	26	Nebraska	6.7	44	Utah	5.8	48
Hawaii	8.9	37	Nevada	12.2	23	Vermont	8.5	39
Idaho	6.7	45	New Hampshire	9.3	34	Virginia	10.1	31
Illinois	13.3	20	New Jersey	10.3	30	Washington	16.1	10
Indiana	14.2	14	New Mexico	21.6	4	West Virginia	8.4	40
Iowa	9.7	32	New York	5.3	49	Wisconsin	11.7	25
Kansas	9.4	33	North Carolina	9.1	35	Wyoming	8.7	38

[1]Percentage of uninsured drivers, as measured by the ratio of uninsured motorists (UM) claims to bodily injury (BI) claim frequencies.
[2]Rank calculated from unrounded data.
[3]In Florida, compulsory auto laws apply to personal injury protection (PIP) and physical damage but not to third party bodily injury coverage.

Source: Insurance Research Council.

Auto: Laws

Automobile Financial Responsibility Laws

Most states require motor vehicle owners to buy a minimum amount of bodily injury and property damage liability insurance before they can legally drive their vehicle. All states have financial responsibility laws, which means that people involved in an accident will be required to furnish proof of financial responsibility up to a certain amount. To comply with these laws, most drivers purchase liability insurance. Despite these laws a significant percentage of drivers are uninsured.

Motorcycle insurance is compulsory in every state except Hawaii, Montana, New Hampshire and Washington state. Minimum liability limits and the insurance required by state law are the same for motorcycles as for autos and other motor vehicles.

The chart below shows mandatory requirements for bodily injury (BI), property damage (PD) liability, no-fault personal injury protection (PIP), and uninsured (UM) and underinsured (UIM) motorists coverage. It also indicates which states have only financial responsibility (FR) laws.

AUTOMOBILE FINANCIAL RESPONSIBILITY LIMITS BY STATE

State	Insurance required	Minimum liability limits[1]
Alabama	BI & PD Liab	25/50/25
Alaska	BI & PD Liab	50/100/25
Arizona	BI & PD Liab	15/30/10
Arkansas	BI & PD Liab, PIP	25/50/25
California	BI & PD Liab	15/30/5[2]
Colorado	BI & PD Liab	25/50/15
Connecticut	BI & PD Liab	20/40/10
Delaware	BI & PD Liab, PIP	15/30/10
D.C.	BI & PD Liab, UM	25/50/10
Florida	PD Liab, PIP	10/20/10[3]
Georgia	BI & PD Liab	25/50/25
Hawaii	BI & PD Liab, PIP	20/40/10
Idaho	BI & PD Liab	25/50/15
Illinois	BI & PD Liab, UM, UIM	20/50/20
Indiana	BI & PD Liab	25/50/10
Iowa	BI & PD Liab	20/40/15
Kansas	BI & PD Liab, PIP, UM, UIM	25/50/10
Kentucky	BI & PD Liab, PIP	25/50/10[3]
Louisiana	BI & PD Liab	15/30/25
Maine	BI & PD Liab, UM, UIM	50/100/25[4]
Maryland	BI & PD Liab, PIP, UM, UIM	30/60/15
Massachusetts	BI & PD Liab, PIP, UM, UIM	20/40/5
Michigan	BI & PD Liab, PIP	20/40/10
Minnesota	BI & PD Liab, PIP, UM, UIM	30/60/10
Mississippi	BI & PD Liab	25/50/25
Missouri	BI & PD Liab, UM	25/50/10
Montana	BI & PD Liab	25/50/10
Nebraska	BI & PD Liab, UM, UIM	25/50/25

(table continues)

AUTOMOBILE FINANCIAL RESPONSIBILITY LIMITS BY STATE (Cont'd)

State	Insurance required	Minimum liability limits[1]
Nevada	BI & PD Liab	15/30/10
New Hampshire	FR only, UM	25/50/25[4]
New Jersey	BI & PD Liab, PIP, UM, UIM	15/30/5[5]
New Mexico	BI & PD Liab	25/50/10
New York	BI & PD Liab, PIP, UM	25/50/10[6]
North Carolina	BI & PD Liab, UIM[7]	30/60/25
North Dakota	BI & PD Liab, PIP, UM, UIM	25/50/25
Ohio	BI & PD Liab	25/50/25
Oklahoma	BI & PD Liab	25/50/25
Oregon	BI & PD Liab, PIP, UM, UIM	25/50/20
Pennsylvania	BI & PD Liab, PIP	15/30/5
Rhode Island	BI & PD Liab	25/50/25[3]
South Carolina	BI & PD Liab, UM	25/50/25
South Dakota	BI & PD Liab, UM, UIM	25/50/25
Tennessee	BI & PD Liab	25/50/15[3]
Texas	BI & PD Liab	30/60/25
Utah	BI & PD Liab, PIP	25/65/15[3]
Vermont	BI & PD Liab, UM, UIM	25/50/10
Virginia	BI & PD Liab[8], UM, UIM	25/50/20
Washington	BI & PD Liab	25/50/10
West Virginia	BI & PD Liab, UM	25/40/10
Wisconsin	BI & PD Liab, UM, UIM	25/50/10
Wyoming	BI & PD Liab	25/50/20

[1]The first two numbers refer to bodily injury (BI) liability limits and the third number to property damage (PD) liability. For example, 20/40/10 means coverage up to $40,000 for all persons injured in an accident, subject to a limit of $20,000 for one individual, and $10,000 coverage for property damage. [2]Low-cost policy limits for low-income drivers in the California Automobile Assigned Risk Plan are 10/20/3. [3]Instead of policy limits, policyholders can satisfy the requirement with a combined single limit policy. Amounts vary by state. [4]In addition, policyholders must carry coverage for medical payments. Amounts vary by state. [5]Basic policy (optional) limits are 10/10/5. Uninsured and underinsured motorist coverage not available under the basic policy but uninsured and underinsured motorist coverage is required under the standard policy. [6]In addition, policyholders must have 50/100 for wrongful death coverage.
[7]UIM mandatory in policies with UM limits exceeding 30/60. [8]Compulsory to buy insurance or pay an uninsured motorists vehicle (UMV) fee to the state Department of Motor Vehicles.

Source: Property Casualty Insurers Association of America; state departments of insurance.

State Auto Insurance Laws Governing Liability Coverage

State auto insurance laws governing liability coverage fall into four broad categories: no-fault, choice no-fault, tort liability and add-on. The major differences are whether there are restrictions on the right to sue and whether the policyholder's own insurer pays first-party (i.e., the insured's) benefits, up to the state maximum amount, regardless of who is at fault in the accident.

- **No-fault:** The no-fault system is intended to lower the cost of auto insurance by taking small claims out of the courts. Each insurance company compensates its own policyholders for the cost of minor injuries regardless of who was at fault in the accident. These first-party benefits, known as personal injury protection (PIP), are a mandatory coverage in no-fault states but benefits vary by state. In states with the most comprehensive benefits, a policyholder receives compensation for medical fees, lost wages, funeral costs and other out-of-pocket expenses. The term "no-fault" can be confusing because it is often used to denote any auto insurance system in which each driver's own insurance company pays for certain losses, regardless of fault. In its strict form, the term no-fault applies only to states where insurance companies pay first-party benefits and where there are restrictions on the right to sue.

  Drivers in no-fault states may sue for severe injuries if the case meets certain conditions. These conditions are known as the tort liability threshold, and may be expressed in verbal terms such as death or significant disfigurement (verbal threshold) or in dollar amounts of medical bills (monetary threshold).

- **Choice no-fault:** In choice no-fault states, drivers may select one of two options: a no-fault auto insurance policy, usually with a verbal threshold, or a traditional tort liability policy.

- **Tort liability:** In traditional tort liability states, there are no restrictions on lawsuits. A policyholder at fault in a car crash can be sued by the other driver and by the other driver's passengers for the pain and suffering the accident caused as well as for out-of-pocket expenses such as medical costs.

- **Add-on:** In add-on states, drivers can purchase medical coverage and other first-party benefits from their own insurance company as they do in no-fault states but there are no restrictions on lawsuits. The term "add-on" is used because in these states first-party benefits have been added on to the traditional tort liability system. In add-on states, first-party coverage may not be mandatory and the benefits may be lower than in true no-fault states.

In the following 28 states auto liability is based on the traditional tort liability system. In these states, there are no restrictions on lawsuits:

Alabama
Alaska
Arizona
California
Colorado
Connecticut
Georgia
Idaho
Illinois
Indiana
Iowa
Louisiana
Maine
Mississippi
Missouri
Montana
Nebraska
Nevada
New Mexico
North Carolina
Ohio
Oklahoma
Rhode Island
South Carolina
Tennessee
Vermont
West Virginia
Wyoming

STATE AUTO INSURANCE LAWS GOVERNING LIABILITY COVERAGE

"True" no-fault	First-party benefits (PIP)[1]		Restrictions on lawsuits		Thresholds for lawsuits	
	Compulsory	Optional	Yes	No	Monetary	Verbal
Florida	X		X			X
Hawaii	X		X		X	
Kansas	X		X		X	
Kentucky	X		X	X[2]	X[2]	
Massachusetts	X		X		X	
Michigan	X		X			X
Minnesota	X		X		X	
New Jersey	X		X	X[2]		X[2,3]
New York	X		X			X
North Dakota	X		X		X	
Pennsylvania	X		X	X[2]		X[2]
Puerto Rico	X		X		X	
Utah	X		X		X	
Add-on						
Arkansas	X			X		
Delaware	X			X		
D.C.		X	X[4]	X[4]		
Maryland	X			X		
New Hampshire		X		X		
Oregon	X			X		
South Dakota		X		X		
Texas		X		X		
Virginia		X		X		
Washington		X		X		
Wisconsin		X		X		

[1]Personal injury protection.
[2]"Choice" no-fault state. Policyholder can choose a policy based on the no-fault system or traditional tort liability.
[3]Verbal threshold for the Basic Liability Policy, the Special Policy and the Standard Policy where the policyholder chooses no-fault. The Basic and Special Policies contain lower amounts of coverage.
[4]The District of Columbia is neither a true no-fault nor add-on state. Drivers are offered the option of no-fault or fault-based coverage, but in the event of an accident a driver who originally chose no-fault benefits has 60 days to decide whether to receive those benefits or file a claim against the other party.

Source: Property Casualty Insurers Association of America.

Seatbelt Laws

Thirty-three states and the District of Columbia have a primary seatbelt enforcement law, which allows law enforcement officers to stop a car for noncompliance with seatbelt laws. The other states have secondary laws; officials can only issue seatbelt violations if they stop motorists for other infractions. New Hampshire, the only state that does not have a seatbelt law that applies to adults, has a child restraint law. Seatbelt use was 87 percent nationwide in 2013; states with primary seatbelt laws had an average 91 percent usage rate, 11 points higher than the 78 percent in states with secondary laws.

STATE SEATBELT USE LAWS

State	2012 usage rate	Primary/ secondary enforcement[1]	Age requirements	Maximum fine, first offense	Damages reduced[2]
Alabama	89.5%	P	15+ yrs. in front seat	$25	
Alaska	88.1	P	16+ yrs. in all seats	15	X
Arizona	82.2	S	8+ yrs. in front seat; 8-15 in all seats	10	X
Arkansas	71.9	P	15+ yrs. in front seat	25	
California	95.5	P	16+ yrs. in all seats	20	X
Colorado	80.7	S	16+ yrs. in front seat	71	X
Connecticut	86.8	P	7+ yrs. in front seat	15	
Delaware	87.9	P	16+ yrs. in all seats	25	
D.C.	92.4	P	16+ yrs. in all seats	50	
Florida	87.4	P	6+ yrs. in front seat; 6-17 yrs. in all seats	30	X
Georgia	92.0	P	8-17 yrs. in all seats; 18+ yrs. in front seat	15	
Hawaii	93.4	P	8+ yrs. in all seats	45	
Idaho	79.0	S	7+ yrs. in all seats	10	
Illinois	93.6	P	16+ yrs. in all seats	25	
Indiana	93.6	P	16+ yrs. in all seats	25	
Iowa	92.4	P	18+ yrs. in front seat	25	X
Kansas	79.5	P	14+ yrs. in all seats	10-60	
Kentucky	83.7	P	6 and younger and more than 50 inches tall in all seats; 7+ yrs. in all seats	25	X
Louisiana	79.3	P	13+ yrs. in all seats	25-45	
Maine	84.4	P	18+ yrs. in all seats	50	
Maryland	91.1	P	16+ yrs. in all seats	50	
Massachusetts	72.7	S	13+ yrs. in all seats	25	
Michigan	93.6	P	16+ yrs. in front seat	25	X
Minnesota	93.6	P	7 and younger and more than 57 inches tall in all seats; 8+ in all seats	25	

(table continues)

STATE SEATBELT USE LAWS (Cont'd)

State	2012 usage rate	Primary/ secondary enforcement[1]	Age requirements	Maximum fine, first offense	Damages reduced[2]
Mississippi	83.2%	P	7+ yrs. in front seat	$25	
Missouri	79.4	3	16+ yrs. in front seat	10	X
Montana	76.3	S	6+ yrs. in all seats	20	
Nebraska	78.6	S	18+ yrs. in front seat	25	X
Nevada	90.5	S	6+ yrs. in all seats	25	
New Hampshire	68.6	no law for adults			
New Jersey	88.3	P[4]	7 yrs. and younger and more than 80 lbs.; 8+ yrs. in all seats	20	X
New Mexico	91.4	P	18+ yrs. in all seats	25	
New York	90.4	P	16+ yrs. in front seat	50	X
North Carolina	87.5	P[4]	16+ yrs. in all seats	25, 20	
North Dakota	80.9	S	18+ yrs. in front seat	20	X
Ohio	82.0	S	8-14 yrs. in all seats; 15+ yrs. in front seat	30 driver/20 passenger	X
Oklahoma	83.8	P	13+ yrs. in front seat	20	X
Oregon	96.8	P	16+ yrs. in all seats	110	X
Pennsylvania	83.5	3	8-17 yrs. in all seats; 18+ yrs. in front seat	10	
Rhode Island	77.5	P	18+ yrs. in all seats	40	
South Carolina	90.5	P	6+ yrs. in all seats	25	
South Dakota	66.5	S	18+ yrs. in front seat	20	
Tennessee	83.7	P	16+ yrs. in front seat	50	
Texas	94.0	P	7 yrs. and younger who are 57 inches or taller; 8+ yrs. in all seats	200	
Utah	81.9	3	16+ yrs. in all seats	45	
Vermont	84.2	S	18+ yrs. in all seats	25	
Virginia	78.4	S	18+ yrs. in front seat	25	
Washington	96.9	P	16+ yrs. in all seats	124	
West Virginia	84.0	P	8+ yrs. in front seat; 8-17 yrs. in all seats	25	X
Wisconsin	79.9	P	8+ yrs. in all seats	10	X
Wyoming	77.0	S	9+ yrs. in all seats	25 driver/ 10 passenger	
United States	**86.0%**				

[1]Primary enforcement means police may stop a vehicle and issue a fine for noncompliance with seatbelt laws. Secondary enforcement means that police may issue a fine for not wearing a seatbelt only if the vehicle has been stopped for other traffic violations. [2]Court awards for compensation for injury may be reduced if seatbelt laws were violated. [3]Primary enforcement for children; ages vary. [4]Secondary for rear seat occupants.

Source: U.S. Department of Transportation, National Highway Traffic Safety Administration (NHTSA); Insurance Institute for Highway Safety.

Drunk Driving Laws

There were 10,322 deaths in the U.S. in alcohol-impaired crashes in 2012, up 4.6 percent from 9,865 in 2011. This uptick came in spite of numbers that have been falling since 2003, when 13,096 deaths were reported. (See page 178.) A major factor in the long-term downward trend is the enactment, beginning in the 1980s, of state laws designed to deter drunk driving. By 2004 every state and the District of Columbia had lowered the limit defining drunk driving from 0.10 percent blood alcohol concentration (BAC) to 0.08 percent. All states have more stringent restrictions for drivers under the legal drinking age (21 years old in all states).

STATE LAWS CURBING DRUNK DRIVING

State	License revocation		Open container law[4]	Mandatory ignition interlocks[1]			
	Admin. license rev./ susp.[2]	Mandatory 90-day license rev./ susp.[3]		All offenders	First offenders		
					All	High-BAC offenders only[5]	Repeat offenders
Alabama	X	X	X				X
Alaska	X	X	X	X	X		X
Arizona	X	X	X	X	X		X
Arkansas	X	X		X	X		X
California	X	X	X	in 4 counties	in 4 counties		X
Colorado	X	X	X	X	X		X
Connecticut	X	X		X	X		X
Delaware	X	X			X	X	X
D.C.	X		X				
Florida	X	X	X			X	X
Georgia	X	X	X				X
Hawaii	X	X	X	X	X		X
Idaho	X	X	X				X
Illinois	X	X	X	X	X		X
Indiana	X	X	X				
Iowa	X	X	X				
Kansas	X		X	X	X		X
Kentucky			X				X
Louisiana	X	X	X	X	X		X
Maine	X	X	X	X	X		X
Maryland	X		X			X	X
Massachusetts	X	X	X				X
Michigan			X			X	X
Minnesota	X	X	X	X	X		X

(table continues)

STATE LAWS CURBING DRUNK DRIVING (Cont'd)

State	License revocation		Open container law[4]	All offenders	Mandatory ignition interlocks[1]		
	Admin. license rev./susp.[2]	Mandatory 90-day license rev./susp.[3]			First offenders		Repeat offenders
					All	High-BAC offenders only[5]	
Mississippi	X	X		X	X		X
Missouri	X			X	X		X
Montana			X				X
Nebraska	X	X	X	X	X		X
Nevada	X	X	X			X	X[6]
New Hampshire	X	X	X			X	X
New Jersey			X			X	X
New Mexico	X	X	X	X	X		X
New York	[7]		X	X	X		X
North Carolina	X		X			X	X
North Dakota	X	X	X				
Ohio	X	X	X				
Oklahoma	X	X	X			X	X
Oregon	X	X	X	X	X		X
Pennsylvania			X				X
Rhode Island			X			X	X
South Carolina			X			X	X
South Dakota			X				
Tennessee			X		X		X
Texas	X	X	X			X	X
Utah	X	X	X	X	X		X
Vermont	X	X	X	X	X		
Virginia	X	X	X	X	X		X
Washington	X	X	X	X	X		X
West Virginia	X	X	X	X	X		X
Wisconsin	X	X	X			X	X
Wyoming	X	X	X			X	X

[1]Ignition interlock devices analyze a driver's breath for alcohol and disable the ignition if a driver has been drinking. States identified mandate the devices on offenders' vehicles. [2]On-the-spot drivers license suspension or revocation if BAC is over the legal limit or the driver refuses to take a BAC test. [3]Mandatory penalty for violation of the implied consent law, which means that drivers who refuse to take a breath alcohol test when stopped or arrested for drunk driving will have their license revoked or suspended. [4]Prohibits unsealed alcohol containers in motor vehicle passenger compartments for all occupants. Arresting officer not required to witness consumption. [5]Usually 0.15 percent BAC or higher. [6]High-BAC repeat offenders only. [7]Administrative license suspension lasts until prosecution is complete.

Note: BAC=Blood alcohol concentration.

Source: Insurance Institute for Highway Safety; Property Casualty Insurers Association of America.

Alcohol Server Liability Laws

Most states have enacted liquor liability laws which hold businesses and/or people who serve liquor liable for the damage a drunk driver causes.

STATUTES OR COURT CASES HOLDING ALCOHOLIC BEVERAGE SERVERS LIABLE

State	Commercial servers Statute[1]	Court[2]	Social hosts Statute[3]	Court	State	Commercial servers Statute[1]	Court[2]	Social hosts Statute[3]	Court
Alabama	X		X	X	Montana	X	X	X	
Alaska	X		X		Nebraska			X	
Arizona	X	X	X	X	Nevada			X[4]	
Arkansas	X	X			New Hampshire	X		X	X
California	X		X[4]		New Jersey	X		X	X
Colorado	X	X	X		New Mexico	X		X	X
Connecticut	X	X		X[4,5]	New York	X		X	
Delaware					North Carolina	X	X	X	X[4]
D.C.		X[4]			North Dakota	X		X	
Florida	X		X	X	Ohio	X	X	X	X[4]
Georgia	X		X		Oklahoma	X	X		
Hawaii		X	X		Oregon	X		X	
Idaho	X	X	X		Pennsylvania	X	X		X[4]
Illinois	X		X	X	Rhode Island	X			
Indiana	X	X	X	X	South Carolina	X	X	X	X[4]
Iowa	X	X	X	X[4]	South Dakota				
Kansas					Tennessee	X			
Kentucky	X	X		X[4]	Texas	X	X	X	X
Louisiana	X	X	X	X	Utah	X		X	X
Maine	X		X		Vermont	X		X	X
Maryland					Virginia				
Massachusetts	X	X	X	X	Washington	X	X	X	X[4]
Michigan	X		X	X[4]	West Virginia	X	X[4]		
Minnesota	X		X	X	Wisconsin	X	X	X	X
Mississippi	X	X	X	X	Wyoming	X		X	X
Missouri	X								

[1]Indicates some form of liability is permitted by statute. [2]States where common-law liability has not been specifically overruled by statute or where common-law actions are specifically recognized in addition to statutory liability. [3]Indicates that language is capable of being read broadly enough to include noncommercial servers. [4]For guests under the age of 21. [5]Only if host purveyed or supplied alcohol.

Source: Property Casualty Insurers Association of America.

Older Drivers

In 2012, 14 percent of the total U.S. resident population (43.1 million people) were 65 years old and older. Such motorists accounted for 17 percent of all traffic fatalities in 2012. Recognizing the need for older drivers to retain their mobility and independence, some states issue restricted licenses. Depending on ability, older drivers may be limited to driving during daylight hours or on nonfreeway types of roads. In most states, restrictions such as these can be placed on anyone's drivers license, regardless of age, if his or her medical condition warrants it.

STATE DRIVERS LICENSE RENEWAL LAWS INCLUDING REQUIREMENTS FOR OLDER DRIVERS

| State | Length of regular renewal cycle (years) | Renewal for older drivers | | Require older drivers to pass tests | | Require doctors to report medical conditions[1] | Age limits on mail renewal |
		Length (years)	Age	Age	Type of test		
Alabama	4						
Alaska	5						69
Arizona	none before age 65	5	65	65	vision[2]		70
Arkansas	4						
California	5					X[3]	70
Colorado	10	5	61				66
Connecticut	6						65
Delaware	8					X	
D.C.	8			70	vision, medical		
Florida	8	6	80	80	vision		
Georgia	5 or 8	5	60	64	vision	X	
Hawaii	8	2	72				
Idaho	4 or 8	4	63				
Illinois	4	2	81[4]	75	road		
Indiana	6	3	75[4]				75
Iowa	5 or 8	2	72				70
Kansas	6	4	65				
Kentucky	4						
Louisiana	4						70
Maine	6	4	65	40 and 62	vision		
Maryland	8			40	vision		
Massachusetts	5						75
Michigan	4						
Minnesota	4						

(table continues)

STATE DRIVERS LICENSE RENEWAL LAWS INCLUDING REQUIREMENTS FOR OLDER DRIVERS (Cont'd)

State	Length of regular renewal cycle (years)	Renewal for older drivers Length (years)	Renewal for older drivers Age	Require older drivers to pass tests Age	Require older drivers to pass tests Type of test	Require doctors to report medical conditions[1]	Age limits on mail renewal
Mississippi	4 or 8						
Missouri	6	3	70[4]				
Montana	8	4	75				
Nebraska	5						72
Nevada	4 or 8		65	70	medical[2]	X	
New Hampshire	5						
New Jersey	4					X	
New Mexico	4 or 8	4	67[4]				
New York	8						
North Carolina	8	5	66				
North Dakota	6	4	78				
Ohio	4						
Oklahoma	4						
Oregon	8			50	vision	X	
Pennsylvania	4					X	
Rhode Island	5	2	75				
South Carolina	10	5	65	65	vision		
South Dakota	5			65	vision[2]		
Tennessee	5						
Texas	6	2	85				79
Utah	5			65	vision	X	
Vermont	4						
Virginia	8	5	75	75	vision		75
Washington	5						
West Virginia	8					X	
Wisconsin	8						
Wyoming	4						

[1]Physicians must report physical conditions that might impair driving skills.
[2]If renewing by mail.
[3]Specifically requires doctors to report a diagnosis of dementia.
[4]These states have special renewal requirements for other age groups. Illinois (1 year for drivers 87 and older); Indiana (2 years for drivers 85 and older); Missouri (3 years for drivers age 21 and younger); and New Mexico (1 year for drivers 75 and older).
Note: Specific requirements vary by state; contact state department of motor vehicles for more information.

Source: Insurance Institute for Highway Safety.

Cellphone Laws

Most states have passed laws to address the problem of using a cellphone while driving. Fourteen states—California, Connecticut, Delaware, Hawaii, Illinois, Maryland, Nevada, New Hampshire, New Jersey, New York, Oregon, Vermont, Washington state, West Virginia—and the District of Columbia have a law banning the use of hand-held cellphones behind the wheel for all drivers. The use of all cellphones by novice drivers is restricted in 37 states and the District of Columbia, according to the Insurance Institute for Highway Safety. Washington state was the first state to ban the practice of texting with a cellphone while driving. Text messaging is now banned for all drivers in 44 states and the District of Columbia.

Young Driver Laws

Young drivers account for a disproportionate number of motor vehicle crashes. States are increasingly adopting laws to help lower the crash rate. One approach has been to lower blood alcohol concentration (BAC) limits so those young drivers who drink even small amounts of alcohol will be penalized. Another has been to require a more rigorous learning period before granting young drivers the privilege of a drivers license. This requires young drivers between the ages of 15 and 18 to apply for a graduated drivers license (GDL) to help them improve their driving skills and habits before receiving full driving privileges.

Graduated licensing as defined by the National Highway Traffic Safety Administration consists of three stages. Stage 1 (learners permit) requirements and recommendations include a vision test, a road knowledge test, driving accompanied by a licensed adult, seatbelt use by all vehicle occupants, a zero BAC level, and six months with no crashes or convictions for traffic violations. Stage 2 (intermediate license) includes the completion of Stage 1, a behind-the-wheel road test, advanced driver education training, driving accompanied by a licensed adult at night and 12 consecutive months with no crashes or convictions for traffic offenses before reaching Stage 3 (full license).

Driverless Cars

As automotive technology has advanced, a number of companies have begun working on proto-types of driverless cars, in which the vehicle goes from point to point without guidance. In May 2012 Nevada became the first state to approve a license to test self-driving cars on public roads. California, Florida, Michigan and the District of Columbia have passed similar laws and other states are considering them.

STATE YOUNG DRIVER LAWS[1]

State	Learners permit required for a minimum period	Graduated licensing		Driver may not operate a cellphone in learner and/ or intermediate stages[4]
		Intermediate phase		
		Restrictions on night driving[2]	Passenger restrictions[3]	
Alabama	6 months	X	X	talk
Alaska	6 months	X	X	
Arizona	6 months	X	X	
Arkansas	6 months	X	X	talk
California	6 months	X	X	talk
Colorado	12 months	X	X	talk
Connecticut	6 months	X	X	talk
Delaware	6 months	X	X	talk
D.C.	6 months	X	X	talk
Florida	12 months	X		
Georgia	12 months	X	X	talk
Hawaii	6 months	X	X	talk
Idaho	6 months	X	X	
Illinois	9 months	X	X	talk
Indiana	6 months	X	X	talk
Iowa	12 months	X		talk
Kansas	12 months	X	X	talk
Kentucky	6 months	X	X	talk
Louisiana	6 months	X	X	talk
Maine	6 months	X	X	talk
Maryland	9 months	X	X	talk
Massachusetts	6 months	X	X	talk
Michigan	6 months	X	X	talk
Minnesota	6 months	X	X	talk
Mississippi	12 months	X		text
Missouri	6 months	X	X	text
Montana	6 months	X	X	
Nebraska	6 months	X	X	talk
Nevada	6 months	X	X	
New Hampshire	none[5]	X	X	
New Jersey	6 months	X	X	talk
New Mexico	6 months	X	X	talk

(table continues)

STATE YOUNG DRIVER LAWS[1] (Cont'd)

State	Learners permit required for a minimum period	Graduated licensing		Driver may not operate a cellphone in learner and/ or intermediate stages[4]
		Intermediate phase		
		Restrictions on night driving[2]	Passenger restrictions[3]	
New York	6 months	X	X	
North Carolina	12 months	X	X	talk
North Dakota	6-12 months[6]	X		talk
Ohio	6 months	X	X	talk
Oklahoma	6 months	X	X	talk, text[7]
Oregon	6 months	X	X	talk
Pennsylvania	6 months	X	X	
Rhode Island	6 months	X	X	talk
South Carolina	6 months	X	X	
South Dakota	6 months	X		talk, text
Tennessee	6 months	X	X	talk
Texas	6 months	X	X	talk, text
Utah	6 months	X	X	talk
Vermont	12 months		X	talk
Virginia	9 months	X	X	talk
Washington	6 months	X	X	talk
West Virginia	6 months	X	X	talk
Wisconsin	6 months	X	X	talk
Wyoming	10 days	X	X	talk

[1]Designed to aid young novice drivers between the ages of 15 and 18 gain driving experience. To date they apply only to drivers under the age of 18. All states have lower blood alcohol content laws for under-21 drivers which range from none to 0.02 percent, in contrast with 0.08 percent for drivers over the age of 21 in all states. Includes graduated licensing as defined by the National Highway Traffic Safety Administration. Every state has a graduated licensing law.

[2]Intermediate stage; varies by state with regard to age of driver, night hours that driving is restricted, who must accompany driver during night hours and how long and what stage the restrictions are lifted. Exceptions may be made for work, school or religious activities and emergencies.

[3]Intermediate stage; limits the number of teenage passengers a young driver may have in the vehicle.

[4]Only includes states with restrictions on the use of cellphones for talking or texting by young drivers. Does not reference cellphone laws such as bans on handheld cellphones that apply to all drivers in some states.

[5]New Hampshire does not issue learners permits.

[6]Under age 16: 12 months; 16-18: 6 months.

[7]Banned for nonlife threatening purposes.

Source: Insurance Institute for Highway Safety; U.S. Department of Transportation, National Highway Traffic Safety Administration; National Conference of State Legislatures; Insurance Information Institute.

Homeowners Insurance

Homeowners insurance accounts for 15.1 percent of all property/casualty (P/C) insurance premiums and 29.4 percent of personal property/casualty lines insurance.

Homeowners insurance is a package policy, providing both property and personal liability insurance. The typical policy covers the house, garage and other structures on the property—as well as personal property inside the house—against a wide variety of perils, such as fire, windstorm, vandalism and accidental water damage. The typical homeowners policy includes theft coverage on personal property anywhere in the world and liability coverage for accidental harm caused to others. It also reimburses the policyholder for the additional cost of living elsewhere while his or her house is being repaired or rebuilt after a fire or other disaster.

Earthquake damage and flood damage caused by external flooding are not covered by standard homeowners policies but special policies can be purchased separately. Flood coverage is provided by the federal government's National Flood Insurance Program and some private insurers.

HOMEOWNERS PREMIUMS AS A PERCENT OF ALL P/C PREMIUMS, 2013

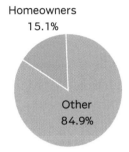

Homeowners 15.1%

Other 84.9%

Source: SNL Financial LC.

HOMEOWNERS MULTIPLE PERIL INSURANCE, 2004-2013
($000)

Year	Net premiums written[1]	Annual percent change	Combined ratio[2]	Annual point change[3]
2004	$49,980,419	8.8%	96.2	-2.2 pts.
2005	53,010,922	6.1	105.1	8.9
2006	55,822,275	5.3	89.5	-15.6
2007	57,053,137	2.2	93.9	4.4
2008	57,375,139	0.6	115.4	21.5
2009	58,478,195	1.9	105.7	-9.7
2010	61,659,466	5.4	106.0	0.3
2011	64,131,058	4.0	121.0	15.0
2012	67,847,033	5.8	103.0	-18.1
2013	72,773,216	7.3	89.6	-13.4

[1]After reinsurance transactions, excludes state funds.
[2]After dividends to policyholders. A drop in the combined ratio represents an improvement; an increase represents a deterioration.
[3]Calculated from unrounded data.

Source: SNL Financial LC.

Property/Casualty Insurance by Line

Homeowners: Premiums/High-Risk Markets

TOP TEN WRITERS OF HOMEOWNERS INSURANCE BY DIRECT PREMIUMS WRITTEN, 2013
($000)

Rank	Group/company	Direct premiums written[1]	Market share[2]
1	State Farm Mutual Automobile Insurance	$17,073,508	20.8%
2	Allstate Corp.	7,428,694	9.1
3	Liberty Mutual	5,236,892	6.4
4	Farmers Insurance Group of Companies[3]	5,029,555	6.1
5	USAA Insurance Group	4,328,005	5.3
6	Travelers Companies Inc.	3,368,962	4.1
7	Nationwide Mutual Group	3,092,293	3.8
8	American Family Mutual	2,272,519	2.8
9	Chubb Corp.	1,972,793	2.4
10	Citizens Property Insurance Corp. (Florida)	1,272,336	1.6

[1]Before reinsurance transactions, includes state funds.
[2]Based on U.S. total, includes territories.
[3]Data for Farmers Insurance Group of Companies and Zurich Financial Group (which owns Farmers' management company) are reported separately by SNL Financial.

Source: SNL Financial LC.

Homeowners: High-Risk Markets

TOP TEN STATES, BY POPULATION CHANGE IN COASTAL COUNTIES, 1960-2010

- The Atlantic Coast, the Gulf of Mexico and the Hawaiian Islands are home to the U.S. counties most vulnerable to hurricanes. These counties accounted for nearly two-thirds of the nation's coastline population in 2008, according to the U.S. Census Bureau.

	By number change			By percent change	
Rank	State	Number change	Rank	State	Percent change
1	California	13,130,000	1	Florida	270.1%
2	Florida	10,360,000	2	Alaska	239.8
3	Texas	3,732,000	3	New Hampshire	198.0
4	Washington	2,578,000	4	Texas	161.9
5	Virginia	1,903,000	5	Virginia	150.8
6	New York	1,400,000	6	Washington	144.4
7	New Jersey	1,275,000	7	South Carolina	125.1
8	Maryland	938,000	8	Hawaii	115.2
9	Massachusetts	826,000	9	North Carolina	114.4
10	Hawaii	728,000	10	California	107.2

Source: U.S. Department of Commerce, Census Bureau (www.census.gov/dataviz/visualizations/039/508.php).

From 1960 to 2008, five of the 11 most hurricane-prone counties were in Louisiana; three were in Florida and three were in North Carolina. In Florida, 75.7 percent of the state's population resides in coastal counties, compared with 32.3 percent in Louisiana and 9.9 percent in North Carolina. In the United States as a whole, 52 percent of the population resides in coastal counties outside of Alaska, according to the U.S. Census Bureau. The population of most counties along the Pacific, Atlantic and Gulf coasts grew between 2000 and 2010, creating an almost unbroken chain of coastal counties with population densities of 319 people per square mile or more running from New Hampshire through northern Virginia, according to the U.S. Census Bureau.

TOP COASTAL COUNTIES MOST FREQUENTLY HIT BY HURRICANES: 1960 TO 2008

County	State	Coastline region	Number of hurricanes	Percent change in population, 1960 to 2008
Monroe County	Florida	Gulf of Mexico	15	50.8%
Lafourche Parish	Louisiana	Gulf of Mexico	14	67.2
Carteret County	North Carolina	Atlantic	14	104.3
Dare County	North Carolina	Atlantic	13	465.9
Hyde County	North Carolina	Atlantic	13	10.1
Jefferson Parish	Louisiana	Gulf of Mexico	12	108.9
Palm Beach County	Florida	Atlantic	12	454.7
Miami-Dade County	Florida	Atlantic	11	156.5
St. Bernard Parish	Louisiana	Gulf of Mexico	11	17.2
Cameron Parish	Louisiana	Gulf of Mexico	11	4.8
Terrebonne Parish	Louisiana	Gulf of Mexico	11	78.7

Source: U.S. Department of Commerce, Census Bureau, Decennial Census of Population and Housing: 1960 to 2000; Population Estimates Program: 2008.

Coastal Area Growth

A report by AIR Worldwide on the insured value of properties in coastal areas of the U.S. (the cost of rebuilding) shows that over the past five years the compound annual growth rate slowed from 7 percent to 4 percent, due to the sharp decrease in the number of housing starts which, in turn, kept the cost of labor and building materials in check. But as the economy recovers, particularly the demand for new housing, AIR expects the growth rate to accelerate. Among the 18 coastal states studied, New York has the highest coastal property values, but Florida has the largest proportion of total value in coastal counties, at 79 percent, compared with 62 percent for New York. The total insured value of residential and commercial properties in U.S. coastal counties exceeds $10 trillion, with New York and Florida accounting for nearly $3 trillion each. Of the $10.6 trillion in insured coastal properties, $4.7 trillion, or 44 percent, were residential and $5.9 trillion, or 56 percent, were commercial.

VALUE OF INSURED RESIDENTIAL COASTAL EXPOSURE, 2012
($ billions)

■ Total U.S. insured residential coastal exposure totaled $4.7 trillion in 2012.

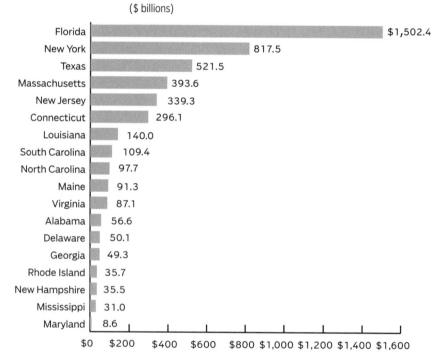

State	$ billions
Florida	$1,502.4
New York	817.5
Texas	521.5
Massachusetts	393.6
New Jersey	339.3
Connecticut	296.1
Louisiana	140.0
South Carolina	109.4
North Carolina	97.7
Maine	91.3
Virginia	87.1
Alabama	56.6
Delaware	50.1
Georgia	49.3
Rhode Island	35.7
New Hampshire	35.5
Mississippi	31.0
Maryland	8.6

Source: AIR Worldwide.

ESTIMATED VALUE OF INSURED COASTAL PROPERTIES VULNERABLE TO HURRICANES BY STATE, 2012[1]
($ billions)

Rank	State	Coastal	Total exposure[2]	Coastal as a percent of total
1	New York	$2,923.1	$4,724.2	62%
2	Florida	2,862.3	3,640.1	79
3	Texas	1,175.3	4,580.7	26
4	Massachusetts	849.6	1,561.4	54
5	New Jersey	713.9	2,129.9	34
6	Connecticut	567.8	879.1	65
7	Louisiana	293.5	823.0	36
8	South Carolina	239.3	843.6	28
9	Virginia	182.3	1,761.7	10
10	Maine	164.6	285.5	58
11	North Carolina	163.5	1,795.1	9
12	Alabama	118.2	917.8	13
13	Georgia	106.7	1,932.2	6
14	Delaware	81.9	208.9	39
15	New Hampshire	64.0	278.7	23
16	Mississippi	60.6	468.5	13
17	Rhode Island	58.3	207.5	28
18	Maryland	17.3	1,293.4	1
	All states above	**$10,642.2**	**$28,331.4**	**38%**
	Total U.S.	**$10,642.2**	**$64,624.3**	**16%**

- The insured value of properties in coastal areas in the United States totaled $10.6 trillion in 2012, according to AIR Worldwide.

[1]Includes residential and commercial properties, as of December 31, 2012. Ranked by value of insured coastal property.
[2]Total exposure is an estimate of the actual total value of all property in the state that is insured or can be insured, including the full replacement value of structures and their contents, additional living expenses and the time value of business interruption coverage.
Source: AIR Worldwide.

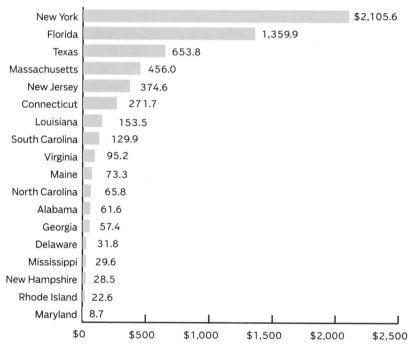

VALUE OF INSURED COMMERCIAL COASTAL EXPOSURE, 2012
($ billions)

- Total U.S. insured commercial exposure totaled $5.9 trillion in 2012.

State	Value
New York	$2,105.6
Florida	1,359.9
Texas	653.8
Massachusetts	456.0
New Jersey	374.6
Connecticut	271.7
Louisiana	153.5
South Carolina	129.9
Virginia	95.2
Maine	73.3
North Carolina	65.8
Alabama	61.6
Georgia	57.4
Delaware	31.8
Mississippi	29.6
New Hampshire	28.5
Rhode Island	22.6
Maryland	8.7

Source: AIR Worldwide.

Residual Market Property Plans

A myriad of different programs in place across the United States provide insurance to high-risk policyholders who may have difficulty obtaining coverage from the standard market. So-called residual, shared or involuntary market programs make basic insurance coverage more readily available. Today, property insurance for the residual market is provided by Fair Access to Insurance Requirements (FAIR) Plans, Beach and Windstorm Plans, and two state-run insurance companies in Florida and Louisiana: Florida's Citizens Property Insurance Corporation and Louisiana's Citizens Property Insurance Corporation. Established in the late 1960s to ensure the continued provision of insurance in urban areas, FAIR Plans often provide property insurance in both urban and coastal areas, while Beach and Windstorm Plans cover predominantly wind-only risks in designated coastal areas. Exposure to loss in both FAIR Plans and Beach and Windstorm Plans fell from $696 billion in 2008 to $639 billion in 2013. The number of policies in force grew from 2.61 million to 3.22 million during the same period.

INSURANCE PROVIDED BY FAIR PLANS, FISCAL YEARS 2004-2013[1]

Year	Number of Habitational policies	Number of Commercial policies	Exposure[2] ($000)	Direct premiums written ($000)
2004	1,907,337	138,163	$400,413,034	$2,164,546
2005	1,928,292	117,942	387,780,124	2,234,493
2006	2,389,299	172,070	601,859,916	4,063,324
2007	2,412,252	114,053	684,829,667	4,431,381
2008	2,190,189	90,876	612,749,753	3,727,311
2009	2,043,969	86,575	614,905,551	3,038,712
2010	2,378,736	83,243	662,633,180	3,448,576
2011	2,658,662	51,657	715,289,876	3,942,021
2012	2,518,808	71,776	635,705,150	4,059,446
2013	2,484,816	64,359	445,635,335	3,685,283

[1]Includes the Texas FAIR Plan; Florida's Citizens Property Insurance Corporation, which includes FAIR and Beach Plans; the Louisiana Citizens Property Insurance Corporation, which includes FAIR and Beach Plans for 2004, 2005 and premiums written after 2007; and North Carolina after 2010.
[2]Exposure is the estimate of the aggregate value of all insurance in force in all FAIR Plans in all lines (except liability, where applicable, and crime) for 12 months ending September through December.

Source: Property Insurance Plans Service Office (PIPSO).

INSURANCE PROVIDED BY FAIR PLANS BY STATE, FISCAL YEAR 2013[1]

State	Number of Habitational policies	Number of Commercial policies	Exposure[2] ($000)	Direct premiums written ($000)
California	123,287	5,327	$41,708,503	$69,103
Connecticut	2,829	116	540,843	3,687
Delaware	1,947	73	306,440	629
D.C.	368	63	115,687	393
Florida[3]	1,418,877	40,467	228,887,485	2,761,638
Georgia	33,793	1,792	4,731,530	25,431
Illinois	6,406	94	686,372	7,132
Indiana	2,232	52	243,382	2,190
Iowa	1,133	42	73,477	800
Kansas	11,648	163	623,217	5,540
Kentucky	11,596	589	589,679	7,633
Louisiana[3]	126,708	5,022	17,831,008	179,003

(table continues)

INSURANCE PROVIDED BY FAIR PLANS BY STATE, FISCAL YEAR 2013[1] (Cont'd)

State	Number of Habitational policies	Number of Commercial policies	Exposure[2] ($000)	Direct premiums written ($000)
Maryland	2,225	89	$421,309	$1,408
Massachusetts	215,201	378	77,176,753	275,455
Michigan	24,109	439	3,011,975	26,581
Minnesota	5,465	37	1,259,687	4,257
Mississippi	12,847	4	751,425	8,829
Missouri	4,088	179	234,464	2,209
New Jersey	18,098	529	2,601,010	10,865
New Mexico	10,612	223	70,119	4,038
New York	52,312	3,584	14,449,237	36,996
North Carolina	139,642	2,226	11,204,596	52,429
Ohio	30,727	547	7,116,116	25,857
Oregon	2,332	80	189,989	947
Pennsylvania	20,706	1,463	1,731,758	8,272
Rhode Island	16,643	134	3,997,695	20,933
Texas	155,469	4	20,594,317	122,683
Virginia	32,871	557	4,429,507	19,798
Washington	54	23	21,109	175
West Virginia	591	71	36,646	372
Total	**2,484,816**	**64,359**	**$445,635,335**	**$3,685,283**

[1]Excludes the FAIR Plans of Arkansas, Hawaii and Wisconsin.
[2]Exposure is the estimate of the aggregate value of all insurance in force in all FAIR Plans in all lines (except liability, where applicable, and crime) for 12 months ending September through December.
[3]Citizens Property Insurance Corporation, which combined the FAIR and Beach Plans.
[4]The Mississippi and Texas FAIR Plans do not offer a commercial policy.

Source: Property Insurance Plans Service Office (PIPSO).

Insurance Provided by Beach and Windstorm Plans

Beach and Windstorm Plans ensure that insurance is available against damage from hurricanes and other windstorms. In Georgia, Massachusetts and New York, FAIR Plans provide wind and hail coverage for certain coastal communities. These states do not have Beach and Windstorm Plans.

INSURANCE PROVIDED BY BEACH AND WINDSTORM PLANS, FISCAL YEAR 2013[1]

State	Number of Habitational policies	Number of Commercial policies	Exposure[2] ($000)	Direct premiums written ($000)
Alabama	29,520	96	$5,061,538	$45,393
Mississippi	42,351	1,331	6,891,208	76,509
North Carolina	247,797	12,179	90,074,990	385,460
South Carolina	42,617	861	14,772,689	92,648
Texas	273,097	16,433	76,921,369	472,740
Total	**635,382**	**30,900**	**$193,721,794**	**$1,072,750**

[1]The Florida and Louisiana Beach Plans merged with their FAIR Plans, see chart on page 101. [2]Exposure is the estimate of the aggregate value of all insurance in force in each state's Beach and Windstorm Plan in all lines (except liability, where applicable, and crime) for 12 months ending September through December.

Source: Property Insurance Plans Service Office (PIPSO).

Homeowners: Costs/Expenditures

The average homeowners insurance premium rose by 7.6 percent in 2011, following a 3.3 percent increase in 2010, according to a December 2013 study by the National Association of Insurance Commissioners. The average renters insurance premium rose by 1.1 percent in 2011, after rising 0.5 percent the previous year.

AVERAGE PREMIUMS FOR HOMEOWNERS AND RENTERS INSURANCE, UNITED STATES, 2003-2011

Year	Homeowners[1]	Percent change	Renters[2]	Percent change
2003	$668	12.6%	$192	3.2%
2004	729	9.1	195	1.6
2005	764	4.8	193	-1.0
2006	804	5.2	189	-2.1
2007	822	2.2	182	-3.7
2008	830	1.0	182	[3]
2009	880	6.0	184	1.1
2010	909	3.3	185	0.5
2011	978	7.6	187	1.1

[1]Based on the HO-3 homeowner package policy for owner-occupied dwellings, 1 to 4 family units. Provides "all risks" coverage (except those specifically excluded in the policy) on buildings and broad named-peril coverage on personal property, and is the most common package written. [2]Based on the HO-4 renters insurance policy for tenants. Includes broad named-peril coverage for the personal property of tenants. [3]Less than 0.1 percent.

Source: © 2013 National Association of Insurance Commissioners (NAIC). Reprinted with permission. Further reprint or distribution strictly prohibited without written permission of NAIC.

- A 2014 Insurance Information Institute poll conducted by ORC International found that 95 percent of homeowners had homeowners insurance but only 37 percent of renters had renters insurance.

- The U.S. home ownership rate was 65.1 percent in 2013, down from 65.4 percent in 2012, according to the U.S. Census Bureau. The 2010 Census showed that in some of the largest cities renters outnumbered owners, including New York, where 69.0 percent of households were renter occupied, followed by Los Angeles (61.8 percent), Chicago (55.1 percent) and Houston (54.6 percent).

AVERAGE HOMEOWNERS INSURANCE PREMIUMS RANKED BY STATE, 2011[1]

Rank	State	Average premium	Rank	State	Average premium
1	Florida	$1,933	26	Kentucky	$839
2	Louisiana	1,672	27	Illinois	822
3	Texas[2]	1,578	28	Montana	818
4	Mississippi	1,409	29	New Hampshire	811
5	Oklahoma	1,386	30	Maryland	800
6	Alabama	1,163	31	New Mexico	793
7	Rhode Island	1,139	32	Virginia	782
8	Kansas	1,103	33	Indiana	779
9	New York	1,097	34	Michigan	774
10	Connecticut	1,096	35	Wyoming	770
11	South Carolina	1,091	36	Vermont	748
12	D.C.	1,083	37	Pennsylvania	744
13	Massachusetts	1,072	38	West Virginia	743
14	Minnesota	1,056	39	South Dakota	721
15	Arkansas	1,029	40	Maine	714
16	Missouri	1,022	41	Iowa	713
17	North Dakota	969	42	Nevada	689
18	California[3]	967	43	Arizona	675
19	Colorado	961	44	Delaware	664
20	Nebraska	958	45	Ohio	644
21	Alaska	924	46	Washington	626
22	New Jersey	915	47	Wisconsin	592
22	Tennessee	915	48	Utah	563
23	Hawaii	907	49	Oregon	559
24	Georgia	906	50	Idaho	518
25	North Carolina	869			

[1]Includes policies written by Citizens Property Insurance Corp. (Florida) and Citizens Property Insurance Corp. (Louisiana), Alabama Insurance Underwriting Association, Mississippi Windstorm Underwriting Association, North Carolina Joint Underwriting Association and South Carolina Wind and Hail Underwriting Association. Other southeastern states have wind pools in operation and their data may not be included in this chart. Based on the HO-3 homeowner package policy for owner-occupied dwellings, 1 to 4 family units. Provides "all risks" coverage (except those specifically excluded in the policy) on buildings and broad named-peril coverage on personal property, and is the most common package written.

[2]The Texas Department of Insurance developed home insurance policy forms that are similar but not identical to the standard forms. In addition, due to the Texas Windstorm Association (which writes wind-only policies) classifying HO-1, 2 and 5 premiums as HO-3, the average premium for homeowners insurance is artificially high.

[3]Data provided by the California Department of Insurance.

Note: Average premium=Premiums/exposure per house years. A house year is equal to 365 days of insured coverage for a single dwelling. The NAIC does not rank state average expenditures and does not endorse any conclusions drawn from this data.

Source: ©2013 National Association of Insurance Commissioners (NAIC). Reprinted with permission. Further reprint or distribution strictly prohibited without written permission of NAIC.

AVERAGE PREMIUMS FOR HOMEOWNERS AND RENTERS INSURANCE BY STATE, 2011[1]

State	Homeowners Average premium[2]	Rank[3]	Renters Average premium[4]	Rank[3]	State	Homeowners Average premium[2]	Rank[3]	Renters Average premium[4]	Rank[3]
Alabama	$1,163	6	$230	4	Montana	$818	28	$147	40
Alaska	924	21	171	26	Nebraska	958	20	151	37
Arizona	675	43	200	12	Nevada	689	42	199	13
Arkansas	1,029	15	220	7	New Hampshire	811	29	152	36
California[5]	967	18	208	11	New Jersey	915	22	168	28
Colorado	961	19	175	23	New Mexico	793	31	189	16
Connecticut	1,096	10	196	15	New York	1,097	9	210	10
Delaware	664	44	159	32	North Carolina	869	25	132	42
D.C.	1,083	12	167	29	North Dakota	969	17	117	43
Florida	1,933	1	210	10	Ohio	644	45	183	17
Georgia	906	24	228	5	Oklahoma	1,386	5	235	3
Hawaii	907	23	176	22	Oregon	559	49	170	27
Idaho	518	50	160	31	Pennsylvania	744	37	154	35
Illinois	822	27	172	25	Rhode Island	1,139	7	183	17
Indiana	779	33	179	19	South Carolina	1,091	11	199	14
Iowa	713	41	149	39	South Dakota	721	39	117	43
Kansas	1,103	8	177	21	Tennessee	915	22	213	9
Kentucky	839	26	175	23	Texas[6]	1,578	3	225	6
Louisiana	1,672	2	238	2	Utah	563	48	147	40
Maine	714	40	150	38	Vermont	748	36	155	34
Maryland	800	30	161	30	Virginia	782	32	155	34
Massachusetts	1,072	13	213	8	Washington	626	46	174	24
Michigan	774	34	208	11	West Virginia	743	38	178	20
Minnesota	1,056	14	150	38	Wisconsin	592	47	133	41
Mississippi	1,409	4	252	1	Wyoming	770	35	156	33
Missouri	1,022	16	182	18	**United States**	**$978**		**$187**	

[1]See previous chart for state funds and residual markets included. [2]Based on the HO-3 homeowner package policy for owner-occupied dwellings, 1 to 4 family units. Provides "all risks" coverage (except those specifically excluded in the policy) on buildings and broad named-peril coverage on personal property, and is the most common package written. [3]Ranked from highest to lowest. States with the same premium receive the same rank. [4]Based on the HO-4 renters insurance policy for tenants. Includes broad named-peril coverage for the personal property of tenants. [5]Data provided by the California Department of Insurance. [6]The Texas Department of Insurance developed home insurance policy forms that are similar but not identical to the standard forms. In addition, due to the Texas Windstorm Association (which writes wind-only policies) classifying HO-1, 2 and 5 premiums as HO-3, the average premium for homeowners insurance is artificially high. Note: Average premium=Premiums/exposure per house years. A house year is equal to 365 days of insured coverage for a single dwelling. The NAIC does not rank state average expenditures and does not endorse any conclusions drawn from this data.

Source: ©2013 National Association of Insurance Commissioners (NAIC). Reprinted with permission. Further reprint or distribution strictly prohibited without written permission of NAIC.

HOMEOWNERS INSURANCE INDUSTRY UNDERWRITING EXPENSES, 2013[1]

Expense	Percent of premiums
LOSSES AND RELATED EXPENSE[2]	
Loss and loss adjustment expense (LAE) ratio	**59.6%**
Incurred losses	50.5
Defense and cost containment expenses incurred	1.5
Adjusting and other expenses incurred	7.6
OPERATING EXPENSES[3]	
Expense ratio	**29.5%**
Net commissions and brokerage expenses incurred	12.6
Taxes, licenses and fees	2.7
Other acquisition and field supervision expenses incurred	9.0
General expenses incurred	5.2
DIVIDENDS TO POLICYHOLDERS[2]	**0.5%**
COMBINED RATIO AFTER DIVIDENDS[4]	**89.6%**

[1]After reinsurance transactions.
[2]As a percent of net premiums earned ($70.3 billion in 2013).
[3]As a percent of net premiums written ($72.8 billion in 2013).
[4]Sum of loss and LAE, expense and dividends ratios.

Source: SNL Financial LC.

Claims

- 7.2 percent of insured homes experienced a claim in 2012.

- Homeowners insurance losses, net of reinsurance, fell to $35 billion in 2013, from $41 billion in 2012, according to SNL Financial.

HOMEOWNERS INSURANCE LOSSES, 2008-2012[1]

Year	Total homeowner losses		Year	Total homeowner losses	
	Claim frequency[2]	Claim severity[3]		Claim frequency[2]	Claim severity[3]
2008	6.88	$7,789	2011	9.71	$8,424
2009	6.10	8,400	2012	7.22	8,665
2010	6.63	8,584	**Average[4]**	**7.32**	**$8,384**

[1]For homeowners multiple peril policies. Excludes tenants and condominium policies.
[2]Claims per 100 house years (policies).
[3]Average amount paid per claim; based on accident year incurred losses, excluding loss adjustment expenses, i.e., indemnity costs per accident year incurred claims.
[4]Weighted average, 2008-2012.

Source: ISO®, a Verisk Analytics® company.

Causes of Homeowners Insurance Losses

In 2012, 7.2 percent of insured homes had a claim, according to ISO. Property damage, including theft, accounted for 97.6 percent of those claims. Changes in the percentage of each type of homeowners loss from one year to another are partially influenced by large fluctuations in the number and severity of weather-related events such as hurricanes and winter storms. There are two ways of looking at losses: by the average number of claims filed per 100 policies (frequency) and by the average amount paid for each claim (severity). The loss category "water damage and freezing" includes damage caused by mold, if covered.

HOMEOWNERS INSURANCE LOSSES BY CAUSE, 2008-2012[1]
(Percent of losses incurred)

Cause of loss	2008	2009	2010	2011	2012
Property damage[2]	**94.9%**	**95.0%**	**95.4%**	**97.2%**	**97.6%**
Fire, lightning and debris removal	27.5	27.2	25.5	19.0	25.2
Wind and hail	35.1	31.7	35.6	46.0	47.2
Water damage and freezing	20.6	24.4	21.3	21.7	17.5
Theft	3.0	3.3	3.1	2.4	3.0
All other[3]	8.7	8.5	9.9	8.3	4.7
Liability[4]	**5.1%**	**5.0%**	**4.6%**	**2.8%**	**2.4%**
Bodily injury and property damage	4.9	4.8	4.4	2.6	2.3
Medical payments and other	0.2	0.2	0.2	0.2	0.2
Credit card and other[5]	6	6	6	6	6
Total	**100.0%**	**100.0%**	**100.0%**	**100.0%**	**100.0%**

[1] For homeowners multiple peril policies. Excludes tenants and condominium owners policies.
[2] First party, i.e., covers damage to policyholder's own property.
[3] Includes vandalism and malicious mischief.
[4] Payments to others for which policyholder is responsible.
[5] Includes coverage for unauthorized use of various cards, forgery, counterfeit money and miscellaneous losses.
[6] Less than 0.1 percent.

Source: ISO®, a Verisk Analytics® company.

AVERAGE HOMEOWNERS LOSSES, 2008-2012[1]

(Weighted average, 2008-2012)

In the five-year period, 2008-2012, 7.3 percent of insured homes had a claim. Wind and hail accounted for the largest share of claims, with 3.4 percent of insured homes having such a loss.

Cause of loss	Claim frequency[2]	Claim severity[3]
Property damage[4]	**7.16**	**$8,255**
Fire, lightning and debris removal	0.43	34,306
Wind and hail	3.37	7,307
Water damage and freezing	1.79	7,195
Theft	0.52	3,428
All other[5]	1.04	4,684
Liability[6]	**0.17**	**$14,021**
Bodily injury and property damage	0.12	18,804
Medical payments and other	0.05	2,256
Credit card and other[7]	[8]	**$581**
Average (property damage and liability), 2008-2012	**7.32**	**$8,384**

[1]For homeowners multiple peril policies. Excludes tenants and condominium owners policies. [2]Claims per 100 house years (policies). [3]Accident year incurred losses, excluding loss adjustment expenses, i.e., indemnity costs per accident year incurred claims. [4]First party, i.e., covers damage to policyholder's own property. [5]Includes vandalism and malicious mischief. [6]Payments to others for which policyholder is responsible. [7]Includes coverage for unauthorized use of cards, forgery, counterfeit money and miscellaneous losses. [8]Less than 0.01.

Source: Source: ISO®, a Verisk Analytics® company.

HOMEOWNERS INSURANCE CLAIMS FREQUENCY*

- Homeowners claims related to wind or hail are the most frequent; the costliest are related to fire, lightning or debris removal.
- About one in 15 insured homes have a claim each year.
- About one in 30 insured homes have a property damage claim related to wind or hail each year.
- About one in 55 insured homes have a property damage claim caused by water damage or freezing each year.
- About one in 190 insured homes have a property damage claim due to theft each year.
- About one in 230 insured homes have a property damage claim related to fire, lightning or debris removal every year.
- About one in 830 homeowners policies have a liability claim related to the cost of lawsuits for bodily injury or property damage that the policyholder or family members cause to others.

*I.I.I. calculations, based on ISO®, a Verisk Analytics® company, data for homeowners insurance claims from 2008-2012 (see table above).

Lightning

In 2013 there were 23 lightning fatalities, a record low and 12 fewer than the 10-year average of 35 fatalities, according to the National Oceanic and Atmospheric Administration.

HOMEOWNERS INSURANCE CLAIMS AND PAYOUTS FOR LIGHTNING LOSSES, 2009-2013

	2009	2010	2011	2012	2013	Percent change	
						2012-2013	2009-2013
Number of paid claims	185,789	213,278	186,307	151,000	114,740	-24.0%	-38.2%
Insured losses ($ millions)	$798.1	$1,033.5	$952.5	$969.0	$673.5	-30.5	-15.6
Average cost per claim	$4,296	$4,846	$5,112	$6,400	$5,869	-8.3	36.6

Source: Insurance Information Institute, State Farm®.

TOP TEN STATES FOR HOMEOWNERS INSURANCE LIGHTNING LOSSES BY NUMBER OF CLAIMS, 2013

Rank	State	Number of paid claims	Insured losses ($ millions)	Average cost per claim
1	Georgia	11,184	$56.0	$5,007
2	Texas	6,419	54.2	8,436
3	North Carolina	5,711	34.1	5,965
4	Louisiana	5,547	21.6	3,902
5	Alabama	5,199	34.8	6,702
6	Pennsylvania	4,483	22.4	4,987
7	Tennessee	4,317	23.2	5,381
8	South Carolina	4,011	23.1	5,755
9	Ohio	3,942	17.1	4,344
10	Illinois	3,849	25.6	6,646

Source: Insurance Information Institute, State Farm®.

National Flood Insurance Program

Flood damage is excluded under standard homeowners and renters insurance policies. Flood coverage, however, is available in the form of a separate policy from both the National Flood Insurance Program (NFIP) and from a few private insurers.

Congress created the NFIP in 1968 in response to the rising cost of taxpayer-funded disaster relief for flood victims and the increasing amount of damage caused by floods. The NFIP makes federally backed flood insurance available in communities that agree to adopt and enforce floodplain management ordinances to reduce future flood damage. The NFIP is self-supporting for the average historical loss year. This means that unless there is a widespread disaster, operating expenses and flood insurance claims are financed through premiums collected.

The NFIP provides coverage for up to $250,000 for the structure of the home and $100,000 for personal possessions. Private flood insurance is available for those who need additional insurance protection, known as "excess coverage," over and above the basic policy or for people whose communities do not participate in the NFIP. Some insurers have introduced special policies for high-value properties. These policies may cover homes in noncoastal areas and/or provide enhancements to traditional flood coverage. The comprehensive portion of an auto insurance policy includes coverage for flood damage.

A 2014 poll by the Insurance Information Institute found that 13 percent of American homeowners had a flood insurance policy. This percentage has been at about the same level for the six years since 2009. The percentage of homeowners with flood insurance was highest in the South, at 20 percent, up from 15 percent in 2013. Eleven percent of homeowners in the Northeast had a flood insurance policy, compared with 10 percent in 2013. Eight percent of homeowners in the West had a flood insurance policy, down from 11 percent in 2013, while 7 percent of homeowners in the Midwest had flood insurance, compared with 12 percent in 2013.

- As of November 2014, 81 insurance companies participated in the "Write-Your-Own" program, started in 1983, in which insurers issue policies and adjust flood claims on behalf of the federal government under their own names.

- As of October 2014, 69 percent of NFIP flood insurance policies covered single family homes, 20 percent covered condominiums and 5 percent covered businesses and other non-residential properties. 2 to 4 family units and other residential policies accounted for the remainder.

- Superstorm Sandy, which occurred in October 2012, resulted in $7.8 billion in NFIP payouts as of August 2014, second only to 2005's Hurricane Katrina with $16.3 billion in payouts.

Flood Insurance Losses

National Flood Insurance Program (NFIP) payouts vary widely from year to year. Flood loss payments totaled $441 million in 2013, down significantly from $8.8 billion in 2012, the year of superstorm Sandy. In 2005 loss payments totaled $17.8 billion, the highest amount on record, including losses from hurricanes Katrina, Rita and Wilma. See page 151 for information on flood insurance losses.

The widespread flooding associated with Hurricane Katrina in 2005 set in motion debate about how to improve the NFIP. The Biggert-Waters Flood Insurance Reform Act of 2012 sought to make the federal flood insurance program more financially self-sufficient in part by eliminating rate subsidies. In March 2014 Congress, in response to complaints that the law was making flood insurance unaffordable, passed legislation to restrict many of the rate increases called for in Biggert-Waters.

- There were 128,186 NFIP claims from superstorm Sandy as of August 2014. The average paid loss was $60,484, compared with 167,805 claims from Katrina, with an average paid loss of $97,100.

- In 2013, the average amount of flood coverage was $233,237 and the average premium was $632.

- The average flood claim in 2013 was $26,165, down from $59,189 in 2012, the year of superstorm Sandy.

- NFIP premiums written rose slightly from $3.3 billion in 2012 to $3.5 billion in 2013.

- As of early November, the federal government had declared 26 major flood disasters in 2014, compared with 42 in all of 2013.

NATIONAL FLOOD INSURANCE PROGRAM, 1980-2013

Year	Policies in force at year-end	Losses paid	
		Number	Amount ($000)
1980	2,103,851	41,918	$230,414
1985	2,016,785	38,676	368,239
1990	2,477,861	14,766	167,897
1995	3,476,829	62,441	1,295,578
2000	4,369,087	16,362	251,721
2005	4,962,011	213,290	17,763,189
2006	5,514,895	24,620	641,187
2007	5,655,919	23,169	613,942
2008	5,684,275	74,727	3,485,640
2009	5,700,235	30,996	779,855
2010	5,645,436	29,111	773,526
2011	5,646,144	77,801	2,419,357
2012	5,620,017	148,448	8,786,455
2013	5,580,075	16,864	441,421

Source: U.S. Department of Homeland Security, Federal Emergency Management Agency.

FLOOD INSURANCE IN THE UNITED STATES, 2013[1]

State	Direct NFIP business		WYO business		Total NFIP/WYO	
	Number of policies	Insurance in force[2] ($ millions)	Number of policies	Insurance in force[2] ($ millions)	Number of policies	Insurance in force[2] ($ millions)
Alabama	11,130	$2,182.8	46,594	$10,189.8	57,724	$12,372.6
Alaska	792	176.5	2,271	576.9	3,063	753.4
Arizona	6,504	1,441.6	28,291	6,562.4	34,795	8,004.0
Arkansas	3,979	552.5	16,839	2,630.8	20,818	3,183.3
California	42,225	10,651.9	204,053	54,490.5	246,278	65,142.5
Colorado	4,471	1,020.9	18,516	4,261.7	22,987	5,282.6
Connecticut	3,071	659.2	39,691	9,701.5	42,762	10,360.6
Delaware	5,091	1,300.8	21,116	5,268.8	26,207	6,569.6
D.C.	88	23.8	2,245	382.8	2,333	406.6
Florida	182,359	46,017.3	1,855,348	431,028.3	2,037,707	477,045.6
Georgia	19,239	4,600.4	76,762	19,074.6	96,001	23,675.0
Hawaii	2,547	559.0	57,136	12,171.9	59,683	12,730.9
Idaho	1,300	286.5	5,562	1,256.4	6,862	1,542.9
Illinois	13,521	2,239.5	35,428	6,564.0	48,949	8,803.5
Indiana	7,322	1,112.6	21,728	3,974.3	29,050	5,086.9
Iowa	3,230	471.1	12,953	2,431.0	16,183	2,902.1
Kansas	3,028	460.0	9,599	1,627.9	12,627	2,087.8
Kentucky	4,225	573.6	20,392	3,120.6	24,617	3,694.2
Louisiana	133,122	30,733.8	348,232	82,842.6	481,354	113,576.4
Maine	744	145.1	8,490	1,887.9	9,234	2,033.0
Maryland	8,066	1,871.2	65,531	14,398.9	73,597	16,270.1
Massachusetts	6,096	1,305.9	52,548	12,749.4	58,644	14,055.3
Michigan	5,234	772.8	19,438	3,479.0	24,672	4,251.8
Minnesota	2,199	454.2	9,779	2,112.1	11,978	2,566.3
Mississippi	17,802	3,940.9	55,905	12,497.6	73,707	16,438.5
Missouri	5,101	770.5	20,667	3,587.6	25,768	4,358.1
Montana	1,024	187.1	4,764	875.5	5,788	1,062.6
Nebraska	2,819	403.4	9,620	1,681.1	12,439	2,084.5
Nevada	2,527	562.9	12,260	2,870.6	14,787	3,433.4

(table continues)

FLOOD INSURANCE IN THE UNITED STATES, 2013[1] (Cont'd)

State	Direct NFIP business		WYO business		Total NFIP/WYO	
	Number of policies	Insurance in force[2] ($ millions)	Number of policies	Insurance in force[2] ($ millions)	Number of policies	Insurance in force[2] ($ millions)
New Hampshire	722	$146.3	8,738	$1,800.2	9,460	$1,946.5
New Jersey	23,732	4,460.3	219,917	52,881.0	243,649	57,341.3
New Mexico	2,722	475.5	13,263	2,524.1	15,985	2,999.6
New York	27,949	5,763.7	167,164	43,438.8	195,113	49,202.5
North Carolina	16,949	4,028.9	121,732	28,798.7	138,681	32,827.6
North Dakota	2,509	608.5	11,250	2,792.6	13,759	3,401.1
Ohio	8,458	1,179.9	32,444	5,601.2	40,902	6,781.1
Oklahoma	3,998	667.3	13,539	2,521.5	17,537	3,188.8
Oregon	7,386	1,654.1	26,161	6,046.3	33,547	7,700.4
Pennsylvania	12,635	1,804.0	60,453	11,779.0	73,088	13,583.0
Rhode Island	659	154.5	15,280	3,801.8	15,939	3,956.2
South Carolina	26,878	7,137.9	178,032	43,716.4	204,910	50,854.3
South Dakota	1,095	209.8	4,306	922.9	5,401	1,132.7
Tennessee	6,297	1,373.8	26,033	5,889.9	32,330	7,263.7
Texas	120,495	31,095.7	506,658	129,156.2	627,153	160,251.9
Utah	767	162.9	3,710	868.5	4,477	1,031.4
Vermont	518	70.4	4,002	846.7	4,520	917.1
Virginia	19,960	4,800.7	94,920	23,378.1	114,880	28,178.8
Washington	6,940	1,504.4	37,162	8,875.1	44,102	10,379.5
West Virginia	5,512	605.3	15,106	2,092.1	20,618	2,697.4
Wisconsin	2,418	374.9	13,436	2,444.7	15,854	2,819.6
Wyoming	516	103.7	1,959	429.2	2,475	532.9
Guam	182	33.0	80	16.8	262	49.8
N. Mariana Islands	10	0.4	1	1.0	11	1.4
Puerto Rico	738	36.0	39,083	3,603.8	39,821	3,639.8
Virgin Islands	306	57.1	1,757	301.9	2,063	359.0
United States	**799,207**	**$183,986.6**	**4,697,944**	**$1,098,824.8**	**5,497,151**	**$1,282,811.4**

[1]Direct and WYO business may not add to total due to rounding.
[2]Total limits of liability for all policies in force.

Source: U.S. Department of Homeland Security, Federal Emergency Management Agency.

Property/Casualty Insurance by Line

Earthquake Insurance

Standard homeowners, renters and business insurance policies do not cover damage from earthquakes. Coverage is available either in the form of an endorsement or as a separate policy. Earthquake insurance provides protection from the shaking and cracking that can destroy buildings and personal possessions. Coverage for other kinds of damage that may result from earthquakes, such as fire and water damage due to burst gas and water pipes, is provided by standard home and business insurance policies. Earthquake coverage is available mostly from private insurance companies. In California, homeowners can also get coverage from the California Earthquake Authority (CEA), a privately funded, publicly managed organization. Only about 10 percent of California residents currently have earthquake coverage, down from about 30 percent in 1996, two years after the Northridge, California, earthquake.

Seven percent of homeowners responding to a 2014 poll by the Insurance Information Institute said they have earthquake insurance. Homeowners in the West were most likely to buy earthquake coverage, 10 percent; followed by the Midwest, 7 percent; the South, 6 percent; and the Northeast, 2 percent. See page 155 for information on earthquake insurance losses.

EARTHQUAKE INSURANCE, 2004-2013
($000)

Year	Net premiums written[1]	Annual percent change	Combined ratio[2]	Annual point change[3]
2004	$1,098,441	4.7%	48.6	-7.4 pts.
2005	1,106,671	0.7	50.9	2.3
2006	1,315,423	18.9	40.4	-10.5
2007	1,246,538	-5.2	30.0	-10.4
2008	1,259,872	1.1	33.5	3.5
2009	1,288,353	2.3	36.3	2.8
2010	1,443,598	12.0	41.4	5.1
2011	1,467,372	1.6	55.8	14.4
2012	1,593,451	8.6	36.3	-19.5
2013	1,586,985	-0.4	30.3	-6.0

[1]After reinsurance transactions, excludes state funds
[2]After dividends to policyholders. A drop in the combined ratio represents an improvement; an increase represents a deterioration.
[3]Calculated from unrounded data.

Source: SNL Financial LC.

Leading Writers of Earthquake Insurance

The California Earthquake Authority (CEA), a publicly managed, largely privately funded organization that sells its policies through participating private insurance companies, was the leading writer of earthquake insurance in the United States, based on direct premiums written in 2013, according to data from SNL Financial. The CEA had $574 million in direct premiums written in 2013, all of which covered residential California properties. In 2013 the CEA accounted for 35 percent of the California earthquake insurance market and 20 percent of the total U.S. earthquake insurance market. The nine other largest earthquake insurers in 2013 were all private insurance companies.

TOP TEN WRITERS OF EARTHQUAKE INSURANCE BY DIRECT PREMIUMS WRITTEN, 2013
($000)

Rank	Group/company	Direct premiums written[1]	Market share[2]
1	California Earthquake Authority	$573,960	20.0%
2	State Farm Mutual Automobile Insurance	228,898	8.0
3	Zurich Insurance Group[3]	217,978	7.6
4	American International Group	150,861	5.3
5	Travelers Companies Inc.	143,022	5.0
6	GeoVera Insurance Holdings Ltd.	118,128	4.1
7	Liberty Mutual	100,496	3.5
8	ACE Ltd.	86,556	3.0
9	Swiss Re Ltd.	84,249	2.9
10	Chubb Corp.	58,990	2.1

[1]Before reinsurance transactions, includes state funds.
[2]Based on U.S. total, includes territories.
[3]Data for Farmers Group and Zurich Financial Group (which owns Farmers' management company) are reported separately by SNL Financial LC.

Source: SNL Financial LC.

Property/Casualty Insurance by Line

Commercial Lines

The commercial lines sector of the property/casualty insurance industry generally provides insurance products for businesses as opposed to the personal lines sector, which offers products for individuals. However, the division between commercial and personal coverages is not precise. For example, inland marine insurance, which is included in the commercial lines sector, may cover some personal property such as expensive jewelry and fine art.

Leading Companies

TOP TEN WRITERS OF COMMERCIAL LINES INSURANCE BY DIRECT PREMIUMS WRITTEN, 2013
($000)

Rank	Group/company	Direct premiums written[1]	Market share[2]
1	American International Group	$16,503,438	6.1%
2	Travelers Companies Inc.	16,126,917	5.9
3	Liberty Mutual	14,535,081	5.3
4	Zurich Insurance Group[3]	10,816,040	4.0
5	ACE Ltd.	8,691,889	3.2
6	CNA Financial Corp.	8,440,261	3.1
7	Hartford Financial Services	7,370,550	2.7
8	Chubb Corp.	7,343,526	2.7
9	Nationwide Mutual Group	7,338,123	2.7
10	American Financial Group Inc.	4,819,736	1.8

[1]Before reinsurance transactions, includes state funds. [2]Based on U.S. total, includes territories. [3]Data for Farmers Insurance Group of Companies and Zurich Financial Group (which owns Farmers' management company) are reported separately by SNL Financial.

Source: SNL Financial LC.

TOP TEN COMMERCIAL INSURANCE BROKERS OF U.S. BUSINESS BY REVENUES, 2013[1]
($ millions)

Rank	Company	Brokerage revenues
1	Aon P.L.C.	$5,561
2	Marsh & McLennan Cos. Inc.[2]	5,522
3	Arthur J. Gallagher & Co.[2]	2,111
4	Willis Group Holdings P.L.C.	1,744
5	BB&T Insurance Holdings Inc.[2]	1,582
6	Brown & Brown Inc.	1,356
7	Wells Fargo Insurance Services USA Inc.	1,350
8	Lockton Cos. L.L.C.[3]	826
9	USI Holdings Corp.[2]	782
10	Hub International Ltd.[2]	769

[1]Companies that derive less than 50 percent of revenues from commercial retail brokerage or employee benefits are not ranked. [2]Reported U.S. acquisitions in 2013. [3]Fiscal year ending April 30.

Source: Business Insurance, July 21, 2014.

Workers Compensation Insurance

Workers compensation insurance provides for the cost of medical care and rehabilitation for injured workers and lost wages and death benefits for the dependents of persons killed in work-related accidents. Workers compensation systems vary from state to state. Workers compensation combined ratios are expressed in two ways. Calendar year results reflect claim payments and changes in reserves for accidents that happened in that year or earlier. Accident year results only include losses from a particular year.

WORKERS COMPENSATION INSURANCE, 2004-2013
($000)

| Year | Net premiums written[2] | Annual percent change | Combined ratio[1] | | | |
			Calendar year[3]	Annual point change[4]	Accident year[5]	Annual point change
2004	$36,735,582	11.7%	106.9	-3.6 pts.	88	-10 pts.
2005	38,981,699	6.1	102.1	-4.8	87	-1
2006	41,820,419	7.3	95.4	-6.7	86	-1
2007	40,610,991	-2.9	101.7	6.3	99	13
2008	36,939,016	-9.0	101.5	-0.2	106	7
2009	32,247,870	-12.7	107.9	6.4	110	4
2010	31,643,087	-1.9	116.1	8.2	118	8
2011	35,664,230	12.7	117.6	1.5	113	-5
2012	38,747,594	8.6	110.4	-7.3	107	-6
2013	40,896,983	5.5	103.0	-7.4	99[6]	-8

[1]After dividends to policyholders. A drop in the combined ratio represents an improvement; an increase represents a deterioration.
[2]After reinsurance transactions, excludes state funds. [3]Calendar year data are from SNL Financial. [4]Calculated from unrounded data.
[5]Accident year data are from the National Council on Compensation Insurance (NCCI). [6]Estimated by NCCI.
Source: SNL Financial LC; ©National Council on Compensation Insurance.

Excess Workers Compensation

Excess workers compensation, a coverage geared to employers that self-insure for workers compensation, comes into play when claims exceed a designated dollar amount.

EXCESS WORKERS COMPENSATION INSURANCE, 2008-2013
($000)

Year	Net premiums written[1]	Annual percent change	Combined ratio[2]	Annual point change[3]
2008	$926,487	NA	148.3	NA
2009	941,117	1.6%	34.8	-113.5 pts.
2010	799,733	-15.0	50.9	16.0
2011	816,435	2.1	134.7	83.8
2012	815,770	-0.1	153.6	18.9
2013	844,098	3.5	69.3	-84.3

[1]After reinsurance transactions, excludes state funds. [2]After dividends to policyholders. A drop in the combined ratio represents an improvement; an increase represents a deterioration. [3]Calculated from unrounded data. NA=Data not available. Source: SNL Financial LC.

WORKERS COMPENSATION MEDICAL COSTS, 2004-2013

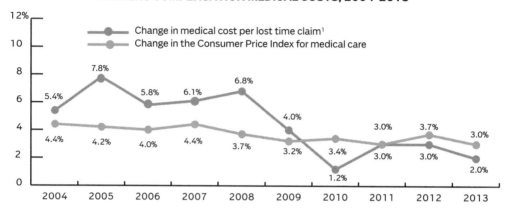

● Change in medical cost per lost time claim[1]
● Change in the Consumer Price Index for medical care

Change in medical cost per lost time claim: 2004: 5.4%, 2005: 7.8%, 2006: 5.8%, 2007: 6.1%, 2008: 6.8%, 2009: 4.0%, 2010: 1.2%, 2011: 3.0%, 2012: 3.7%, 2013: 2.0%

Change in the Consumer Price Index for medical care: 2004: 4.4%, 2005: 4.2%, 2006: 4.0%, 2007: 4.4%, 2008: 3.7%, 2009: 3.2%, 2010: 3.4%, 2011: 3.0%, 2012: 3.0%, 2013: 3.0%

[1]Based on states where the National Council on Compensation Insurance provides ratemaking services. Represents costs for injuries that resulted in time off from work. Data for 2013 are preliminary.

Source: U.S. Bureau of Labor Statistics; ©National Council on Compensation Insurance.

WORKERS COMPENSATION BENEFITS, COVERAGE AND COSTS, 2011-2012

	2011	2012	Percent change
Covered workers (000)	125,833	127,904	1.6%
Covered wages ($ billions)	$6,049	$6,309	4.3
Workers compensation benefits paid ($ billions)	61.0	61.9	1.3
Medical benefits	30.6	30.8	0.9
Cash benefits	30.5	31.0	1.8
Employer costs for workers compensation ($ billions)	77.8	83.2	6.9

Source: Workers Compensation: Benefits, Coverage, and Costs, 2012, National Academy of Social Insurance.

Liability Insurance

"Other liability" insurance is a commercial coverage that protects the policyholder from legal liability arising from negligence, carelessness or a failure to act that causes property damage or personal injury to others. It encompasses a wide variety of coverages including errors and omissions, umbrella liability and liquor liability. It does not include products liability, which is a separate line of insurance. Products liability protects the manufacturer, distributor or seller of a product from legal liability resulting from a defective condition that caused personal injury or damage associated with the use of the product.

OTHER LIABILITY INSURANCE, 2004-2013
($000)

Year	Net premiums written[1]	Annual percent change	Combined ratio[2]	Annual point change[3]	Year	Net premiums written[1]	Annual percent change	Combined ratio[2]	Annual point change[3]
2004	$39,676,116	9.8%	114.1	1.9 pts.	2009	$36,184,065	-6.3%	105.5	11.7pts.
2005	39,266,103	-1.0	110.5	-3.6	2010	35,802,772	-1.1	108.1	2.6
2006	42,229,148	7.5	94.8	-15.8	2011	36,511,575	2.0	96.1	-12.0
2007	40,997,132	-2.9	99.2	4.4	2012	38,307,679	4.9	103.2	7.0
2008	38,602,734	-5.8	93.8	-5.4	2013	42,053,059	9.8	96.8	-6.4

[1]After reinsurance transactions, excludes state funds. [2]After dividends to policyholders. A drop in the combined ratio represents an improvement; an increase represents a deterioration. [3]Calculated from unrounded data.

Source: SNL Financial LC.

PRODUCTS LIABILITY INSURANCE, 2004-2013
($000)

Year	Net premiums written[1]	Annual percent change	Combined ratio[2]	Annual point change[3]
2004	$3,401,867	24.8%	152.4	-13.5 pts.
2005	3,546,009	4.2	131.1	-21.3
2006	3,621,671	2.1	77.8	-53.3
2007	3,265,035	-9.8	99.8	22.0
2008	2,777,587	-14.9	124.0	24.2
2009	2,365,681	-14.8	124.0	[4]
2010	2,050,619	-13.3	157.1	33.1
2011	2,320,540	13.2	160.0	2.9
2012	2,575,225	11.0	102.7	-57.3
2013	2,718,879	5.6	155.3	52.6

[1]After reinsurance transactions, excludes state funds. [2]After dividends to policyholders. A drop in the combined ratio represents an improvement; an increase represents a deterioration. [3]Calculated from unrounded data. [4]Less than 0.1 point.

Source: SNL Financial LC.

Commercial and Farmowners Multiple Peril Insurance

Commercial multiple peril insurance is a package policy that includes property, boiler and machinery, crime and general liability coverages. Farmowners multiple peril insurance, similar to homeowners insurance, provides coverage to farmowners and ranchowners against a number of named perils and liabilities. It covers a dwelling and its contents, as well as barns, stables and other structures.

COMMERCIAL MULTIPLE PERIL INSURANCE, 2004-2013

Year	Total ($000)		Year		
	Net premiums written[1]	Annual percent change		Net premiums written[1]	Annual percent change
2004	$29,011,421	5.9%	2009	$28,926,363	-4.6%
2005	29,577,004	1.9	2010	28,913,516	[2]
2006	31,856,902	7.7	2011	29,995,201	3.7
2007	31,261,039	-1.9	2012	31,502,689	5.0
2008	30,306,109	-3.1	2013	33,244,677	5.5

Year	Nonliability portion ($000)				Year				
	Net premiums written[1]	Annual percent change	Combined ratio[3]	Annual point change[4]		Net premiums written[1]	Annual percent change	Combined ratio[3]	Annual point change[4]
2004	$16,942,080	3.8%	98.3	8.9 pts.	2009	$17,927,074	-1.7%	98.3	-9.4 pts.
2005	17,672,953	4.3	95.3	-2.9	2010	18,210,612	1.6	102.9	4.5
2006	18,250,773	3.3	83.9	-11.5	2011	18,657,799	2.5	119.1	16.2
2007	18,334,139	0.5	89.6	5.7	2012	19,513,568	4.6	113.9	-5.1
2008	18,235,095	-0.5	107.7	18.1	2013	21,058,405	7.9	93.3	-20.6

Year	Liability portion ($000)				Year				
	Net premiums written[1]	Annual percent change	Combined ratio[3]	Annual point change[4]		Net premiums written[1]	Annual percent change	Combined ratio[3]	Annual point change[4]
2004	$12,069,341	9.1%	105.5	-9.5 pts.	2009	$10,999,289	-8.9%	94.2	-3.2 pts.
2005	11,904,051	-1.4	102.9	-2.7	2010	10,702,904	-2.7	96.0	1.8
2006	13,606,129	14.3	104.0	1.1	2011	11,337,402	5.9	101.8	5.8
2007	12,926,900	-5.0	95.4	-8.6	2012	11,989,121	5.7	94.1	-7.7
2008	12,071,014	-6.6	97.5	2.1	2013	12,186,272	1.6	103.8	9.7

[1]After reinsurance transactions, excludes state funds. [2]Less than 0.1 percent. [3]After dividends to policyholders. A drop in the combined ratio represents an improvement; an increase represents a deterioration. [4]Calculated from unrounded data.

Source: SNL Financial LC.

FARMOWNERS MULTIPLE PERIL INSURANCE, 2004-2013
($000)

Year	Net premiums written[1]	Annual percent change	Combined ratio[2]	Annual point change[3]
2004	$2,118,097	5.9%	92.1	-7.4 pts.
2005	2,258,489	6.6	95.2	3.1
2006	2,300,728	1.9	123.2	28.0
2007	2,413,562	4.9	98.1	-25.0
2008	2,586,861	7.2	119.5	21.3
2009	2,612,262	1.0	107.9	-11.6
2010	2,754,955	5.5	108.2	0.3
2011	2,932,576	6.4	117.4	9.2
2012	3,277,423	11.8	99.5	-17.9
2013	3,511,651	7.1	93.9	-5.6

[1]After reinsurance transactions, excludes state funds. [2]After dividends to policyholders. A drop in the combined ratio represents an improvement; an increase represents a deterioration. [3]Calculated from unrounded data.

Source: SNL Financial LC.

Medical Malpractice Insurance

Medical malpractice insurance covers facilities, doctors and other professionals in the medical field for liability claims arising from the treatment of patients.

MEDICAL MALPRACTICE INSURANCE, 2004-2013
($000)

Year	Net premiums written[1]	Annual percent change	Combined ratio[2]	Annual point change[3]
2004	$9,124,240	4.2%	109.0	-30.1 pts.
2005	8,619,612	-5.5	95.3	-13.7
2006	10,378,325	20.4	90.6	-4.7
2007	9,958,513	-4.0	84.7	-5.9
2008	9,521,113	-4.4	79.2	-5.5
2009	9,206,794	-3.3	85.5	6.3
2010	9,096,345	-1.2	88.9	3.4
2011	8,833,365	-2.9	88.0	-1.0
2012	8,713,595	-1.4	93.1	5.2
2013	8,530,830	-2.1	89.4	-3.8

[1]After reinsurance transactions, excludes state funds. [2]After dividends to policyholders. A drop in the combined ratio represents an improvement; an increase represents a deterioration. [3]Calculated from unrounded data.

Source: SNL Financial LC.

Fire and Allied Lines Insurance

Fire insurance provides coverage against losses caused by fire and lightning. It is usually sold as part of a package policy such as commercial multiple peril. Allied lines insurance includes property insurance that is usually bought in conjunction with a fire insurance policy. Allied lines includes coverage for wind and water damage and vandalism.

FIRE INSURANCE, 2004-2013
($000)

Year	Net premiums written[1]	Annual percent change	Combined ratio[2]	Annual point change[3]
2004	$8,025,042	-4.4%	73.2	-6.5 pts.
2005	7,934,584	-1.1	83.3	10.1
2006	9,365,050	18.0	78.0	-5.3
2007	9,664,054	3.2	85.6	7.6
2008	9,906,059	2.5	92.3	6.7
2009	10,109,161	2.1	78.6	-13.7
2010	10,199,101	0.9	80.2	1.7
2011	10,317,968	1.2	94.1	13.9
2012	10,795,612	4.6	87.4	-6.7
2013	11,229,431	4.0	79.1	-8.3

[1]After reinsurance transactions, excludes state funds. [2]After dividends to policyholders. A drop in the combined ratio represents an improvement; an increase represents a deterioration. [3]Calculated from unrounded data.

Source: SNL Financial LC.

ALLIED LINES INSURANCE, 2004-2013
($000)

Year	Net premiums written[1]	Annual percent change	Combined ratio[2]	Annual point change[3]
2004	$5,979,859	-2.8%	120.0	41.9 pts.
2005	5,944,151	-0.6	153.1	33.1
2006	6,593,122	10.9	94.6	-58.6
2007	6,889,750	4.5	53.5	-41.1
2008	7,691,004	11.6	128.1	74.6
2009	7,744,256	0.7	93.6	-34.5
2010	7,494,281	-3.2	98.9	5.3
2011	7,800,211	4.1	132.7	33.8
2012	8,161,346	4.6	138.0	5.3
2013	9,250,527	13.3	90.2	-47.7

[1]After reinsurance transactions, excludes state funds. [2]After dividends to policyholders. A drop in the combined ratio represents an improvement; an increase represents a deterioration. [3]Calculated from unrounded data.

Source: SNL Financial LC.

Inland Marine and Ocean Marine Insurance

Inland marine insurance covers bridges and tunnels, goods in transit, movable equipment, unusual property, and communications-related structures as well as expensive personal property. Ocean marine insurance provides coverage on all types of vessels, for property damage to the vessels and cargo, as well as associated liabilities.

INLAND MARINE INSURANCE, 2004-2013
($000)

Year	Net premiums written[1]	Annual percent change	Combined ratio[2]	Annual point change[3]
2004	$7,937,670	2.0%	84.3	4.1 pts.
2005	8,248,273	3.9	90.4	6.1
2006	9,217,002	11.7	72.7	-17.7
2007	9,775,987	6.1	79.2	6.5
2008	9,408,463	-3.8	92.7	13.5
2009	8,686,660	-7.7	89.2	-3.5
2010	8,527,512	-1.8	86.0	-3.2
2011	8,768,829	2.8	97.6	11.6
2012	9,603,749	9.5	95.9	-1.7
2013	10,147,014	5.7	83.6	-12.4

[1]After reinsurance transactions, excludes state funds. [2]After dividends to policyholders. A drop in the combined ratio represents an improvement; an increase represents a deterioration. [3]Calculated from unrounded data.

Source: SNL Financial LC.

OCEAN MARINE INSURANCE, 2004-2013
($000)

Year	Net premiums written[1]	Annual percent change	Combined ratio[2]	Annual point change[3]
2004	$2,828,685	9.3%	95.5	-7.7 pts.
2005	2,948,604	4.2	114.5	19.0
2006	3,133,674	6.3	97.3	-17.2
2007	3,261,490	4.1	113.6	16.3
2008	3,098,438	-5.0	103.2	-10.5
2009	2,941,486	-5.1	91.8	-11.3
2010	2,740,956	-6.8	96.1	4.3
2011	2,760,853	0.7	100.9	4.8
2012	2,704,665	-2.0	109.1	8.2
2013	2,863,507	5.9	98.1	-11.0

[1]After reinsurance transactions, excludes state funds. [2]After dividends to policyholders. A drop in the combined ratio represents an improvement; an increase represents a deterioration. [3]Calculated from unrounded data.

Source: SNL Financial LC.

Surety and Fidelity

Surety bonds provide monetary compensation in the event that a policyholder fails to perform certain acts such as the proper fulfillment of a construction contract within a stated period. They are required for public projects in order to protect taxpayers. Fidelity bonds, which are usually purchased by an employer, protect against losses caused by employee fraud or dishonesty.

SURETY BONDS, 2004-2013
($000)

Year	Net premiums written[1]	Annual percent change	Combined ratio[2]	Annual point change[3]
2004	$3,802,893	12.6%	120.6	-0.5 pts.
2005	3,817,496	0.4	102.1	-18.5
2006	4,434,780	16.2	81.5	-20.6
2007	4,779,117	7.8	72.2	-9.3
2008	4,960,250	3.8	67.0	-5.2
2009	4,835,409	-2.5	79.5	12.6
2010	4,851,328	0.3	70.7	-8.8
2011	4,849,480	[4]	72.9	2.2
2012	4,695,782	-3.2	76.8	3.9
2013	4,868,847	3.7	72.7	-4.0

[1]After reinsurance transactions, excludes state funds. [2]After dividends to policyholders. A drop in the combined ratio represents an improvement; an increase represents a deterioration. [3]Calculated from unrounded data. [4]Less than 0.1 percent.

Source: SNL Financial LC.

FIDELITY BONDS, 2004-2013
($000)

Year	Net premiums written[1]	Annual percent change	Combined ratio[2]	Annual point change[3]
2004	$1,309,344	9.9%	79.8	8.9 pts.
2005	1,216,647	-7.1	85.1	5.3
2006	1,240,822	2.0	87.2	2.1
2007	1,239,760	-0.1	76.5	-10.7
2008	1,140,617	-8.0	84.2	7.7
2009	1,098,372	-3.7	105.4	21.2
2010	1,082,534	-1.4	95.8	-9.6
2011	1,098,225	1.4	102.0	6.2
2012	1,096,406	-0.2	99.4	-2.6
2013	1,124,199	2.5	92.9	-6.5

[1]After reinsurance transactions, excludes state funds. [2]After dividends to policyholders. A drop in the combined ratio represents an improvement; an increase represents a deterioration. [3]Calculated from unrounded data.

Source: SNL Financial LC.

Mortgage Guaranty Insurance

Private mortgage insurance (PMI), also known as mortgage guaranty insurance, guarantees that, in the event of a default, the insurer will pay the mortgage lender for any loss resulting from a property foreclosure, up to a specific amount. PMI, which is purchased by the borrower but protects the lender, is sometimes confused with mortgage life insurance, a life insurance product that pays off the mortgage if the borrower dies before the loan is repaid. Banks generally require PMI for all borrowers with down payments of less than 20 percent of the home price. The industry's combined ratio, a measure of profitability, deteriorated (i.e., rose) significantly in 2007 and 2008, reflecting the economic downturn and the subsequent rise in mortgage defaults, and remained at high levels through 2012. In 2013 the combined ratio fell to 98.0, the lowest level since 2006.

MORTGAGE GUARANTY INSURANCE, 2004-2013
($000)

Year	Net premiums written[1]	Annual percent change	Combined ratio[2]	Annual point change[3]
2004	$4,323,071	0.9%	75.6	8.0 pts.
2005	4,454,711	3.0	75.2	-0.4
2006	4,565,899	2.5	71.0	-4.2
2007	5,192,104	13.7	129.0	58.1
2008	5,371,878	3.5	219.8	90.8
2009	4,564,406	-15.0	201.9	-17.9
2010	4,248,798	-6.9	198.4	-3.6
2011	4,242,340	-0.2	219.0	20.7
2012	3,965,896	-6.5	189.7	-29.4
2013	4,329,947	9.2	98.0	-91.7

[1]After reinsurance transactions, excludes state funds. [2]After dividends to policyholders. A drop in the combined ratio represents an improvement; an increase represents a deterioration. [3]Calculated from unrounded data.

Source: SNL Financial LC.

**TOP TEN WRITERS OF MORTGAGE GUARANTY INSURANCE
BY DIRECT PREMIUMS WRITTEN, 2013**
($000)

Rank	Group/company	Direct premiums written[1]	Market share[2]
1	Radian Group Inc.	$1,032,326	22.7%
2	American International Group	994,646	21.9
3	MGIC Investment Corp.	989,915	21.8
4	Genworth Financial Inc.	583,010	12.8
5	PMI Group Inc.	375,545	8.3
6	Old Republic International Corp.	285,062	6.3
7	Essent US Holdings Inc.	186,201	4.1
8	Arch Capital Group Ltd.	99,245	2.2
9	NMI Holdings Inc.	3,541	0.1
10	ACE Ltd.	138	[3]

[1]Before reinsurance transactions.
[2]Based on U.S. total, includes territories.
[3]Less than 0.1 percent.

Source: SNL Financial LC.

Financial Guaranty Insurance

Financial guaranty insurance, also known as bond insurance, helps expand the financial markets by increasing borrower and lender leverage. Starting in the 1970s, surety bonds began to be used to guarantee the principal and interest payments on municipal obligations. This made the bonds more attractive to investors and at the same time benefited bond issuers because having the insurance lowered their borrowing costs. Initially, financial guaranty insurance was considered a special category of surety. It became a separate line of insurance in 1986.

Financial guaranty insurers are specialized, highly capitalized companies that traditionally had the highest rating. The insurer's high rating attached to the bonds, lowering the riskiness of the bonds to investors. With their credit rating thus enhanced, municipalities can issue bonds that pay a lower interest rate, enabling them to borrow more for the same outlay of funds. The combined ratio climbed to 421.4 in 2008 at the height of the economic downturn. In 2013 the combined ratio fell below zero as several companies reduced loss reserves by more than $2 billion combined as a result of strains created by the financial crisis. Over the years financial guaranty insurers have expanded their reach beyond municipal bonds and now insure a wide array of products, including mortgage-backed securities, pools of credit default swaps and other structured transactions.

FINANCIAL GUARANTY INSURANCE, 2004-2013[1]
($000)

Year	Net premiums written[2]	Annual percent change	Combined ratio[3]	Annual point change[4]
2004	$2,133,599	-14.9%	44.3	14.9 pts.
2005	2,014,467	-5.6	29.8	-14.5
2006	2,163,324	7.4	47.7	17.8
2007	3,038,889	40.5	152.4	104.8
2008	3,171,560	4.4	421.4	268.9
2009	1,793,410	-43.5	100.6	-320.7
2010	1,371,908	-23.5	228.4	127.8
2011	968,898	-29.4	219.0	-9.4
2012	692,541	-28.5	181.6	-37.4
2013	710,480	2.6	-3.4	-184.9

[1]Based on insurance expense exhibit (IEE) data. Ambac did not file an IEE from 2004 to 2006; Financial Guaranty Insurance Co. did not file an IEE in 2012. Several companies in 2013 reduced loss reserves as a result of strains from the financial crisis, creating a negative combined ratio.
[2]After reinsurance transactions, excludes state funds.
[3]After dividends to policyholders. A drop in the combined ratio represents an improvement; an increase represents a deterioration.
[4]Calculated from unrounded data.

Source: SNL Financial LC.

TOP TEN WRITERS OF FINANCIAL GUARANTY INSURANCE
BY DIRECT PREMIUMS WRITTEN, 2013
($000)

Rank	Group/company	Direct premiums written[1]	Market share[2]
1	Assured Guaranty Ltd.	$305,915	45.3%
2	MBIA Inc.	143,989	21.3
3	Ambac Financial Group Inc.	95,536	14.2
4	Financial Guaranty Insurance Co.	37,969	5.6
5	Syncora Holdings Ltd.	33,873	5.0
6	Radian Group Inc.	18,086	2.7
7	CIFG Assurance North America Inc.	15,604	2.3
8	Build America Mutual Assurance Co.	13,560	2.0
9	Berkshire Hathaway Inc.	7,033	1.0
10	Stonebridge Casualty Insurance Co.	3,000	0.4

[1]Before reinsurance transactions.
[2]Based on U.S. total, includes territories.

Source: SNL Financial LC.

Burglary and Theft and Boiler and Machinery Insurance

Burglary and theft insurance covers the loss of property, money and securities due to burglary, robbery or larceny. Boiler and machinery insurance is also known as mechanical breakdown, equipment breakdown or systems breakdown coverage. Among the types of equipment covered by this insurance are heating, cooling, electrical, telephone/communications and computer equipment.

BURGLARY AND THEFT INSURANCE, 2004-2013
($000)

Year	Net premiums written[1]	Annual percent change	Combined ratio[2]	Annual point change[3]
2004	$138,307	11.8%	68.3	1.5 pts.
2005	120,170	-13.1	63.6	-4.7
2006	143,132	19.1	64.3	0.7
2007	160,703	12.3	56.4	-7.9
2008	160,434	-0.2	48.2	-8.3
2009	152,197	-5.1	59.6	11.5
2010	167,152	9.8	69.4	9.8
2011	194,661	16.5	61.6	-7.8
2012	220,831	13.4	58.6	-3.0
2013	205,239	-7.1	42.0	-16.6

[1]After reinsurance transactions, excludes state funds. [2]After dividends to policyholders. A drop in the combined ratio represents an improvement; an increase represents a deterioration. [3]Calculated from unrounded data.
Source: SNL Financial LC.

BOILER AND MACHINERY INSURANCE, 2004-2013
($000)

Year	Net premiums written[1]	Annual percent change	Combined ratio[2]	Annual point change[3]
2004	$1,572,195	-1.2%	67.1	-1.3 pts.
2005	1,582,964	0.7	60.2	-6.9
2006	1,675,347	5.8	73.1	12.9
2007	1,741,099	3.9	73.1	4
2008	1,728,595	-0.7	87.7	14.6
2009	1,803,376	4.3	71.7	-16.1
2010	1,721,764	-4.5	71.5	-0.2
2011	1,810,941	5.2	75.0	3.5
2012	1,887,625	4.2	80.8	5.8
2013	1,979,514	4.9	72.2	-8.6

[1]After reinsurance transactions, excludes state funds. [2]After dividends to policyholders. A drop in the combined ratio represents an improvement; an increase represents a deterioration. [3]Calculated from unrounded data. [4]Less than 0.1 point.
Source: SNL Financial LC.

Crop Insurance

There are two kinds of crop insurance: crop-hail, which is provided by the private market and covers just hail, fire and wind; and federally sponsored multiple peril crop insurance, which is sold and serviced by the private market but subsidized and reinsured by the federal government.

CROP-HAIL INSURANCE, 2004-2013
($000)

Year	Direct premiums written[1]	Annual percent change	Loss ratio[2]	Annual point change
2004	$427,567	1.3%	58	2 pts.
2005	434,711	1.7	44	-14
2006	405,254	-6.8	50	6
2007	489,649	20.8	48	-2
2008	669,436	36.7	83	35
2009	621,322	-7.2	91	8
2010	682,188	9.8	67	-24
2011	843,801	23.7	116	49
2012	958,163	13.6	74	-42
2013	959,912	0.2	68	-6

[1]Before reinsurance transactions, total for all policyholders of crop-hail insurance.
[2]The percentage of each premium dollar spent on claims and associated costs. A drop in the loss ratio represents an improvement; an increase represents a deterioration.

Source: National Crop Insurance Services.

MULTIPLE PERIL CROP INSURANCE, 2004-2013
($000)

Year	Net premiums written[1]	Annual percent change	Combined ratio[2]	Annual point change[3]
2004	$2,203,143	29.4%	76.1	-33.8 pts.
2005	2,234,630	1.4	91.3	15.2
2006	2,824,769	26.4	77.9	-13.3
2007	3,648,996	29.2	74.7	-3.2
2008	5,077,625	39.2	90.1	15.3
2009	3,964,690	-21.9	79.7	-10.4
2010	3,501,631	-11.7	73.9	-5.8
2011	5,456,991	55.8	90.6	16.8
2012	5,321,811	-2.5	104.0	13.3
2013	4,942,547	-7.1	103.3	-0.7

[1]After reinsurance transactions, excludes state funds. [2]After dividends to policyholders. A drop in the combined ratio represents an improvement; an increase represents a deterioration. [3]Calculated from unrounded data.

Source: SNL Financial LC.

TOP TEN WRITERS OF MULTIPLE PERIL CROP INSURANCE BY DIRECT PREMIUMS WRITTEN, 2013
($000)

Rank	Group/company	Direct premiums written[1]	Market share[2]
1	Wells Fargo & Co.	$2,335,794	20.0%
2	ACE Ltd.	2,145,182	18.4
3	QBE Insurance Group Ltd.	1,531,478	13.1
4	American Financial Group Inc.	987,301	8.5
5	Endurance Specialty Holdings	896,077	7.7
6	CUNA Mutual Insurance Group	571,750	4.9
7	GuideOne Insurance	537,315	4.6
8	Farmers Mutual Hail Insurance Company of Iowa	501,193	4.3
9	John Deere Insurance Co.	435,899	3.7
10	Archer-Daniels-Midland Co.	354,342	3.0

[1]Before reinsurance transactions, includes some state funds.
[2]Based on U.S. total, includes territories.

Source: SNL Financial LC.

Warranty Insurance

Warranty insurance coverage compensates for the cost of repairing or replacing defective products past the normal warranty period provided by manufacturers.

WARRANTY INSURANCE, 2008-2013
($000)

Year	Net premiums written[1]	Annual percent change	Combined ratio[2]	Annual point change[3]
2008	$2,086,935	NA	94.3	NA
2009	1,757,247	-15.8%	97.9	3.6 pts.
2010	1,864,139	6.1	106.4	8.5
2011	1,695,799	-9.0	97.1	-9.3
2012	1,386,404	-18.2	99.5	2.5
2013	1,155,338	-16.7	104.2	4.7

[1]After reinsurance transactions, excludes state funds.
[2]After dividends to policyholders. A drop in the combined ratio represents an improvement; an increase represents a deterioration.
[3]Calculated from unrounded data.

NA=Data not available.

Source: SNL Financial LC.

Overview

In addition to Social Security and private savings, a large number of Americans rely on investments in formal plans to prepare for retirement. Employer-sponsored retirement plans, individual retirement accounts (IRAs) and annuities play an important role in the U.S. retirement system. Such retirement assets totaled $23.0 trillion at year-end 2013, up 15.6 percent from year-end 2012, according to the Investment Company Institute (ICI). The largest components of retirement assets were IRAs and employer-sponsored defined contribution plans, holding $6.5 trillion and $5.9 trillion, respectively, at year-end 2013. An ICI report found that 67 percent of U.S. households (or 82 million households) reported that they had employer-sponsored retirement plans, IRAs or both in 2013.

U.S. RETIREMENT ASSETS, 2009 AND 2013
($ trillions, year-end)

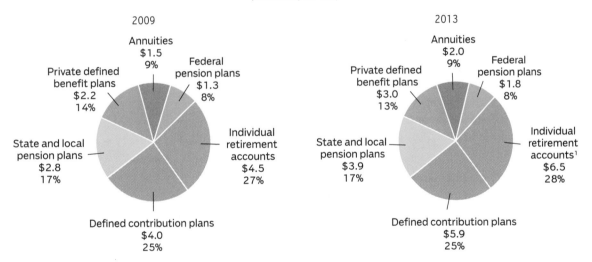

2009

Annuities $1.5 9%

Federal pension plans $1.3 8%

Private defined benefit plans $2.2 14%

State and local pension plans $2.8 17%

Individual retirement accounts $4.5 27%

Defined contribution plans $4.0 25%

2013

Annuities $2.0 9%

Federal pension plans $1.8 8%

Private defined benefit plans $3.0 13%

State and local pension plans $3.9 17%

Individual retirement accounts[1] $6.5 28%

Defined contribution plans $5.9 25%

[1]Estimated.

Source: Investment Company Institute, *The U.S. Retirement Market, Fourth Quarter 2013.*

Defined Benefit and Defined Contribution Retirement Plans

There are two basic types of workplace pension plans: defined benefit and defined contribution plans. In a defined benefit plan, the income the employee receives in retirement is guaranteed, based on predetermined benefits formulas. In a defined contribution plan, a type of savings plan in which taxes on earnings are deferred until funds are withdrawn, the amount of retirement income depends on the contributions made and the earnings generated by the securities purchased. The employer generally matches the employee contribution up to a certain level, and the employee selects investments from among the options the employer's plan offers. 401(k) plans fall into this category, as do 403(b) plans for nonprofit organizations and 457 plans for government workers.

- In defined benefit plans, equities held the largest share by type of investment in 2013, with 40 percent, followed by credit market instruments, with 24 percent, and mutual funds, with 15 percent.

- In defined contribution plans, mutual funds held the largest share, with 50 percent. Equities ranked second, with 26 percent, followed by other assets (such as guaranteed investment contracts) with 15 percent.

RETIREMENT FUNDS ASSET MIX, 2013

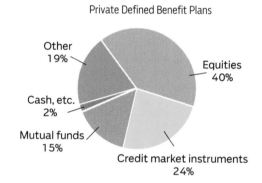

Private Defined Benefit Plans

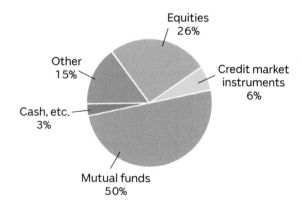

Private Defined Contribution Plans

Source: Board of Governors of the Federal Reserve System, June 5, 2014.

Individual Retirement Accounts (IRAs)

An individual retirement account, or IRA, is a personal savings plan that allows individuals to set aside money for retirement, while offering tax advantages. Traditional IRAs are defined as those first allowed under the Employee Retirement Income Security Act of 1974. Amounts in a traditional IRA, including earnings, generally are not taxed until distributed to the holder. Roth IRAs were created by the Taxpayer Relief Act of 1997. Unlike traditional IRAs, Roth IRAs do not allow holders to deduct contributions. However, qualified distributions are tax-free. Other variations include Simplified Employee Pensions (SEP), which enable businesses to contribute to traditional IRAs set up for their workers, Savings Incentive Match Plans for Employees (SIMPLE) plans, a similar arrangement for small businesses and Keogh plans for the self-employed. According to the Investment Company Institute, 46 million households (or almost 40 percent of U.S. households) had at least one type of IRA as of mid-2013. Of these, 36 million households had traditional IRAs, 19.1 million had Roth IRAs and 9.2 million had a SEP, SIMPLE or other employer-sponsored IRA.

IRA MARKET SHARES BY HOLDER, 2009 AND 2013

(Market value, end of year)

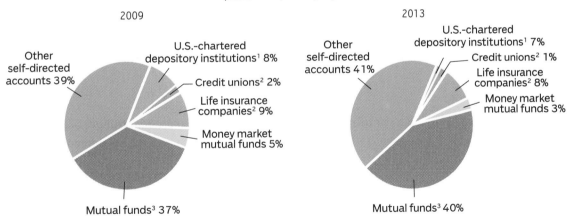

2009

Other self-directed accounts 39%

U.S.-chartered depository institutions[1] 8%

Credit unions[2] 2%

Life insurance companies[2] 9%

Money market mutual funds 5%

Mutual funds[3] 37%

2013

Other self-directed accounts 41%

U.S.-chartered depository institutions[1] 7%

Credit unions[2] 1%

Life insurance companies[2] 8%

Money market mutual funds 3%

Mutual funds[3] 40%

[1]Includes savings banks, commercial banks and Keogh accounts.
[2]Includes Keogh accounts.
[3]Excludes variable annuities.

Source: Board of Governors of the Federal Reserve System, June 5, 2014.

401(k)s

A 401(k) plan is a defined-contribution retirement plan offered by an employer to its workers, allowing employees to set aside tax deferred income for retirement purposes. (See page 132.) With $4.2 trillion in assets at year-end 2013, 401(k) plans held the largest share of employer-sponsored defined contribution plan assets. At the end of 2013, employer-sponsored defined contribution plans, including 401(k) plans held an estimated $5.9 trillion in assets.

AVERAGE ASSET ALLOCATION FOR ALL 401(k) PLAN BALANCES, 2012[1]

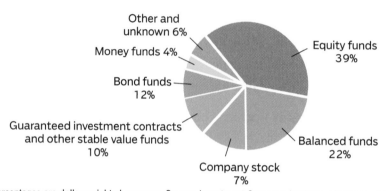

Other and unknown 6%

Money funds 4%

Bond funds 12%

Guaranteed investment contracts and other stable value funds 10%

Company stock 7%

Equity funds 39%

Balanced funds 22%

[1]Percentages are dollar-weighted averages. Source: Investment Company Institute, *ICI Research Perspective, 19 no. 12.*

Mutual Funds

Mutual funds held in defined contribution plans and IRAs accounted for $6.5 trillion, or 28 percent, of the $23 trillion U.S. retirement market at the end of 2013, according to the Investment Company Institute.

MUTUAL FUND RETIREMENT ASSETS BY TYPE OF PLAN, 2013[1]
($ billions, end of year)

- Of the total $6.5 trillion in mutual fund assets held by retirement plans at the end of 2013, 58 percent were invested in equity funds, including 45 percent in domestic funds and 13 percent in foreign funds.

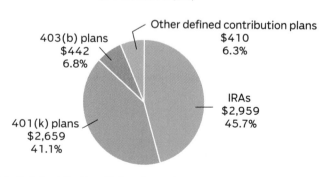

403(b) plans
$442
6.8%

Other defined contribution plans
$410
6.3%

IRAs
$2,959
45.7%

401(k) plans
$2,659
41.1%

[1]Preliminary data. Excludes defined benefit plans. Source: Investment Company Institute, *2014 Investment Company Factbook.*

Sales of Fixed and Variable Annuities

Annuities play an important role in retirement planning by helping individuals guard against outliving their assets. In its most general sense, an annuity is an agreement for an entity (generally a life insurance company) to pay another a stream or series of payments. While there are many types of annuities, key features can include tax savings, protection from creditors, investment options, lifetime income and benefits to heirs.

There are many types of annuities. Among the most common are fixed and variable. Fixed annuities guarantee the principal and a minimum rate of interest. Generally, interest credited and payments made from a fixed annuity are based on rates declared by the company, which can change only yearly. In contrast, variable annuity account values and payments are based on the performance of a separate investment portfolio, thus their value may fluctuate daily.

There is a variety of fixed annuities and variable annuities. One type of fixed annuity, the equity indexed annuity, contains features of fixed and variable annuities. It provides a base return, just as other fixed annuities do, but its value is also based on the performance of a specified stock index. The return can go higher if the index rises. The 2010 Dodd-Frank Act included language keeping equity indexed annuities under state insurance regulation. Variable annuities are subject to both state insurance regulation and federal securities regulation. Fixed annuities are not considered securities and are only subject to state regulation.

Annuities can be deferred or immediate. Deferred annuities generally accumulate assets over a long period of time, with withdrawals taken as a single sum or as an income payment beginning at retirement. Immediate annuities allow purchasers to convert a lump sum payment into a stream of income that begins right away. Annuities can be written on an individual or group basis. (See the Premiums by Line table, page 35.)

Annuities can be used to fund structured settlements, arrangements in which an injury victim in a lawsuit receives compensation in a number of tax-free payments over time, rather than as a lump sum.

INDIVIDUAL ANNUITY CONSIDERATIONS, 2009-2013[1]
($ billions)

Individual variable annuity sales in the U.S. fell 1.4 percent in 2013, following a 6.6 percent drop the previous year. Fixed annuity sales grew 16.6 percent in 2013, after a 10.2 percent drop in 2012.

Year	Variable	Fixed	Total Amount	Total Percent change from prior year
2009	$128.0	$110.6	$238.6	-10.0%
2010	140.5	81.9	222.4	-6.8
2011	157.9	80.5	238.4	7.2
2012	147.4	72.3	219.7	-7.8
2013	145.3	84.3	229.6	4.5

[1]Based on LIMRA's estimates of the total annuity sales market. Includes some considerations (i.e., premiums) that though bought in group settings involve buying decisions.

Source: LIMRA Secure Retirement Institute.

DEFFERED ANNUITY ASSETS, 2004-2013
($ billions, end of year)

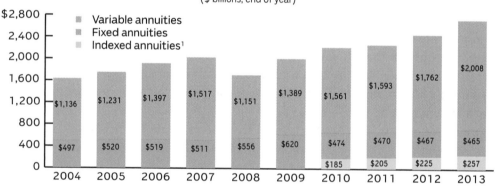

- Variable annuities
- Fixed annuities
- Indexed annuities[1]

	2004	2005	2006	2007	2008	2009	2010	2011	2012	2013
Variable	$1,136	$1,231	$1,397	$1,517	$1,151	$1,389	$1,561	$1,593	$1,762	$2,008
Fixed	$497	$520	$519	$511	$556	$620	$474	$470	$467	$465
Indexed							$185	$205	$225	$257

[1]Not reported before 2010.

Source: LIMRA Secure Retirement Institute.

INDIVIDUAL IMMEDIATE ANNUITY SALES, 2009-2013[1]
($ billions)

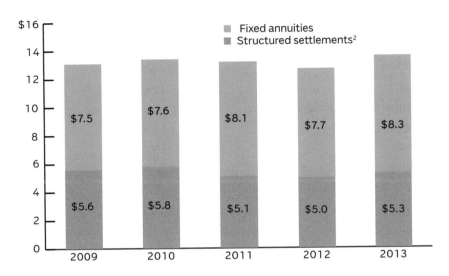

[1]Includes variable individual annuities sales which were less than $0.1 billion.
[2]Single premium contracts bought by property/casualty insurers to distribute awards in personal injury or wrongful death lawsuits over a period of time, rather than as lump sums.

Source: LIMRA Secure Retirement Institute.

TOP TEN WRITERS OF ANNUITIES BY DIRECT PREMIUMS WRITTEN, 2013[1]
($000)

Rank	Group/company	Direct premiums written	Market share[2]
1	Jackson National Life Group	$23,286,433	9.6%
2	Lincoln National Corp.	18,107,029	7.5
3	American International Group	17,978,751	7.4
4	MetLife Inc.	14,336,625	5.9
5	Prudential Financial Inc.	13,195,131	5.5
6	TIAA-CREF	12,413,403	5.1
7	Voya Financial Inc.	10,777,665	4.5
8	AXA	9,723,630	4.0
9	Guggenheim Capital LLC	9,719,980	4.0
10	New York Life Insurance Group	9,243,127	3.8

[1]Includes individual and group annuities.
[2]Based on U.S. total, includes territories.

Source: SNL Financial LC.

TOP TEN WRITERS OF INDIVIDUAL ANNUITIES BY DIRECT PREMIUMS WRITTEN, 2013
($000)

Rank	Group/company	Direct premiums written	Market share[1]
1	Jackson National Life Group	$20,590,959	10.8%
2	Lincoln National Corp.	15,174,309	8.0
3	Prudential Financial Inc.	11,580,012	6.1
4	MetLife Inc.	10,604,859	5.6
5	American International Group	10,347,212	5.4
6	Guggenheim Capital LLC	9,255,038	4.9
7	Allianz Group	9,075,854	4.8
8	New York Life Insurance Group	8,993,626	4.7
9	AEGON	8,548,350	4.5
10	AXA	7,332,020	3.8

[1]Based on U.S. total, includes territories.

Source: SNL Financial LC.

TOP TEN WRITERS OF GROUP ANNUITIES BY DIRECT PREMIUMS WRITTEN, 2013
($000)

Rank	Group/company	Direct premiums written	Market share[1]
1	Voya Financial Inc.	$8,820,053	17.2%
2	American International Group	7,631,540	14.9
3	TIAA-CREF	5,374,186	10.5
4	Great-West Insurance Group	4,751,377	9.3
5	MetLife Inc.	3,731,766	7.3
6	Lincoln National Corp.	2,932,720	5.7
7	Jackson National Life Group	2,695,474	5.3
8	OneAmerica Financial Partners	2,520,110	4.9
9	AXA	2,391,610	4.7
10	Prudential Financial Inc.	1,615,119	3.2

[1]Based on U.S. total, includes territories.

Source: SNL Financial LC.

World Insurance Losses

Natural catastrophes and man-made disasters resulted in $45 billion in insured losses in 2013, down from $78 billion in 2012 mainly because of a quiet hurricane season in the United States, according to Swiss Re. Worldwide weather-related natural catastrophes caused $37 billion in insured losses. Europe experienced the two most expensive natural disasters of 2013—massive flooding in central and eastern Europe in May and June that resulted in extensive damage in Germany, the Czech Republic, Hungary and Poland, and hailstorms that hit France and Germany in July. Germany bore the brunt of these storms, which caused insured losses of $3.8 billion, the largest worldwide for a hail event on record. Asia was the hardest hit region by natural catastrophes such as Typhoon Haiyan, which struck the Philippines with some of the strongest winds ever recorded, killed about 7,500 people and left more than 4 million homeless.

THE FIFTEEN MOST COSTLY WORLD INSURANCE LOSSES, 2013[1]
($ millions)

Rank	Date	Country	Event	Insured loss in U.S. dollars
1	May 27	Germany, et al.	Floods	$4,134
2	Jul. 27	Germany, France	Hailstorms	3,838
3	Jun. 19	Canada	Floods	1,882
4	May 18	U.S.	Severe thunderstorms, tornadoes (EF5 tornado in Moore, OK)	1,776
5	Mar. 18	U.S.	Thunderstorms, tornadoes, hail	1,615
6	Nov. 8	Phillipines, et al.	Typhoon Haiyan, storm surge	1,486
7	Oct. 27	Germany, et al.	Windstorm Christian (St. Jude)	1,471
8	May 28	U.S.	Severe thunderstorms, tornadoes, large hail	1,425
9	Apr. 7	U.S.	Winter storm, ice, tornadoes, heavy rains	1,204
10	Sep. 29	China, Japan	Typhoon Fitow	1,133
11	Apr. 2	Argentina	Large fire at refinery	NA
12	Dec. 5	U.K., et al.	Windstorm Xaver	1,034
13	Jan. 21	Australia	Floods caused by cyclone Oswald	983
14	Sep. 13	Mexico	Hurricane Manuel	947
15	Nov. 17	U.S.	Thunderstorms, tornadoes (2 EF4) with winds up to 305 km/h	931

[1]Property and business interruption losses, excluding life and liability losses. Includes flood losses in the U.S. insured via the National Flood Insurance Program. Loss data shown here may differ from figures shown elsewhere for the same event due to differences in the date of publication, the geographical area covered and other criteria used by organizations collecting the data.

NA=Data not available.

Source: Swiss Re, sigma, No. 1/2014; The Property Claim Services® (PCS®) unit of ISO®, a Verisk Analytics® company, insured losses for natural catastrophes in the United States.

WORLD INSURED CATASTROPHE LOSSES, 2004-2013[1]
(2013 $ millions)

Year	Weather-related natural catastrophes	Earthquakes/tsunamis	Man-made disasters	Total
2004	$51,954	$3,278	$4,221	$59,453
2005	120,755	279	6,559	127,594
2006	14,293	94	5,897	20,284
2007	25,530	548	6,536	32,614
2008	45,196	456	9,086	54,739
2009	23,330	662	4,575	28,568
2010	30,601	14,415	5,101	50,118
2011	67,281	55,562	6,180	129,024
2012	70,493	1,865	6,049	78,408
2013	37,002	45	7,870	44,917

[1]In order to maintain comparability of the data over the course of time, the minimum threshold for losses was adjusted annually to compensate for inflation in the United States. Adjusted to 2013 dollars by Swiss Re.
Source: Swiss Re.

THE TEN MOST COSTLY WORLD INSURANCE LOSSES, 1970-2013[1]
(2013 $ millions)

Rank	Date	Country	Event	Insured loss
1	Aug. 25, 2005	U.S., Gulf of Mexico, Bahamas, North Atlantic	Hurricane Katrina, storm surge, levee failure, damage to oil rigs	$80,373
2	Mar. 11, 2011	Japan	Earthquake (Mw 9.0) triggers tsunami, aftershocks	37,665
3	Oct. 24, 2012	U.S., et al.	Hurricane Sandy, storm surge	36,890
4	Aug. 23, 1992	U.S., Bahamas	Hurricane Andrew, floods	27,594
5	Sep. 11, 2001	U.S.	Terror attacks on WTC, Pentagon and other buildings	25,664
6	Jan. 17, 1994	U.S.	Northridge earthquake (M 6.6)	22,857
7	Sep. 6, 2008	U.S., Caribbean: Gulf of Mexico, et al.	Hurricane Ike, floods, offshore damage	22,751
8	Sep. 2, 2004	U.S., Caribbean; Barbados, et al.	Hurricane Ivan, damage to oil rigs	17,218
9	Jul. 27, 2011	Thailand	Floods caused by heavy monsoon rains	16,519
10	Feb. 22, 2011	New Zealand	Earthquake (Mw 6.3), aftershocks	16,142

[1]Property and business interruption losses, excludes life and liability losses. Includes flood losses in the United States insured via the National Flood Insurance Program. Adjusted to 2013 dollars by Swiss Re. Note: Loss data shown here may differ from figures shown elsewhere for the same event due to differences in the date of publication, the geographical area covered and other criteria used by organizations collecting the data.
Source: Swiss Re, *sigma*, No. 1/2014.

THE TEN DEADLIEST WORLD CATASTROPHES, 2013

Rank	Date	Country	Event	Victims[1]
1	Nov. 8	Philippines, et al.	Typhoon Haiyan, storm surge	7,345
2	Jun. 14	India	Floods caused by heavy monsoon rains	5,748
3	Apr. 24	Bangladesh	Eight-story garment factory collapses	1,127
4	Aug. 6	U.K.	Heat wave	760
5	Apr. 1	India	Heat wave	531
6	Sep. 24	Pakistan	Earthquake Mw 7.7, aftershocks	399
7	Jan. 1	India, et al.	Cold wave	388
8	Oct. 3	Mediterranean Sea, Italy	Boat carrying immigrants catches fire and capsizes	366
9	Aug. 24	Peru	Heavy snowfall, freezing temperatures	275
10	Jan. 17	Mozambique, Zimbabwe	Floods caused by heavy seasonal rains	246

[1]Dead and missing.

Source: Swiss Re, *sigma*, No. 1/2014.

THE TEN DEADLIEST WORLD CATASTROPHES, 1970-2013

Rank	Date	Country	Event	Victims[1]
1	Nov. 14, 1970	Bangladesh, Bay of Bengal	Storm and flood catastrophe	300,000
2	Jul. 28, 1976	China	Earthquake (Mw 7.5)	255,000
3	Jan. 12, 2010	Haiti	Earthquake (Mw 7.0)	222,570
4	Dec. 26, 2004	Indonesia, Thailand et al.	Earthquake (Mw 9), tsunami in Indian Ocean	220,000
5	May 2, 2008	Myanmar (Burma), Bay of Bengal	Tropical cyclone Nargis, Irrawaddy Delta flooded	138,300
6	Apr. 29, 1991	Bangladesh	Tropical cyclone Gorky	138,000
7	May 12, 2008	China	Earthquake (Mw 7.9) in Sichuan, aftershocks	87,449
8	Oct. 8, 2005	Pakistan, India, Afghanistan	Earthquake (Mw 7.6), aftershocks, landslides	73,300
9	May 31, 1970	Peru	Earthquake (M 7.7), rock slides	66,000
10	Jun. 15, 2010	Russia	Heat wave in Russia	55,630

[1]Dead and missing.

Source: Swiss Re, *sigma*, No. 1/2014.

THE TEN MOST COSTLY WORLD EARTHQUAKES AND TSUNAMIS BY INSURED LOSSES, 1980-2013[1]

($ millions)

Rank	Date	Location	Losses when occurred Overall	Insured[2]	Fatalities
1	Mar. 11, 2011	Japan: Honshu, Aomori, Tohoku; Miyagi, Sendai; Fukushima, Mito; Ibaraki; Tochigi, Utsunomiya. Includes tsunami.	$210,000	$40,000	15,880
2	Jan. 17, 1994	USA: CA: Northridge, Los Angeles, San Fernando Valley, Ventura, Orange	44,000	15,300	61
3	Feb. 22, 2011	New Zealand: South Island, Canterbury, Christchurch, Lyttelton	20,000	14,600	185
4	Feb. 27, 2010	Chile: Bio Bio, Concepcion, Talcahuano, Coronel, Dichato, Chillan; Del Maule, Talca, Curico. Includes tsunami.	30,000	8,000	520
5	Sep. 4, 2010	New Zealand: Canterbury, Christchurch, Avonside, Omihi, Timaru, Kaiapoi, Lyttelton	7,400	5,900	NA
6	Jan. 17, 1995	Japan: Prefecture Hyogo, Kobe, Osaka, Kyoto	100,000	3,000	6,430
7	Jun. 13, 2011	New Zealand: Canterbury, Christchurch, Lyttelton	2,500	2,000	1
8	May 5 and May 29, 2012	Italy: Emilia-Romagna, San Felice del Panaro, Cavezzo, Rovereto di Novi, Carpi, Concordia, Bologna. Multiple earthquakes.	16,000	1,600	18
9	Dec. 26, 2004	Sri Lanka: Indonesia; Thailand; India; Bangladesh; Myanmar; Maldives; Malaysia. Multiple earthquakes, includes tsunami.	10,000	1,000	220,000
10	Oct. 17, 1989	USA: CA: Loma Prieta, Santa Cruz, San Francisco, Oakland, Berkeley, Silicon Valley	10,000	960	68

[1]As of February 2014. Ranked on insured losses when occurred. [2]Based on property losses including, if applicable, agricultural, offshore, marine, aviation and National Flood Insurance Program losses in the United States and may differ from data shown elsewhere. NA=Data not available. Source: © 2014 Munich Re, Geo Risks Research, NatCatSERVICE.

Major Catastrophes: United States

Property Claim Services (PCS), a division of Verisk Analytics, defines a catastrophe as an event that causes $25 million or more in insured property losses and affects a significant number of property/casualty policyholders and insurers. PCS estimates represent anticipated insured losses from natural and man-made catastrophes on an industrywide basis, reflecting the total net insurance payment for personal and commercial property lines of insurance covering fixed property, vehicles, boats, related-property items, business interruption and additional living expenses. They exclude loss-adjustment expenses. Property/casualty insurance industry catastrophes losses in the United States plummeted to $12.9 billion in 2013 from $35.0 billion in 2012, the lowest since 2009's $10.5 billion, according to PCS. While insured catastrophe losses and the number of claims fell well below the 10-year average in 2013, the number of catastrophes rose to 28 from 26 in 2012. Munich Re estimates shown on the next page are for natural catastrophes only.

NATURAL CATASTROPHE LOSSES IN THE UNITED STATES, 2013[1]

($ millions)

Event	Number of events	Fatalities	Estimated overall losses	Estimated insured losses[2]
Severe thunderstorm	69	110	$16,341	$10,274
Winter storm	11	43	2,935	1,895
Flood	19	23	1,929	240
Earthquake and geophysical	6	1	Minor	Minor
Tropical cyclone	1	1	Minor	Minor
Wildfire, heat and drought	22	29	620	385
Total	**128**	**207**	**$21,825**	**$12,794**

[1]As of December 31, 2013.
[2]Based on property losses including, if applicable, agricultural, offshore, marine, aviation and National Flood Insurance Program losses and may differ from data shown elsewhere.
Source: ©2014 Munich Re, NatCatSERVICE. As of January 2014.

CATASTROPHES BY QUARTER, 2013[1]

($ millions)

Quarter	Estimated insured losses	Number of catastrophes
1	$2,755	4
2	7,199	13
3	1,889	8
4	1,023	3
Full year	**$12,866**	**28**

[1]Includes catastrophes causing insured property losses of at least $25 million in 1997 dollars and affecting a significant number of policyholders and insurers. Excludes losses covered by the federally administered National Flood Insurance Program.
Source: The Property Claim Services® (PCS®) unit of ISO®, a Verisk Analytics® company.

TOP TEN STATES BY INSURED CATASTROPHE LOSSES, 2013[1]

($ millions)

Rank	State	Estimated insured loss	Number of Events	Rank	State	Estimated insured loss	Number of Events
1	Oklahoma	$1,995	6	6	Mississippi	$805	1
2	Texas	1,541	10	7	Nebraska	773	1
3	Illinois	1,169	6	8	Georgia	762	4
4	Minnesota	942	2	9	Indiana	684	7
5	Colorado	907	4	10	Louisiana	593	2

[1]Includes catastrophes causing insured property losses of at least $25 million in 1997 dollars and affecting a significant number of policyholders and insurers. Excludes losses covered by the federally administered National Flood Insurance Program.
Source: The Property Claim Services® (PCS®) unit of ISO®, a Verisk Analytics® company.

ESTIMATED INSURED PROPERTY LOSSES, U.S. CATASTROPHES, 2004-2013[1]

Year	Number of catastrophes	Number of claims (millions)	Dollars when occurred ($ billions)	In 2013 dollars[2] ($ billions)
2004	22	3.4	$27.5	$32.9
2005	24	4.4	62.3	72.2
2006	31	2.3	9.2	10.4
2007	23	1.2	6.7	7.3
2008	36	4.1	27.0	29.0
2009	27	2.2	10.5	11.2
2010	33	2.4	14.3	15.1
2011	30	4.9	33.6	34.7
2012	26	4.0	35.0	35.5
2013	28	1.8	12.9	12.9

[1]Includes catastrophes causing insured property losses of at least $25 million in 1997 dollars and affecting a significant number of policyholders and insurers. Excludes losses covered by the federally administered National Flood Insurance Program.
[2]Adjusted for inflation through 2013 by ISO using the GDP implicit price deflator.

Source: The Property Claim Services® (PCS®) unit of ISO®, a Verisk Analytics® company.

THE TEN MOST COSTLY CATASTROPHES, UNITED STATES[1]
($ millions)

Rank	Date	Peril	Estimated Insured property losses	
			Dollars when occurred	In 2013 dollars[2]
1	Aug. 2005	Hurricane Katrina	$41,100	$47,622
2	Sep. 2001	Fire, explosion: World Trade Center, Pentagon terrorist attacks	18,779	23,895
3	Aug. 1992	Hurricane Andrew	15,500	23,386
4	Oct. 2012	Hurricane Sandy	18,750	19,033
5	Jan. 1994	Northridge, CA earthquake	12,500	18,038
6	Sep. 2008	Hurricane Ike	12,500	13,426
7	Oct. 2005	Hurricane Wilma	10,300	11,934
8	Aug. 2004	Hurricane Charley	7,475	8,939
9	Sep. 2004	Hurricane Ivan	7,110	8,502
10	Apr. 2011	Flooding, hail and wind including the tornadoes that struck Tuscaloosa and other locations	7,300	7,540

[1]Property coverage only. Excludes flood damage covered by the federally administered National Flood Insurance Program.
[2]Adjusted for inflation through 2013 by ISO using the GDP implicit price deflator.

Source: The Property Claim Services® (PCS®) unit of ISO®, a Verisk Analytics® company.

INFLATION-ADJUSTED U.S. INSURED CATASTROPHE LOSSES BY CAUSE OF LOSS, 1994-2013[1]

(2013 $ billions)

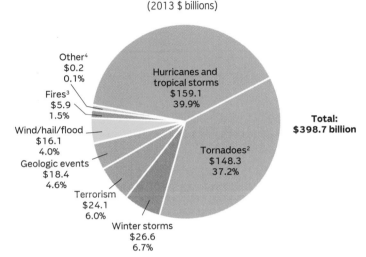

Other[4]
$0.2
0.1%

Fires[3]
$5.9
1.5%

Wind/hail/flood
$16.1
4.0%

Geologic events
$18.4
4.6%

Terrorism
$24.1
6.0%

Winter storms
$26.6
6.7%

Hurricanes and
tropical storms
$159.1
39.9%

Tornadoes[2]
$148.3
37.2%

Total:
$398.7 billion

[1]Adjusted for inflation through 2013 by ISO using the GDP implicit price deflator. Excludes catastrophes causing direct losses less than $25 million in 1997 dollars. Excludes flood damage covered by the federally administered National Flood Insurance Program. [2]Includes other wind, hail, and/or flood losses associated with catastrophes involving tornadoes. [3]Includes wildland fires. [4]Includes losses from civil disorders, water damage, utility service disruptions, and any workers compensation catastrophes generating losses in excess of PCS's threshold after adjusting for inflation.

Source: The Property Claim Services® (PCS®) unit of ISO®, a Verisk Analytics® company.

TOP THREE STATES BY INFLATION-ADJUSTED INSURED CATASTROPHE LOSSES, 1983-2013[1]

(2013 $ billions)

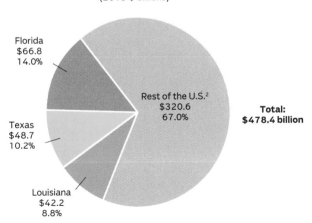

Florida
$66.8
14.0%

Texas
$48.7
10.2%

Louisiana
$42.2
8.8%

Rest of the U.S.[2]
$320.6
67.0%

Total:
$478.4 billion

[1]Adjusted for inflation through 2013 by ISO using the GDP implicit price deflator. Excludes catastrophes causing direct losses less than $25 million in 1997 dollars. Excludes flood damage covered by the federally administered National Flood Insurance Program. [2]Includes the other 47 states plus Washington, D.C., Puerto Rico, and the U.S. Virgin Islands.

Source: The Property Claim Services® (PCS®) unit of ISO®, a Verisk Analytics® company.

Major Catastrophes: Hurricanes

Hurricanes are tropical cyclones. A hurricane's winds revolve around a center of low pressure, expressed in millibars (mb) or inches of mercury. Hurricanes are categorized on the Saffir-Simpson Hurricane Wind Scale, which has a range of from 1 to 5, based on the hurricane's intensity at the time of landfall at the location experiencing the strongest winds. The scale provides examples of the type of damage and impacts in the United States associated with winds of the indicated intensity, but does not address the potential for other hurricane-related phenomena such as storm surge, rain-fall-induced floods and tornadoes. The Saffir-Simpson Hurricane Wind Scale, which was introduced in 2009 and modified in 2010 and 2012, replaced the Saffir-Simpson Scale which tied specific storm surge and flooding effects to each category of hurricane. The National Oceanic and Atmospheric Administration found that storm surge values varied widely, depending on the size of the storm, among several other factors, and thus often fell significantly outside the ranges suggested in the original scale.

Insured losses from hurricanes rose in the past decade as hurricane activity intensified. When adjusted for inflation, eight of the 10 most costly hurricanes in U.S. history have struck since 2004. In addition to the increase in storm activity, building along the Gulf and East Coasts has continued to develop and property values have increased, leaving higher property values exposed to a storm.

THE SAFFIR-SIMPSON HURRICANE WIND SCALE

Category	Sustained wind speeds (mph)	Wind damage	Historical example
1	74-95	Very dangerous winds will produce some damage	Hurricane Dolly, 2008, South Padre Island, Texas
2	96-110	Extremely dangerous winds will cause extensive damage	Hurricane Frances, 2004, Port St. Lucie, Florida
3	111-129	Devastating damage will occur	Hurricane Ivan, 2004, Gulf Shores, Alabama
4	130-156	Catastrophic damage will occur	Hurricane Charley, 2004, Punta Gorda, Florida
5	More than 157	Catastrophic damage will occur	Hurricane Andrew, 1992, Cutler Ridge, Florida

Source: U.S. Department of Commerce, National Oceanic and Atmospheric Administration, National Hurricane Center.

The 2013 and 2014 Atlantic Hurricane Seasons

The 2013 Atlantic hurricane season produced 13 tropical storms, two of which became hurricanes, according to the National Oceanographic and Atmospheric Administration. Neither of these became major hurricanes, which is defined as a storm that reaches Category 3 or higher. It was the first year with no major hurricanes since 1994, and it had the fewest hurricanes since 1982. Also, 2013 had no U.S. hurricanes that met Property Claim Service's (PCS) catastrophe threshold of at least $25 million in insured property losses. The first hurricane of the season, Humberto, reached hurricane force on September 11, but did not make landfall. It is topped only by 2002's Hurricane Gustav as the latest forming first hurricane. Ingrid, the second 2013 hurricane, made landfall in Mexico on September 16. Together with Pacific Tropical Storm Manuel, it caused massive flooding and over 40 deaths. Andrea, an Atlantic tropical storm, made landfall in Florida on June 6 and caused one death. Losses from Andrea did not reach PCS's catastrophe threshold.

By early November 2014, eight Atlantic named storms had formed, six of which became hurricanes. Only Hurricane Arthur, the first hurricane of the 2014 Atlantic hurricane season, made landfall. Arthur was also the first hurricane to make landfall on the U.S. mainland since Isaac in August 2012 and the first Category 2 hurricane in the U.S. since Ike in 2008, according to the National Weather Service. Arthur became a hurricane on July 3 and made landfall over Shackleford Banks, North Carolina. The storm weakened as it passed Cape Cod and New England.

The Pacific hurricane season has been particularly active in 2014 with 20 named storms, 14 of which became hurricanes by early November. Iselle hit Hawaii in August as a tropical storm, and Odile hit the Baja California area of Mexico as a Category 3 hurricane, killing about 15 people. Odile inflicted extensive damage on two airports in Mexico in addition to causing damage in California, Texas and New Mexico.

CATASTROPHIC HURRICANE LOSSES IN THE UNITED STATES, 2004-2013
(\$ billions)

Year	Number of catastrophic hurricanes[1]	Estimated Insured loss		Year	Number of catastrophic hurricanes[1]	Estimated Insured loss	
		Dollars when occurred	In 2013 dollars[2]			Dollars when occurred	In 2013 dollars[2]
2004	5	$22.9	$27.0	2009	0[3]	NA	NA
2005	6	58.3	67.6	2010	0[3]	NA	NA
2006	0[3]	NA	NA	2011	1	$4.3	$4.4
2007	0[3]	NA	NA	2012	2	19.7	20.0
2008	3	15.2	16.3	2013	0[3]	NA	NA

[1]Hurricanes causing insured property losses of at least $25 million in 1997 dollars and affecting a significant number of policyholders and insurers. Excludes losses covered by the federally administered National Flood Insurance Program. [2]Adjusted for inflation through 2013 by ISO using the GDP implicit price deflator. [3]No hurricane met the PCS definition of a catastrophe. NA=Not applicable.

Source: The Property Claim Services® (PCS®) unit of ISO®, a Verisk Analytics® company.

Losses

Major Catastrophes: Hurricanes

The following chart from PCS ranks historic hurricanes based on their insured losses, adjusted for inflation. The chart beneath it, from AIR Worldwide, estimates insured property losses from notable hurricanes from past years, if they were to hit the nation again today with the same meteorological parameters.

TOP TEN MOST COSTLY HURRICANES IN THE UNITED STATES[1]
($ millions)

Rank	Date	Location	Hurricane	Estimated insured loss[2]	
				Dollars when occurred	In 2013 dollars[3]
1	Aug. 25-30, 2005	AL, FL, GA, LA, MS, TN	Hurricane Katrina	$41,100	$47,622
2	Aug. 24-26, 1992	FL, LA	Hurricane Andrew	15,500	23,386
3	Oct. 28-31, 2012	CT, DC, DE, MA, MD, ME, NC, NH, NJ, NY, OH, PA, RI, VA, VT, WV	Hurricane Sandy	18,750	19,033
4	Sep. 12-14, 2008	AR, IL, IN, KY, LA, MO, OH, PA, TX	Hurricane Ike	12,500	13,426
5	Oct. 24, 2005	FL	Hurricane Wilma	10,300	11,934
6	Aug. 13-14, 2004	FL, NC, SC	Hurricane Charley	7,475	8,939
7	Sep. 15-21, 2004	AL, DE, FL, GA, LA, MD, MS, NC, NJ, NY, OH, PA, TN, VA, WV	Hurricane Ivan	7,110	8,502
8	Sep. 17-22, 1989	GA, NC, PR, SC, U.S. Virgin Islands, VA	Hurricane Hugo	4,195	6,937
9	Sep. 20-26, 2005	AL, AR, FL, LA, MS, TN, TX	Hurricane Rita	5,627	6,520
10	Sep. 3-9, 2004	FL, GA, NC, NY, SC	Hurricane Frances	4,595	5,495

[1]Includes hurricanes occurring through 2013. [2]Property coverage only. Excludes flood damage covered by the federally administered National Flood Insurance Program. [3]Adjusted for inflation through 2013 by ISO using the GDP implicit price deflator.
Source: The Property Claim Services® (PCS®) unit of ISO®, a Verisk Analytics® company.

ESTIMATED INSURED LOSSES FOR THE TOP TEN HISTORICAL HURRICANES BASED ON CURRENT EXPOSURES[1]
($ billions)

Rank	Date	Event	Category	Insured loss (current exposures)
1	Sep. 18, 1926	Miami Hurricane	4	$125
2	Aug. 24, 1992	Hurricane Andrew	5	57
3	Sep. 17, 1947	1947 Fort Lauderdale Hurricane	4	53
4	Sep. 17, 1928	Great Okeechobee Hurricane	5	51
5	Aug. 29, 2005	Hurricane Katrina	3[2]	45
6	Sep. 9, 1965	Hurricane Betsy	3	45
7	Sep. 9, 1900	Galveston Hurricane of 1900	4	41
8	Sep. 10, 1960	Hurricane Donna	4	35
9	Sep. 21, 1938	The Great New England Hurricane	3	33
10	Sep. 15, 1950	Hurricane Easy	3	23

[1]Modeled loss to property, contents, and business interruption and additional living expenses for residential, mobile home, commercial, and auto exposures as of December 31, 2011. Losses include demand surge. [2]Refers to Katrina's second landfall in Louisiana.
Source: AIR Worldwide Corporation.

HURRICANES AND RELATED DEATHS IN THE UNITED STATES, 1994-2013

Year	Total hurricanes	Made landfall as hurricane in the U.S.	Deaths[1]	Year	Total hurricanes	Made landfall as hurricane in the U.S.	Deaths[1]	Year	Total hurricanes	Made landfall as hurricane in the U.S.	Deaths[1]
1994	1	0	8	2001	9	0	42	2008	8	4[3]	41
1995	3	3	29	2002	4	1	5	2009	3	1[4]	6
1996	3	2	59	2003	7	2	24	2010	12	0	11
1997	1	1	6	2004	9	6[2]	59	2011	7	1	44
1998	10	3	23	2005	15	7	1,518	2012	10	1[5]	83
1999	8	2	60	2006	5	0	0	2013	2	0	1
2000	8	0	4	2007	6	1	1				

[1]Includes fatalities from high winds of less than hurricane force from tropical storms.
[2]One hurricane (Alex) is considered a strike but not technically a landfall.
[3]Includes Hurricane Hanna, which made landfall as a tropical storm.
[4]Hurricane Ida, which made landfall as a tropical storm.
[5]Excludes Huricane Sandy, which made landfall as a post-tropical storm.

Source: Insurance Information Institute from data supplied by the U.S. Department of Commerce, National Oceanic and Atmospheric Administration, National Hurricane Center.

THE TEN DEADLIEST MAINLAND U.S. HURRICANES[1]

Rank	Year	Hurricane	Category	Deaths
1	1900	Texas (Galveston)	4	8,000[2]
2	1928	Florida (Southeast; Lake Okeechobee)	4	2,500[3]
3	2005	Hurricane Katrina (Southeast Louisiana; Mississippi)	3	1,200
4	1893	Louisiana (Cheniere Caminanda)	4	1,100-1,400[4]
5	1893	South Carolina; Georgia (Sea Islands)	3	1,000-2,000
6	1881	Georgia; South Carolina	2	700
7	1957	Hurricane Audrey (Southwest Louisiana; North Texas)	4	416
8	1935	Florida (Keys)	5	408
9	1856	Louisiana (Last Island)	4	400
10	1926	Florida (Miami, Pensacola); Mississippi; Alabama	4	372

[1]Based on a National Hurricane Center analysis of mainland U.S. tropical cyclones from 1851-2010.
[2]Could be as high as 12,000.
[3]Could be as high as 3,000.
[4]Total including offshore deaths is near 2,000.

Source: U.S. Department of Commerce, National Oceanic and Atmospheric Administration, National Hurricane Center.

THE FIFTEEN MOST COSTLY U.S. WINTER EVENTS BY INSURED LOSSES, 1980-2013[1]
($ millions)

Rank	Date	Event	Location	Losses when occurred Overall	Insured [2]	Deaths
1	Mar. 11-14, 1993	Blizzard	24 states affected	$5,000	$1,980	270
2	Apr. 13-17, 2007	Winter storm, tornadoes, floods	Northeast, Southeast, South, CT; DE; D.C.; GA; LA; MA; MD; ME; MS; NC; NH; NJ; NY; PA; RI; SC; TX; VA; VT; WV	2,000	1,575	19
3	Apr. 7-11, 2013	Winter storm	CA; IN; KS; MO; NE; SD; WI	1,500	1,200	NA
4	Dec. 10-13, 1992	Winter storm	Northeast, Midwest, VA; MD; DE; PA; NJ; NY; CT; RI; MA; NE	3,000	1,000	19
5	Jan. 31-Feb. 3, 2011	Winter storm, snowstorms, winter damage	TX; CT; MA; IL; NY; OK; OH; PA; RI; IN	1,300	975	36
6	Dec. 17-30, 1983	Winter damage, cold wave	FL; GA; ID; IL; IN; IA; KS; KY; LA; MD; MA; MI; MN; MS; MO; MT; NE; NJ; NY; NC; ND; OH; OK; OR; PA; RI; SC; SD; TN; TX; UT; VA; WA; WV; WI; WY	1,000	880	500
7	Jan. 17-20, 1994	Winter damage, cold wave	PA; NJ; NY; OH; MA; IN; NC; VA; WV; KY; MD; NH; DE; ME; RI; VT; CT; IL; TN; SC	1,000	800	70
8	Feb. 10-12, 1994	Winter damage	South, Southeast, TX; OK; AR; LA; MS; AL; TN; GA; SC; NC; VA	3,000	800	9
9	Jan. 1-4, 1999	Winter storm	South, Midwest, Southeast, Northeast, TX; OK; AR; MO; LA; MS; AL; GA; FL; SC; NC; TN; IL; IN; OH; PA; WV; VA; MD; DE; NJ; NY; CT; RI; MA; ME	1,000	775	25
10	Jan. 4-9, 2008	Winter storm	South, Southwest, Midwest, North, Northeast, Northwest, AR; CA; CO; IL; IN; KS; MI; MO; NY; OH; OK; OR; WA; WI; NV	1,000	745	12
11	Jan. 31-Feb. 6, 1996	Winter damage	31 states affected	1,500	735	16
12	Feb. 24-25, 2013	Blizzard, winter damage	LA; OK; TX	1,000	690	1
13	Oct. 28-31, 2011	Winter storm, winter damage	CT; NJ; MA; NY; PA; NH	900	665	28
14	Jan. 6-9, 1996	Snowstorm	Midwest, Northeast	1,200	600	85
15	Feb. 9-14, 2010	Winter storm, blizzards, winter damage	VA; KY; SC; MS; MD; DC; DE; PA; NJ; NY; RI; MA; OH; IL; IA; TX; OK; NC; WV	800	600	NA

[1]Most costly U.S. blizzards and winter storms/damages based on insured losses when occurred. [2]Based on property losses including, if applicable, agricultural, offshore, marine, aviation and National Flood Insurance Program losses in the United States and may differ from data shown elsewhere. NA=Data not available.

Source: © 2014 Munich Re, Geo Risks Research, NatCatSERVICE.

THE TEN MOST SIGNIFICANT FLOOD EVENTS
BY NATIONAL FLOOD INSURANCE PROGRAM PAYOUTS[1]

Rank	Date	Event	Location	Number of paid losses	Amount paid ($ millions)	Average paid loss
1	Aug. 2005	Hurricane Katrina	AL, FL, GA, LA, MS, TN	167,805	$16,294	$97,100
2	Oct. 2012	Superstorm Sandy	CT, DC, DE, MA, MD, ME, NC, NH, NJ, NY, OH, PA, RI, VA, VT, WV	128,186	7,753	60,484
3	Sep. 2008	Hurricane Ike	AR, IL, IN, KY, LA, MO, OH, PA, TX	46,522	2,679	57,581
4	Sep. 2004	Hurricane Ivan	AL, DE, FL, GA, LA, MD, MS, NJ, NY, NC, OH, PA, TN, VA, WV	28,264	1,608	56,897
5	Aug. 2011	Hurricane Irene	CT, DC, DE, MA, MD, ME, NC, NH, NJ, NY, PA, RI, VA, VT	44,147	1,330	30,126
6	Jun. 2001	Tropical Storm Allison	FL, LA, MS, NJ, PA, TX	30,778	1,106	35,931
7	May 1995	Louisiana Flood	LA	31,343	585	18,667
8	Aug. 2012	Tropical Storm Isaac	AL, FL, LA, MS	11,966	543	45,408
9	Sep. 2003	Hurricane Isabel	DE, MD, NJ, NY, NC, PA, VA, WV	19,868	493	24,833
10	Sep. 2005	Hurricane Rita	AL, AR, FL, LA, MS, TN, TX	9,519	474	49,765

[1]Includes events from 1978 to August 31, 2014, as of November 3, 2014. Stated in dollars when occurred. Source: U.S. Department of Homeland Security, Federal Emergency Management Agency; U.S. Department of Commerce, National Oceanic and Atmospheric Administration, National Hurricane Center.

Tornadoes

A tornado is a violently rotating column of air that extends from a thunderstorm and comes into contact with the ground, according to the National Oceanic and Atmospheric Administration (NOAA). In an average year about 1,000 tornadoes are reported nationwide, according to NOAA. Tornado intensity is measured by the enhanced Fujita (EF) scale. The scale rates tornadoes on a scale of 0 through 5, based on the amount and type of wind damage. It incorporates 28 different "damage indicators," based on damage to a wide variety of structures ranging from trees to shopping malls.

THE FUJITA SCALE FOR TORNADOES

Category	Damage	Original F scale[1] Wind speed (mph)	Enhanced F scale[2] 3-second gust (mph)
F-0	Light	40-72	65-85
F-1	Moderate	73-112	86-110
F-2	Considerable	113-157	111-135
F-3	Severe	158-207	136-165
F-4	Devastating	208-260	166-200
F-5	Incredible	261-318	Over 200

[1]Original scale: wind speeds represent fastest estimated speeds over ¼ mile. [2]Enhanced scale: wind speeds represent maximum 3-second gusts. Implemented on February 1, 2007. Source: U.S. Department of Commerce, National Oceanic and Atmospheric Administration.

Tornado Losses

Tornadoes accounted for 37.2 percent of insured catastrophe losses over the 20-year period from 1994 to 2013, according to Property Claim Services (PCS). In 2013 insured losses from U.S. tornadoes/thunderstorms totaled $10.3 billion, down from $15 billion in 2012, according to Munich Re. The number of tornadoes dropped to 908 in 2013 from 939 in 2012, according to the National Oceanic and Atmospheric Administration (NOAA). There were 55 direct fatalities from tornadoes in 2013, down from 70 in 2012, according to NOAA. May was the top month for tornadoes in 2013, with 268 tornadoes. These figures do not include tornadoes that cross state lines. The U.S. experiences more tornadoes than any other country, according to a 2013 report by Lloyd's of London.

Preliminary NOAA data show that there were 831 tornadoes in 2014 through October 27, compared with 811 during the same period the previous year. On April 27, 30 tornadoes formed in at least seven states (Arkansas, Iowa, Nebraska, Kansas, Oklahoma, Mississippi and Louisiana). Nineteen fatalities were reported. Many homes and buildings were damaged or destroyed in Arkansas, Oklahoma and Kansas, according to the Federal Emergency Management Agency.

- The costliest U.S. catastrophe involving tornadoes occurred in April 2011, when a spate of twisters hit Tuscaloosa, Alabama, and other areas, causing $7.5 billion in insured losses (in 2013 dollars).

- The second costliest were the tornadoes that struck Joplin, Missouri, and other locations in May 2011, resulting in $7.1 billion in insured losses in 2013 dollars.

THE TEN MOST COSTLY U.S. CATASTROPHES INVOLVING TORNADOES[1]
($ millions)

Rank	Date	Location	Estimated insured loss[2]	
			Dollars when occurred	In 2013 dollars[3]
1	Apr. 22-28, 2011	AL, AR, GA, IL, KY, LA, MO, MS, OH, OK, TN, TX, VA	$7,300	$7,540
2	May 20-27, 2011	AR, GA, IA, IL, IN, KS, KY, MI, MN, MO, NC, NE, NY, OH, OK, PA, TN, TX, VA, WI	6,900	7,127
3	May 2-11, 2003	AL, AR, CO, GA, IA, IL, IN, KS, KY, MO, MS, NC, NE, OH, OK, SC, SD, TN	3,205	3,938
4	Oct. 4-6, 2010	AZ	2,700	2,843
5	Apr. 6-12, 2001	AR, CO, IA, IL, IN, KS, KY, MI, MN, MO, NE, OH, OK, PA, TX, WI	2,200	2,799
6	Mar. 2-3, 2012	AL, GA, IN, KY, OH, TN	2,500	2,538
7	Apr. 28-29, 2012	IL, IN, KY, MO, TX	2,500	2,538
8	May 12-16, 2010	IL, MD, OK, PA, TX	2,000	2,106
9	Apr. 27-May 3, 2002	AR, GA, IL, IN, KS, KY, MD, MO, MS, NC, NY, OH, PA, TN, TX, VA, WV	1,675	2,099
10	Apr. 13-15, 2006	IA, IL, IN, WI	1,850	2,080

[1]Based on data available as of July 8, 2014. [2]Property coverage only. In addition to losses due to tornadoes themselves, amounts may include losses due to hail, wind and flooding during the same events. [3]Adjusted for inflation through 2013 by ISO using the GDP implicit price deflator.

Source: The Property Claim Services® (PCS®) unit of ISO®, a Verisk Analytics® company.

NUMBER OF TORNADOES AND RELATED DEATHS PER MONTH, 2013[1]

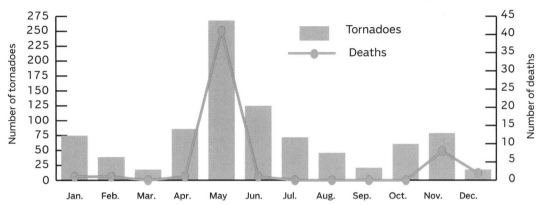

[1]Excludes Puerto Rico. Counts tornadoes crossing state lines as one event.

Source: U.S. Department of Commerce, Storm Prediction Center, National Weather Service.

TORNADOES AND RELATED DEATHS IN THE UNITED STATES, 1994-2013[1]

Year	Tornadoes	Deaths	Year	Tornadoes	Deaths	Year	Tornadoes	Deaths
1994	1,082	69	2001	1,216	40	2008	1,692	126
1995	1,234	30	2002	941	55	2009	1,156	21
1996	1,173	25	2003	1,376	54	2010	1,282	45
1997	1,148	67	2004	1,819	36	2011	1,691	553
1998	1,424	130	2005	1,264	38	2012	939	70
1999	1,345	94	2006	1,103	67	2013	908	55
2000	1,071	40	2007	1,098	81			

[1]Excludes Puerto Rico. Counts tornadoes crossing state lines as one event.

Source: U.S. Department of Commerce, Storm Prediction Center, National Weather Service.

TOP TEN STATES, BY NUMBER OF TORNADOES, 2013[1]

Rank	State	Number of tornadoes	Rank	State	Number of tornadoes
1	Illinois	69	6	Missouri	54
2	Nebraska	65	7	Kentucky	50
3	Texas	65	8	Tennessee	43
4	Kansas	58	9	Indiana	41
5	Oklahoma	56	10	Florida	37

[1]Tornadoes that cross state lines are counted as a single event in each state.

Source: U.S. Department of Commerce, Storm Prediction Center, National Weather Service.

TORNADOES AND RELATED DEATHS BY STATE, 2013[1]

State	Tornadoes	Fatalities	Rank[2]	State	Tornadoes	Fatalities	Rank[2]
Alabama	27	0	15	Montana	10	0	25
Alaska	0	0	3	Nebraska	65	0	2
Arizona	1	0	38	Nevada	0	0	3
Arkansas	30	2	13	New Hampshire	0	0	3
California	6	0	31	New Jersey	3	0	33
Colorado	27	0	15	New Mexico	0	0	3
Connecticut	3	0	33	New York	9	0	27
Delaware	1	0	38	North Carolina	12	0	23
D.C.	0	0	3	North Dakota	17	0	19
Florida	37	0	10	Ohio	26	0	15
Georgia	27	1	15	Oklahoma	56	34	5
Hawaii	0	0	3	Oregon	3	0	33
Idaho	5	0	32	Pennsylvania	9	0	27
Illinois	69	8	1	Rhode Island	0	0	3
Indiana	41	0	9	South Carolina	8	0	29
Iowa	30	1	13	South Dakota	15	0	20
Kansas	58	0	4	Tennessee	43	0	8
Kentucky	50	0	7	Texas	65	7	2
Louisiana	34	0	12	Utah	1	0	38
Maine	1	0	38	Vermont	0	0	3
Maryland	10	0	25	Virginia	3	0	33
Massachusetts	1	0	38	Washington	2	0	37
Michigan	13	0	22	West Virginia	0	0	3
Minnesota	11	0	24	Wisconsin	15	0	20
Mississippi	36	2	11	Wyoming	8	0	29
Missouri	54	0	6	**United States**	**942[4]**	**55**	

[1]Ranked by total number of tornadoes.
[2]States with the same number receive the same ranking.
[3]State had no tornadoes in 2013.
[4]The U.S. total will not match data used in other charts because this chart counts a tornado that crosses state lines as more than one event.
Source: U.S. Department of Commerce, Storm Prediction Center, National Weather Service.

Earthquakes

The costliest U.S. earthquake, the 1994 Northridge quake, caused $15.3 billion in insured damages when it occurred (about $24 billion in 2013 dollars). It ranks as the fifth-costliest U.S. disaster, based on insured property losses (in 2013 dollars), topped only by Hurricane Katrina, the attacks on the World Trade Center, Hurricane Andrew and superstorm Sandy. Eight of the costliest U.S. quakes, based on inflation-adjusted insured losses, were in California, according to Munich Re. There were no major earthquakes in the United States in 2013.

THE TEN MOST COSTLY U.S. EARTHQUAKES BY INFLATION-ADJUSTED INSURED LOSSES[1]
($ millions)

Rank	Date	Location	Overall losses when occurred	Insured losses[2]		Fatalities
				Dollars when occurred	In 2013 dollars[3]	
1	Jan. 17, 1994	California: Northridge, Los Angeles, San Fernando Valley, Ventura, Orange	$44,000	$15,300	$24,050	61
2	Apr. 18, 1906	California: San Francisco, Santa Rosa, San Jose	524	180	4,240[4]	3,000
3	Oct. 17, 1989	California: Loma Prieta, Santa Cruz, San Francisco, Oakland, Berkeley, Silicon Valley	10,000	960	1,800	68
4	Feb. 28, 2001	Washington: Olympia, Seattle, Tacoma; Oregon	2,000	300	395	1
5	Mar. 27-28, 1964	Alaska: Anchorage, Kodiak Island, Seward, Valdez, Portage, Whittier, Cordova, Homer, Seldovia; Hawaii; includes tsunami	540	45	340	131
6	Feb. 9, 1971	California: San Fernando Valley, Los Angeles	553	35	200	65
7	Oct. 1, 1987	California: Los Angeles, Whittier	360	75	155	8
8	Apr. 4, 2010	California: San Diego, Calexico, El Centro, Los Angeles, Imperial; Arizona: Phoenix, Yuma	150	100	105	NA
9	Sep. 3, 2000	California: Napa	80	50	68	NA
10	Jun. 28, 1992	California: San Bernardino	100	40	66	1

[1]Costliest U.S. earthquakes occurring from 1950 to 2013, based on insured losses when occurred. Includes the 1906 San Francisco, California, earthquake, for which reliable insured losses are available.
[2]Based on property losses including, if applicable, agricultural, offshore, marine, aviation and National Flood Insurance Program losses in the United States and may differ from data shown elsewhere.
[3]Inflation-adjusted to 2013 dollars by Munich Re.
[4]Inflation-adjusted to 2013 dollars based on 1913 Bureau of Labor Statistics data (earliest year available).
NA=Data not available.

Source: © 2014 Munich Re, Geo Risks Research, NatCatSERVICE.

Losses

The previous chart ranks historic earthquakes based on their total insured property losses, adjusted for inflation. The chart below uses a computer model to measure the estimated impact of historical quakes according to current exposures. The analysis, conducted in 2012, is based on AIR Worldwide's U.S. earthquake model. It makes use of the firm's property exposure database and takes into account the current number and value of exposed properties.

ESTIMATED INSURED LOSSES FOR THE TOP TEN HISTORICAL EARTHQUAKES BASED ON CURRENT EXPOSURES[1]
($ billions)

Rank	Date	Location	Magnitude	Insured loss (current exposures)
1	Feb. 7, 1812	New Madrid, MO	7.7	$112
2	Apr. 18, 1906	San Francisco, CA	7.8	93
3	Aug. 31, 1886	Charleston, SC	7.3	44
4	Jun. 1, 1838	San Francisco, CA	7.4	30
5	Jan. 17, 1994	Northridge, CA	6.7	23
6	Oct. 21, 1868	Hayward, CA	7.0	23
7	Jan. 9, 1857	Fort Tejon, CA	7.9	8
8	Oct. 17, 1989	Loma Prieta, CA	6.3	7
9	Mar. 10, 1933	Long Beach, CA	6.4	5
10	Jul. 1, 1911	Calaveras, CA	6.4	4

[1]Modeled loss to property, contents, business interruption and additional living expenses for residential, mobile home, commercial and auto exposures as of December 31, 2011. Losses include demand surge and fire following earthquake. Policy conditions and earthquake insurance take-up rates are based on estimates by state insurance departments and client claims data.

Source: AIR Worldwide Corporation.

Terrorism

A total of 2,976 people perished in the September 11, 2001, terrorist attacks in New York, Washington and Pennsylvania, excluding the 19 hijackers. Total insured losses from the terrorist attacks on the World Trade Center in New York City and the Pentagon are about $42.7 billion (in 2013 dollars), including property, life and liability insurance claim costs. Loss estimates may differ from estimates calculated by other organizations. It is the worst terrorist attack on record in terms of fatalities and insured property losses, which totaled about $24.7 billion (in 2013 dollars). The April 15, 2013, Boston Marathon bombing, which killed four people and injured 264, marked the first successful terrorist attack on U.S. soil since the September 11 tragedy. As of April 2014 selected health, property/casualty and workers compensation companies have paid or are projected to pay a total of $24.9 million for medical claims and property damage claims associated with the bombings, according to the Massachusetts Division of Insurance.

THE TWENTY MOST COSTLY TERRORIST ACTS BY INSURED PROPERTY LOSSES
(2013 $ millions)

Rank	Date	Country	Location	Event	Insured property loss[1]	Fatalities
1	Sep. 11, 2001	U.S.	New York, Washington, DC, Pennsylvania	Hijacked airliners crash into World Trade Center and Pentagon	$24,721[2]	2,982
2	Apr. 24, 1993	U.K.	London	Bomb explodes near NatWest tower in the financial district	1,193	1
3	Jun. 15, 1996	U.K.	Manchester	Irish Republican Army (IRA) car bomb explodes near shopping mall	980	0
4	Apr. 10, 1992	U.K.	London	Bomb explodes in financial district	883	3
5	Feb. 26, 1993	U.S.	New York	Bomb explodes in garage of World Trade Center	822	6
6	Jul. 24, 2001	Sri Lanka	Colombo	Rebels destroy 3 airliners, 8 military aircraft and heavily damage 3 civilian aircraft	525	20
7	Feb. 9, 1996	U.K.	London	IRA bomb explodes in South Key Docklands	341	2
8	Jun. 23, 1985	North Atlantic	Irish Sea	Bomb explodes on board of an Air India Boeing 747	212	329
9	Apr. 19, 1995	U.S.	Oklahoma City, OK	Truck bomb crashes into government building	192	166
10	Sep. 12, 1970	Jordan	Zerqa, Dawson's Field (disused RAF airstrip in desert)	Hijacked Swissair DC-8, TWA Boeing 707, BOAC VC-10 dynamited on ground	167	0
11	Sep. 6, 1970	Egypt	Cairo	Hijacked PanAm B-747 dynamited on ground	145	0
12	Apr. 11, 1992	U.K.	London	Bomb explodes in financial district	127	0
13	Nov. 26, 2008	India	Mumbai	Attack on two hotels; Jewish center	111	172
14	Mar. 27, 1993	Germany	Weiterstadt	Bomb attack on a newly built, still unoccupied prison	93	0
15	Dec. 30, 2006	Spain	Madrid	Bomb explodes in car garage at Barajas Airport	76	2
16	Dec. 21, 1988	U.K.	Lockerbie	Bomb explodes on board of a PanAm Boeing 747	74	270
17	Jul. 25, 1983	Sri Lanka		Riot	62	0
18	Jul. 7, 2005	U.K.	London	Four bombs explode during rush hour in a tube and bus	62	52
19	Nov. 23, 1996	Comoros	Indian Ocean	Hijacked Ethiopian Airlines Boeing 767-260 ditched at sea	60	127
20	Mar. 17, 1992	Argentina	Buenos Aires	Bomb attack on Israel's embassy in Buenos Aires	50	24

[1]Includes bodily injury and aviation hull losses. Updated to 2013 dollars by the Insurance Information Institute using the U.S. Bureau of Labor Statistics CPI Inflation Calculator.

[2]Differs from inflation-adjusted estimates made by other organizations due to the use of different deflators.

Source: Swiss Re.

Major Catastrophes: Nuclear Incidents

The International Atomic Energy Agency (IAEA) rates the severity of nuclear incidents on the International Nuclear and Radiological Event Scale (INES) from one (indicating an anomaly) to seven (indicating a major event). The scale considers an event's impact based on three criteria: its effect on people and the environment; whether it caused unsafe levels of radiation in a facility; and if preventive measures did not function as intended. Scales six and seven designate full meltdowns, where the nuclear fuel reactor core overheats and melts. Partial meltdowns, in which the fuel is damaged, are rated four or five.

Japan's Nuclear and Industrial Safety Agency assigned a rating of seven to the March 2011 accident at Japan's Fukushima Daiichi nuclear power plant. The 1986 Chernobyl accident in the former Soviet Union is the only other incident to rate a seven. The Chernobyl incident killed 56 people directly and thousands of others through cancer and other diseases. The 2011 incident released high amounts of radiation and caused widespread evacuations in affected areas but no deaths to date.

The 1979 Three Mile Island accident in Harrisburg, Pennsylvania, the worst nuclear accident in the U.S., was designated a five. Insurers paid about $71 million in liability claims and litigation costs associated with the accident. In addition to the liability payments to the public under the Price-Anderson Act, $300 million was paid by a pool of insurers to the operator of the damaged nuclear power plant under its property insurance policy.

SELECTED EXAMPLES OF HISTORIC NUCLEAR EVENTS, CLASSIFIED BY THE INES[1]

Level	INES description	Example
1	Anomaly	Breach of operating limits at nuclear facilities
2	Incident	Atucha, Argentina, 2005 - Overexposure of a worker at a power reactor exceeding the annual limit
3	Serious incident	Sellafield, U.K., 2005 - Release of large quantity of radioactive material, contained within the installation
4	Accident with local consequences	Tokaimura, Japan, 1999 - Fatal exposure of workers following an event at a nuclear facility
5	Accident with wider consequences	3 Mile Island, U.S., 1979 - Severe damage to reactor core. Minimal breach of outside environment
6	Serious accident	Kyshtym, Russia, 1957 - Significant release of radioactive material from the explosion of high activity waste tank
7	Major accident	Chernobyl, Ukraine, 1986 - Widespread health and environmental effects from explosion in power plant

[1]International Nuclear and Radiological Event Scale.

Source: International Atomic Energy Agency.

Hail

Hail causes about $1 billion dollars in damage to crops and property each year, according to the National Oceanic Atmospheric Administration (NOAA). Events involving wind, hail or flood accounted for $16.1 billion in insured catastrophe losses in 2013 dollars from 1994 to 2013 (not including payouts from the National Flood Insurance Program), according to the Property Claim Services unit of ISO. There were 5,457 major hail storms in 2013, according to NOAA's Severe Storms database.

A report issued by Verisk Insurance Solutions in August 2014 showed that over the 14 years from 2000 to 2013 U.S. insurers paid almost 9 million claims for hail losses, totaling more than $54 billion. Most of those losses—70 percent—occurred during the past six years. In addition to the higher number of claims, the average claim severity during the past six years was 65 percent higher than the period 2000 through 2007.

HAIL FATALITIES, INJURIES AND DAMAGE, 2009-2013[1]

Year	Fatalities	Injuries	Property damage ($ millions)	Crop damage ($ millions)	Total damage ($ millions)
2009	0	70	$1,440.0	$349.7	$1,789.7
2010	0	42	924.1	99.8	1,023.9
2011	0	31	450.5	81.9	532.4
2012	0	54	2,414.4	93.9	2,508.3
2013	0	4	1,245.5	75.0	1,320.5

[1]Includes the 50 states, Puerto Rico, Guam and the Virgin Islands.
Source: U.S. Department of Commerce, Storm Prediction Center, National Weather Service.

TOP FIVE STATES FOR MAJOR HAIL EVENTS, 2013[1]

Rank	State	Number of hail events
1	Texas	651
2	Kansas	504
3	Nebraska	466
4	Oklahoma	411
5	South Dakota	360
	United States	**5,457**

[1]One inch in diameter or larger.
Source: U.S. Department of Commerce, Storm Prediction Center, National Weather Service.

Fire plays an important role in the life of a forest, clearing away dead wood and undergrowth to make way for younger trees. But for much of the last century, fire-suppression policies have sought to extinguish wildfires as quickly as possible to preserve timber and real estate. This approach has led to the accumulation of brush and other vegetation that is easily ignited and serves as fuel for wildfires. Most of the large fires with significant property damage have occurred in California, where some of the fastest developing counties are in forest areas.

WILDFIRE LOSSES IN THE UNITED STATES, 2004-2013[1]
(2013 $ millions)

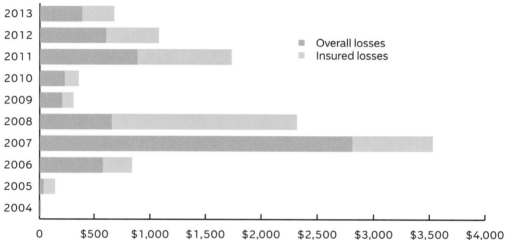

¹Adjusted for inflation.
Source: ©2014 Munich Re, GeoRisks Research, NatCatSERVICE.

2013 and 2014 Wildfires

Between January 1 and October 10, 2014 there were 41,790 wildfires in the U.S., which burned about 3.1 million acres, according to the National Interagency Fire Center. The Happy Camp Complex fire in California burned over 134,056 acres and the Carlton Complex fire in Washington state burned over 256,108 acres and was the largest fire in the state to date.

In 2013, 47,579 wildfires burned over 4 million acres, with California, North Carolina, Oregon, Montana and Arizona experiencing the most wildfires, according to the National Interagency Fire Center. On June 30, 19 firefighters were killed while working to contain the Yarnell Hill Fire in Arizona. This was the deadliest event for firefighters since 9/11 and the third-highest firefighter death toll attributed to wildfires.

TOP TEN STATES FOR WILDFIRES RANKED BY NUMBER OF FIRES AND BY NUMBER OF ACRES BURNED, 2013

Rank	State	Number of fires	Rank	State	Number of acres burned
1	California	9,907	1	Alaska	1,316,876
2	North Carolina	3,514	2	Idaho	722,204
3	Georgia	2,942	3	California	577,675
4	Oregon	2,848	4	Oregon	350,786
5	Arizona	1,756	5	New Mexico	221,951
6	Montana	1,723	6	Colorado	195,145
7	Washington	1,527	7	Nevada	162,907
8	Idaho	1,471	8	Washington	152,603
9	South Carolina	1,337	9	Montana	124,209
10	Alabama	1,284	10	Arizona	105,281

Source: National Interagency Fire Center.

THE TEN MOST COSTLY WILDLAND FIRES IN THE UNITED STATES[1]
($ millions)

Rank	Date	Location	Estimated insured loss	
			Dollars when occurred	In 2013 dollars[2]
1	Oct. 20-21, 1991	Oakland Fire, CA	$1,700	$2,623
2	Oct. 21-24, 2007	Witch Fire, CA	1,300	1,424
3	Oct. 25-Nov. 4, 2003	Cedar Fire, CA	1,060	1,302
4	Oct. 25-Nov. 3, 2003	Old Fire, CA	975	1,198
5	Nov. 2-3, 1993	Los Angeles County Fire, CA	375	553
6	Sep. 4-9, 2011	Bastrop County Complex Fire, TX	530	547
7	Oct. 27-28, 1993	Orange County Fire, CA	350	516
8	Jun. 24-28, 2012	Waldo Canyon Fire, CO	450	457
9	Jun. 27-Jul. 2, 1990	Santa Barbara Fire, CA	265	423
10	Jun. 11-16, 2013	Black Forest Fire, CO	385	385

[1]Property coverage only for catastrophic fires. Effective January 1, 1997, ISO's Property Claim Services (PCS) unit defines catastrophes as events that cause more than $25 million in insured property damage and that affect a significant number of insureds and insurers. From 1982 to 1996, PCS used a $5 million threshold in defining catastrophes. Before 1982, PCS used a $1 million threshold.
[2]Adjusted for inflation through 2013 by ISO using the GDP implicit price deflator.

Source: The Property Claim Services® (PCS®) unit of ISO®, a Verisk Analytics® company.

Fire Losses

Great strides have been made in constructing fire-resistant buildings, reducing the incidence of fires and improving fire suppression techniques. However, in terms of property losses, these advances have been somewhat offset by increases in the number and value of buildings. According to the National Fire Protection Association, in 2013, on average, a fire department responded to a fire every 25 seconds in the United States. A structure fire occurs every 65 seconds; a residential fire occurs every 85 seconds and an outside property fire occurs every 56 seconds.

FIRE LOSSES IN THE UNITED STATES, BY LINE OF INSURANCE, 2013[1]

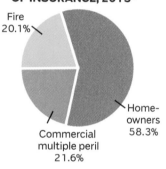

Fire 20.1%

Home-owners 58.3%

Commercial multiple peril 21.6%

[1]Estimated. Includes FAIR plan and uninsured losses.

Source: ISO®, a Verisk Analytics® company.

FIRE LOSSES IN THE UNITED STATES, 2004-2013[1]

Year	Property loss ($ millions)	Loss per capita[2]
2004	$17,344	$59.23
2005	20,427	69.12
2006	20,340	68.17
2007	24,399	81.00
2008	24,734	81.34
2009	22,911	74.68
2010	20,486	66.23
2011	19,511	62.62
2012	23,977	76.39
2013	19,301	61.05

[1]Including allowances for FAIR Plan and uninsured losses.
[2]Calculated by the Insurance Information Institute using ISO property loss and population estimates from the U.S. Census Bureau, Population Division.

Source: ISO®, a Verisk Analytics® company; U.S. Census Bureau, Population Division.

■ Structure fires caused $9.5 billion in damage in 2013, with the majority ($7.0 billion) from residential properties, according to the National Fire Protection Association.

STRUCTURE FIRES, 2004-2013[1]

Year	Number of fires	Year	Number of fires
2004	526,000	2009	480,500
2005	511,000	2010	482,000
2006	524,000	2011	484,500
2007	530,500	2012	480,500
2008	515,000	2013	487,500

[1]Includes public assembly, educational, institutional and residential structures, stores and offices, industry, utility, defense, storage and special structures.

Source: 2012-2013 data reproduced with permission from *Fire Loss in the United States During 2013* by Michael J. Karter, Jr., ©National Fire Protection Association; earlier data from prior reports.

CIVILIAN (NONFIREFIGHTER) FIRE DEATHS AND INJURIES BY PROPERTY USE, 2013

Property use	Civilian fire deaths	Percent change from 2012	Percent of all civilian fire deaths	Civilian fire injuries
Residential	2,785	15.8%	85.9%	12,575
1 and 2 family homes[1]	2,430	21.5	75.0	8,300
Apartments	325	-14.5	10.0	3,900
Other residential[2]	30	20.0	0.9	375
Nonresidential structures[3]	70	7.7	2.2	1,500
Highway vehicles	300	[4]	9.3	925
Other vehicles[5]	20	-20.0	0.6	125
All other fires[6]	65	8.3	2.0	800
Total	**3,240**	**13.5%**	**100.0%**	**15,925**

[1]Includes manufactured homes. [2]Includes hotels and motels, college dormitories, boarding houses, etc. [3]Includes public assembly, educational, institutional, store and office, industry, utility, storage and special structure properties. [4]Less than 0.1 percent. [5]Includes trains, boats, ships, farm vehicles and construction vehicles. [6]Includes outside properties with value, as well as brush, rubbish and other outside locations.

Source: Reproduced with permission from *Fire Loss in the United States During 2013* by Michael J. Karter, Jr., ©National Fire Protection Association.

STRUCTURE FIRES BY TYPE OF USE, 2013[1]

Property use	Estimated number of fires	Percent change from 2012	Property loss[2] ($ millions)	Percent change from 2012
Public assembly	12,500	4.2%	$369	31.3%
Educational	5,500	10.0	66	-3.1
Institutional	6,000	[3]	42	20.0
Residential	387,000	1.6	6,969	-3.2
1 and 2 family homes[4]	271,500	1.3	5,626	-3.3
Apartments	98,000	1.0	1,166	-2.2
Other[5]	17,500	9.4	177	-6.4
Stores and offices	18,000	2.9	611	-5.0
Industry, utility, defense[6]	8,500	-5.6	637	-5.8
Storage in structures	26,000	-8.8	692	-7.9
Special structures	24,000	11.6	140	10.2
Total	**487,500**	**1.5%**	**$9,526**	**-2.6%**

[1]Estimates based on data reported by fire departments responding to the 2013 National Fire Experience Survey. May exclude reports from all fire departments. [2]Includes overall direct property loss to contents, structures, vehicles, machinery, vegetation or any other property involved in a fire. Excludes indirect losses, such as business interruption or temporary shelter costs. [3]Less than 0.1 percent. [4]Includes manufactured homes. [5]Includes hotels and motels, college dormitories, boarding houses, etc. [6]Excludes incidents handled only by private brigades or fixed suppression systems.

Source: Reproduced with permission from *Fire Loss in the United States During 2013* by Michael J. Karter, Jr., ©National Fire Protection Association.

THE TEN MOST COSTLY LARGE-LOSS FIRES, 2013
($ millions)

Rank	Month	State	Type of facility	Estimated loss
1	June	Colorado	Wildfire	$421
2	April	Texas	Fertilizer manufacturing	100
3	April	Connecticut	Single-family home	50
4	January	Wisconsin	Egg processing plant	40
5	April	Arkansas	Aluminum die cast manufacturing	30
6	June	Indiana	Warehouse	20
7	July	California	Tunnel	17
8	October	California	Apartment building	15
9	December	California	Wildfire	15
10	February	Missouri	Restaurant	15

Source: Reproduced with permission from *Large-Loss Fires in the United States, 2013* by Stephen G. Badger, ©National Fire Protection Association.

THE TEN MOST COSTLY LARGE-LOSS FIRES IN U.S. HISTORY
($ millions)

Rank	Date	Location/Event	Estimated loss[1]	
			Dollars when occurred	In 2013 dollars[2]
1	Sep. 11, 2001	World Trade Center (terrorist attacks)	$33,400[3]	$44,000[3]
2	Apr. 18, 1906	San Francisco Earthquake and Fire	350	9,000
3	Oct. 8-9, 1871	Great Chicago Fire	168	3,300
4	Oct. 20, 1991	Oakland, CA, fire storm	1,500	2,600
5	Oct. 20, 2007	San Diego County, CA, The Southern California Firestorm	1,800	2,000
6	Nov. 9, 1872	Great Boston Fire	75	1,500
7	Oct. 23, 1989	Pasadena, Texas, polyolefin plant	750	1,400
8	May 4, 2000	Los Alamos, NM, Cerro Grande wildland fire	1,000	1,400
9	Oct. 25, 2003	Julian, CA, Cedar wildland fire	1,100	1,300
10	Feb. 7, 1904	Baltimore, MD, Baltimore Conflagration	50	1,300

[1] Loss estimates are from National Fire Protection Association (NFPA) records. The list is limited to fires for which some reliable dollar loss estimates exists. [2] Adjustment to 2013 dollars made by the NFPA using the Consumer Price Index, including the U.S. Census Bureau's estimates of the index for historical times. [3] Differs from inflation-adjusted estimates made by other organizations due to the use of different deflators.

Source: Reproduced with permission from *Large-Loss Fires in the United States, 2013* by Stephen G. Badger, ©National Fire Protection Association.

THE TEN MOST CATASTROPHIC MULTIPLE-DEATH FIRES, 2013[1]

Rank	Month	State	Type of facility	Deaths
1	June	Arizona	Wildfire	19
2	April	Texas	Fertilizer plant	15
3	July	Pennsylvania	Three-story duplex home	7
4	May	Pennsylvania	Single-family home	6
5	September	Ohio	Single-family home	6
6	October	West Virginia	Single-family home	6
7	January	Kentucky	Single-family home	5
8	February	Indiana	Single-family home	5
9	March	Illinois	Single-family home	5
10	April	Idaho	Single-family home	5

[1]Fires that kill five or more people in home property, or three or more people in nonhome or nonstructural property.

Source: Reproduced with permission from *Catastrophic Multiple-death Fires in 2013* by Stephen G. Badger, ©National Fire Protection Association.

THE TEN MOST CATASTROPHIC MULTIPLE-DEATH FIRES IN U.S. HISTORY[1]

Rank	Date	Location/event	Deaths
1	Sep. 11, 2001	New York, NY, World Trade Center terrorist attack	2,666[2]
2	Apr. 27, 1865	Mississippi River, SS Sultana steamship	1,547
3	Oct. 8, 1871	Peshtigo, WI, forest fire	1,152
4	Jun. 15, 1904	New York, NY, General Slocum steamship	1,030
5	Dec. 30, 1903	Chicago, IL, Iroquois Theater	602
6	Oct. 12, 1918	Cloquet, MN, forest fire	559
7	Nov. 28, 1942	Boston, MA, Cocoanut Grove night club	492
8	Apr. 16, 1947	Texas City, TX, SS Grandcamp and Monsanto Chemical Co. plant	468
9	Sep. 1, 1894	Hinckley, MN, forest fire	418
10	Dec. 6, 1907	Monongha, WV, coal mine explosion	361

[1]Fires that kill five or more people in home property, or three or more people in nonhome or nonstructural property.
[2]Revised to 2,976 by government officials.

Source: ©National Fire Protection Association.

Arson

Arson, the act of deliberately setting fire to a building, car or other property for fraudulent or malicious purposes, is a crime in all states. Church arsons, a major problem in the 1990s, have dropped significantly. Intentional fires in religious and funeral properties fell 82 percent from 1,320 in 1980 to 240 in 2002, the last time such figures were tracked. There were 1,600 structural fires in houses of worship which caused $105 million in property damage on average from 2007 to 2011, according to the National Fire Protection Association. Fires in a larger category, religious and funeral properties, averaged 1,780 during the same five years. Among those fires, 16 percent, or about 285 each year, were intentional.

- In 2013 property loss from intentionally set structure fires fell 0.7 percent from 2012, according to the National Fire Protection Association, as the number of fires fell 13.5 percent.

- Intentionally set fires in vehicles fell 12.5 percent in 2013. The property loss from those fires fell 82.1 percent to $86 billion from $480 million in 2012. The 2012 figure included $400 million in losses from an intentionally set fire aboard a U.S. submarine.

INTENTIONALLY SET FIRES, 2004-2013

Year	Structures		Vehicles[2]	
	Number of fires	Property loss ($ millions)[1]	Number of fires	Property loss ($ millions)
2004	36,500	$714	36,000	$165
2005	31,500	664	21,000	113
2006	31,100	755	20,500	134
2007	32,500	733	20,500	145
2008	30,500	866	17,500	139
2009	26,500	684	15,000	108
2010	27,500	585	14,000	89
2011	26,500	601	14,000	88
2012	26,000	581	12,500	480[3]
2013	22,500	577	10,500	86

[1]Includes overall direct property loss to contents, structures, vehicles, machinery, vegetation or any other property involved in a fire. Excludes indirect losses, such as business interruption or temporary shelter costs.
[2]Includes highway vehicles, trains, boats, ships, aircraft and farm and construction vehicles.
[3]Includes $400 million in property loss from an intentionally set fire aboard the submarine USS Miami.

Source: 2012-2013 data reproduced with permission from *Fire Loss in the United States During 2013* by Michael J. Karter, Jr., ©National Fire Protection Association; earlier data from prior reports.

Property Crimes

The Federal Bureau of Investigation's (FBI) *Uniform Crime Reports* defines property crime as larceny-theft, motor vehicle theft and burglary. These crimes involve the unlawful taking of money or property without the use of force or threat of force against the victims. Larceny theft involves the successful or attempted taking of property from another; it includes shoplifting, pocket-picking, purse-snatching and bicycle theft. While the theft of motor vehicles is a separate offense category, the thefts of motor vehicle parts and accessories are considered larceny. Burglary involves the unlawful entry into a structure such as a home or business. The burglary rate for renters was about 80 percent higher than for owners in 2011, according to a 2013 Bureau of Justice Statistics report. Home burglaries accounted for 75 percent of burglary offenses in 2012, according to the FBI.

NUMBER AND RATE OF PROPERTY CRIME OFFENSES IN THE UNITED STATES, 2003-2012[1]

Year	Burglary		Larceny-theft	
	Number	Rate	Number	Rate
2003	2,154,834	741.0	7,026,802	2,416.5
2004	2,144,446	730.3	6,937,089	2,362.3
2005	2,155,448	726.9	6,783,447	2,287.8
2006	2,194,993	733.1	6,626,363	2,213.2
2007	2,190,198	726.1	6,591,542	2,185.4
2008	2,228,887	733.0	6,586,206	2,166.1
2009	2,203,313	717.7	6,338,095	2,064.5
2010	2,168,459	701.0	6,204,601	2,005.8
2011	2,185,140	701.3	6,151,095	1,974.1
2012	2,103,787	670.2	6,150,598	1,959.3

Year	Motor vehicle theft		Total property crime[2]	
	Number	Rate	Number	Rate
2003	1,261,226	433.7	10,442,862	3,591.2
2004	1,237,851	421.5	10,319,386	3,514.1
2005	1,235,859	416.8	10,174,754	3,431.5
2006	1,198,245	400.2	10,019,601	3,346.6
2007	1,100,472	364.9	9,882,212	3,276.4
2008	959,059	315.4	9,774,152	3,214.6
2009	795,652	259.2	9,337,060	3,041.3
2010	739,565	239.1	9,112,625	2,945.9
2011	716,508	230.0	9,052,743	2,905.4
2012	721,053	229.7	8,975,438	2,859.2

[1]Rate is per 100,000 inhabitants. [2]Property crimes are the offenses of burglary, larceny-theft and motor vehicle theft.

Source: U.S. Department of Justice, Federal Bureau of Investigation, *Uniform Crime Reports*.

Cybersecurity

As businesses increasingly depend on electronic data and computer networks to conduct their daily operations, growing pools of personal and financial information are being transferred and stored online. This can leave individuals exposed to privacy violations and financial institutions and other businesses exposed to potentially enormous liability, if and when a breach in data security occurs.

In 2000 the Federal Bureau of Investigation, the National White Collar Crime Center and the Bureau of Justice Assistance joined together to create the Internet Crime Complaint Center (IC3) to monitor Internet-related criminal complaints. In 2013 the IC3 received and processed 262,813 complaints, averaging about 22,000 complaints per month. The IC3 reports that 119,457 of these complaints involved a dollar loss, and puts total dollar losses at $782 million. The most common complaints received in 2013 included auto auction, real estate and FBI impersonation email scams.

CYBERCRIME COMPLAINTS, 2009-2013[1]

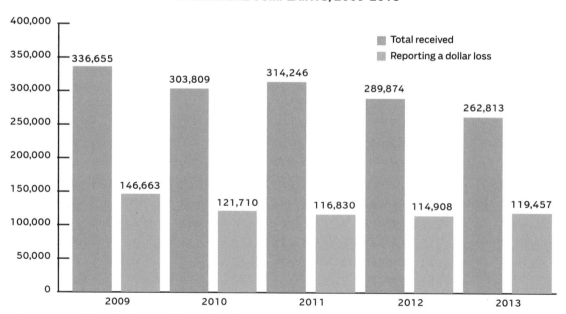

[1]Based on complaints submitted to the Internet Crime Complaint Center.
Source: Internet Crime Complaint Center.

TOP TEN STATES FOR CYBERCRIME, 2013[1]

Rank	State	Percent
1	California	12.13%
2	Florida	7.45
3	Texas	6.74
4	New York	5.29
5	Pennsylvania	3.32
6	New Jersey	3.21
7	Illinois	2.95
8	Virginia	2.84
9	Ohio	2.75
10	Georgia	2.58

[1]Based on complaints submitted to the Internet Crime Complaint Center via its website.

Source: Internet Crime Complaint Center.

Consumer Fraud and Identity Theft

The increase in online shopping in recent years has created new avenues for identity thieves. However, a 2013 study by Travelers Insurance of its 2011 identity fraud claims found that burglary and theft of physical objects led to the majority of identity fraud claims. The study identified the following four top causes of identity fraud:

- Stolen wallet or purse (44 percent)
- Auto burglary (16 percent)
- Online (15 percent)
- Home burglary (12 percent)

The Consumer Sentinel Network, maintained by the Federal Trade Commission (FTC), tracks consumer fraud and identity theft complaints that have been filed with federal, state and local law enforcement agencies and private organizations. Of the over 2 million complaints received in 2013, 55 percent were related to fraud, 14 percent were related to identity theft and 31 percent were for other consumer complaints. The FTC identifies 30 types of complaints. In 2013, for the 14th year in a row, identity theft was the number one type of complaint among the 30 categories, accounting for about 290,000 complaints, followed by debt collection, with about 205,000 complaints. Internet services, with about 50,000 complaints, ranked eleventh.

IDENTITY THEFT AND FRAUD COMPLAINTS, 2011-2013[1]

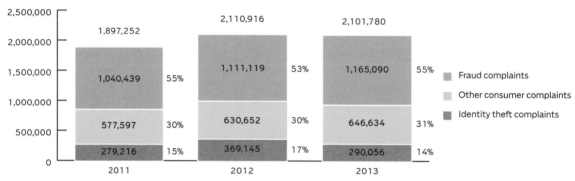

[1]Percentages are based on the total number of Consumer Sentinel Network complaints by calendar year. These figures exclude "Do Not Call" registry complaints.

Source: Federal Trade Commission.

HOW VICTIMS' INFORMATION IS MISUSED, 2013[1]

Type of identity theft fraud	Percent
Government documents or benefits fraud	34%
Credit card fraud	17
Phone or utilities fraud	14
Bank fraud[2]	8
Attempted identity theft	7
Employment-related fraud	6
Loan fraud	4
Other identity theft	24

[1]Percentages are based on the total number of complaints in the Federal Trade Commission's Consumer Sentinel Network (290,056 in 2013). Percentages total to more than 100 because some victims reported experiencing more than one type of identity theft (16% in 2013).

[2]Includes fraud involving checking and savings accounts and electronic fund transfers.

Source: Federal Trade Commission.

IDENTITY THEFT BY STATE, 2013

State	Complaints per 100,000 population[1]	Number of complaints	Rank[2]	State	Complaints per 100,000 population[1]	Number of complaints	Rank[2]
Alabama	74.7	3,610	14	Montana	50.1	509	40
Alaska	52.2	384	37	Nebraska	51.6	965	39
Arizona	91.2	6,043	7	Nevada	97.1	2,708	4
Arkansas	62.1	1,839	29	New Hampshire	51.9	687	38
California	105.4	40,404	3	New Jersey	80.6	7,176	12
Colorado	79.6	4,195	13	New Mexico	69.4	1,448	19
Connecticut	69.4	2,496	19	New York	86.9	17,072	9
Delaware	81.1	751	11	North Carolina	67.8	6,679	24
Florida	192.9	37,720	1	North Dakota	32.1	232	50
Georgia	134.1	13,402	2	Ohio	64.8	7,502	26
Hawaii	37.8	531	48	Oklahoma	60.0	2,309	34
Idaho	49.5	798	43	Oregon	60.3	2,370	33
Illinois	85.9	11,069	10	Pennsylvania	70.0	8,943	18
Indiana	58.5	3,845	35	Rhode Island	60.6	637	31
Iowa	40.4	1,248	46	South Carolina	70.7	3,374	17
Kansas	61.6	1,783	30	South Dakota	33.4	282	49
Kentucky	50.1	2,201	40	Tennessee	68.8	4,468	22
Louisiana	69.3	3,204	21	Texas	88.0	23,266	8
Maine	38.5	511	47	Utah	49.3	1,429	44
Maryland	95.5	5,660	6	Vermont	43.7	274	45
Massachusetts	63.3	4,237	27	Virginia	73.1	6,037	16
Michigan	97.1	9,606	4	Washington	68.0	4,739	23
Minnesota	53.8	2,917	36	West Virginia	60.6	1,124	31
Mississippi	74.7	2,233	14	Wisconsin	63.3	3,635	27
Missouri	67.0	4,052	25	Wyoming	49.6	289	42

[1]Population figures are based on the 2013 U.S. Census population estimates.
[2]Ranked per complaints per 100,000 population. The District of Columbia had 147.9 complaints per 100,000 population and 956 victims.

Source: Federal Trade Commission.

Losses

Motor Vehicles: Crashes

The National Highway Traffic Safety Administration (NHTSA) reports that 33,561 people died in motor vehicle crashes in 2012, up 3.3 percent from 32,479 in 2011. 2012 marked the first year-to-year increase in motor vehicle crash fatalities since 2005. The fatality rate, measured as deaths per 100 million vehicle miles traveled, rose to 1.13 in 2012 from 1.10 in 2011, the highest level since 2009. NHTSA property damage figures shown below are based on accidents reported to the police and exclude fender-benders.

- The number of people injured in motor vehicle crashes rose by 6.3 percent to 2.36 million in 2012 from 2.22 million in 2011. This was the first statistically significant increase in injuries since 1995.

- The injury rate per 100 million vehicle miles traveled was 80 in 2012, up from 75 in the three years ending in 2011.

TRAFFIC DEATHS, 2003-2012

Year	Fatalities	Annual percent change	Fatality rate per 100 million vehicle miles traveled	Fatality rate per 100,000 registered vehicles
2003	42,884	-0.3%	1.48	18.59
2004	42,836	-0.1	1.44	18.00
2005	43,510	1.6	1.46	17.71
2006	42,708	-1.8	1.42	16.99
2007	41,259	-3.4	1.36	16.02
2008	37,423	-9.3	1.26	14.43
2009	33,883	-9.5	1.15	13.08
2010	32,999	-2.6	1.11	12.82
2011	32,479	-1.6	1.10	12.25
2012	33,561	3.3	1.13	12.63

Source: U.S. Department of Transportation, National Highway Traffic Safety Administration.

MOTOR VEHICLE CRASHES, 2003-2012

Year	Fatal	Injury	Property damage only	Total crashes
2003	38,477	1,925,000	4,365,000	6,328,000
2004	38,444	1,862,000	4,281,000	6,181,000
2005	39,252	1,816,000	4,304,000	6,159,000
2006	38,648	1,746,000	4,189,000	5,973,000
2007	37,435	1,711,000	4,275,000	6,024,000
2008	34,172	1,630,000	4,146,000	5,811,000
2009	30,862	1,517,000	3,957,000	5,505,000
2010	30,296	1,542,000	3,847,000	5,419,000
2011	29,757	1,530,000	3,778,000	5,338,000
2012	30,800	1,634,000	3,950,000	5,615,000

Source: U.S. Department of Transportation, National Highway Traffic Safety Administration.

According to the National Highway Traffic Safety Administration, vehicle occupants accounted for 68 percent of traffic deaths in 2012. Motorcycle riders accounted for 15 percent. Pedestrians accounted for another 14 percent; pedalcyclists and other nonoccupants accounted for the remainder.

MOTOR VEHICLE TRAFFIC DEATHS BY STATE, 2011-2012

State	Number of deaths		Percent change	State	Number of deaths		Percent change
	2011	2012			2011	2012	
Alabama	895	865	-3.4%	Montana	209	205	-1.9%
Alaska	72	59	-18.0	Nebraska	181	212	17.0
Arizona	826	825	-0.1	Nevada	246	258	4.9
Arkansas	551	552	0.2	New Hampshire	90	108	20.0
California	2,816	2,857	1.5	New Jersey	627	589	-6.1
Colorado	447	472	5.6	New Mexico	350	365	4.3
Connecticut	221	236	6.8	New York	1,171	1,168	-0.3
Delaware	99	114	15.0	North Carolina	1,230	1,292	5.0
D.C.	27	15	-44.0	North Dakota	148	170	15.0
Florida	2,400	2,424	1.0	Ohio	1,017	1,123	10.0
Georgia	1,226	1,192	-2.8	Oklahoma	696	708	1.7
Hawaii	100	126	26.0	Oregon	331	336	1.5
Idaho	167	184	10.0	Pennsylvania	1,286	1,310	1.9
Illinois	918	956	4.1	Rhode Island	66	64	-3.0
Indiana	751	779	3.7	South Carolina	828	863	4.2
Iowa	360	365	1.4	South Dakota	111	133	20.0
Kansas	386	405	4.9	Tennessee	937	1,014	8.2
Kentucky	720	746	3.6	Texas	3,054	3,398	11.0
Louisiana	680	722	6.2	Utah	243	217	-11.0
Maine	136	164	21.0	Vermont	55	77	40.0
Maryland	485	505	4.1	Virginia	764	777	1.7
Massachusetts	374	349	-6.7	Washington	454	444	-2.2
Michigan	889	938	5.5	West Virginia	338	339	0.3
Minnesota	368	395	7.3	Wisconsin	582	615	5.7
Mississippi	630	582	-7.6	Wyoming	135	123	-8.9
Missouri	786	826	5.1	**United States**	**32,479**	**33,561**	**3.3%**

Source: U.S. Department of Transportation, National Highway Traffic Safety Administration.

VEHICLES INVOLVED IN CRASHES BY VEHICLE TYPE AND CRASH SEVERITY, 2003 AND 2012

	Fatal crashes		Injury crashes		Property damage-only crashes	
	2003	2012	2003	2012	2003	2012
Passenger cars						
Crashes	26,562	18,092	2,129,232	1,683,457	4,355,703	3,875,068
Rate per 100 million vehicle miles traveled	1.65	1.31	132	122	270	281
Rate per 100,000 registered vehicles	20.17	14.24	1,617	1,325	3,308	3,049
Light trucks[1]						
Crashes	22,299	17,254	1,232,615	1,087,044	2,804,228	2,705,815
Rate per 100 million vehicle miles traveled	2.14	1.34	118	84	269	210
Rate per 100,000 registered vehicles	26.21	14.54	1,449	916	3,297	2,280
Motorcycles						
Crashes	3,802	5,080	63,644	88,920	13,575	17,863
Rate per 100 million vehicle miles traveled	39.70	23.85	665	418	142	84
Rate per 100,000 registered vehicles	70.80	60.08	1,185	1,052	253	211

[1]Trucks with 10,000 pounds or less gross vehicle weight. Includes pickups, vans, truck-based station wagons and utility vehicles.

Source: U.S. Department of Transportation (USDOT), National Highway Traffic Safety Administration (NHTSA). Vehicle miles traveled – USDOT, Federal Highway Administration, revised by NHTSA; Registered passenger cars and light trucks – R.L. Polk & Co; Registered motorcycles – USDOT, Federal Highway Administration.

MOTOR VEHICLE DEATHS BY ACTIVITY OF PERSON KILLED, 2012

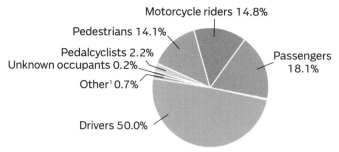

Motorcycle riders 14.8%
Pedestrians 14.1%
Pedalcyclists 2.2%
Unknown occupants 0.2%
Other[1] 0.7%
Passengers 18.1%
Drivers 50.0%

[1]Includes other non-occupants.

Source: U.S. Department of Transportation, National Highway Traffic Safety Administration.

SEX OF DRIVERS INVOLVED IN CRASHES, 2003-2012[1]

	Fatal crashes				Injury crashes			
	Male		Female		Male		Female	
Year	Number	Rate[2]	Number	Rate[2]	Number	Rate[2]	Number	Rate[2]
2003	42,177	42.95	15,106	15.43	1,989,702	2,026	1,524,785	1,557
2004	41,876	42.06	15,272	15.38	1,911,852	1,920	1,482,315	1,493
2005	42,947	42.84	14,967	14.92	1,836,711	1,832	1,425,161	1,421
2006	41,912	41.49	14,661	14.43	1,762,552	1,745	1,387,324	1,366
2007	40,804	39.82	14,099	13.65	1,719,000	1,677	1,339,000	1,296
2008	36,881	35.59	12,568	12.00	1,609,000	1,553	1,280,000	1,223
2009	32,807	31.47	11,825	11.22	1,499,561	1,438	1,224,613	1,162
2010	31,965	30.63	11,811	11.17	1,516,000	1,453	1,265,000	1,196
2011	31,809	30.32	11,209	10.48	1,507,000	1,436	1,244,000	1,163
2012	33,124	31.55	11,509	10.77	1,634,884	1,557	1,314,534	1,230

	Property damage-only crashes				Total crashes			
	Male		Female		Male		Female	
Year	Number	Rate[2]	Number	Rate[2]	Number	Rate[2]	Number	Rate[2]
2003	4,527,515	4,610	3,019,961	3,084	6,559,394	6,679	4,559,852	4,657
2004	4,404,779	4,424	3,037,126	3,058	6,358,507	6,387	4,534,713	4,566
2005	4,357,188	4,347	3,007,038	2,998	6,236,846	6,222	4,447,166	4,435
2006	4,232,184	4,190	2,967,964	2,922	6,036,648	5,976	4,369,949	4,302
2007	4,345,000	4,241	3,066,000	2,968	6,105,000	5,968	4,418,000	4,278
2008	4,174,000	4,028	2,967,000	2,834	5,820,000	5,617	4,260,000	4,069
2009	3,913,473	3,753	2,931,260	2,782	5,445,840	5,223	4,167,698	3,956
2010	3,854,000	3,693	2,862,000	2,707	5,402,000	5,176	4,139,000	3,915
2011	3,675,000	3,503	2,921,000	2,730	5,213,000	4,970	4,176,000	3,904
2012	3,880,163	3,696	3,006,762	3,251	5,548,171	5,285	4,332,806	4,056

[1]Drivers age 16 and over, includes motorcycle riders and restricted and graduated drivers license holders in some states.
[2]Rate per 100,000 licensed drivers.

Source: U.S. Department of Transportation, National Highway Traffic Safety Administration.

Teenage Drivers

Motor vehicle crashes are a leading cause of death among teenagers. The U.S. Department of Transportation (DOT) reports that 1,875 drivers in this age group died and 184,000 were injured in motor vehicle crashes in 2012. Drivers age 15 to 20 accounted for 9 percent of all the drivers involved in fatal crashes and 13 percent of all the drivers involved in all police-reported crashes in 2012. Twenty-eight percent of teen drivers age 15 to 20 who were killed in 2012 had been drinking some amount of alcohol; 24 percent were alcohol-impaired, which is defined by a blood alcohol concentration of 0.08 grams per deciliter or higher. The DOT found that more teenagers are involved in motor vehicle crashes late in the day and at night than at other times of the day. Teens also have a greater chance of getting involved in an accident if other teens are present in the vehicle, according to research from the Children's Hospital of Philadelphia and State Farm.

DRIVERS IN MOTOR VEHICLE CRASHES BY AGE, 2012

Age group	Number of licensed drivers	Percent of total	Drivers in fatal crashes	Involvement rate[1]	Drivers in all crashes	Involvement rate[1]
Under 16	127,283	0.1%	121	95.06	31,562	24,797
16 to 20	11,954,276	5.6	4,211	35.23	1,245,410	10,418
21 to 24	14,229,278	6.7	4,738	33.30	1,140,942	8,018
25 to 34	36,687,339	17.3	8,950	24.40	2,108,045	5,746
35 to 44	36,527,225	17.2	7,311	20.02	1,683,127	4,608
45 to 54	40,594,647	19.2	7,601	18.72	1,601,892	3,946
55 to 64	35,750,452	16.9	5,899	16.50	1,157,852	3,239
65 to 74	21,733,570	10.3	3,212	14.78	564,736	2,598
Over 74	14,210,760	6.7	2,532	17.82	347,352	2,444
Total	**211,814,830**	**100.0%**	**45,337[2]**	**21.40**	**9,881,681[2]**	**4,665**

[1]Per 100,000 licensed drivers.
[2]Includes drivers of unknown age.
Source: U.S. Department of Transportation, National Highway Traffic Safety Administration; Federal Highway Administration.

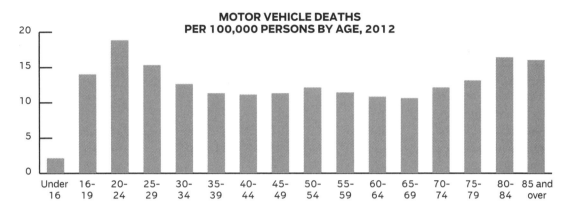

MOTOR VEHICLE DEATHS PER 100,000 PERSONS BY AGE, 2012

Source: Insurance Institute for Highway Safety.

DRIVING BEHAVIORS REPORTED FOR DRIVERS AND MOTORCYCLE OPERATORS INVOLVED IN FATAL CRASHES, 2012

Behavior	Number of drivers	Percent
Driving too fast for conditions or in excess of posted speed limit or racing	9,320	20.6%
Under the influence of alcohol, drugs or medication	6,199	13.7
Failure to keep in proper lane	3,431	7.6
Failure to yield right of way	3,211	7.1
Distracted (phone, talking, eating, etc.)	3,119	6.9
Overcorrecting/oversteering	2,246	5.0
Operating vehicle in a careless manner	2,052	4.5
Failure to obey traffic signs, signals or officer	1,820	4.0
Operating vehicle in erratic, reckless or negligent manner	1,650	3.6
Swerving or avoiding due to wind, slippery surface, other vehicle, object, nonmotorist in roadway, etc.	1,557	3.4
Vision obscured (rain, snow, glare, lights, buildings, trees, etc.)	1,282	2.8
Drowsy, asleep, fatigued, ill or blacked out	1,254	2.8
Driving wrong way in one-way traffic or on wrong side of road	1,004	2.2
Making improper turn	930	2.1
Other factors	5,238	11.6
None reported	14,150	31.2
Unknown	5,146	11.4
Total drivers[1]	**45,337**	**100.0%**

[1]The sum of percentages is greater than total drivers as more than one factor may be present for the same driver.

Source: U.S. Department of Transportation, National Highway Traffic Safety Administration.

ALCOHOL-IMPAIRED CRASH FATALITIES, 2003-2012[1]

- In 2012, 10,322 people were killed in crashes where a driver had a blood alcohol concentration (BAC) of 0.08 percent or higher, up 4.6 percent from 9,865 in 2011.

- The majority of alcohol-impaired crash fatalities in 2012 involved drivers with a BAC of 0.15 or higher—nearly double the legal limit.

Year	Number	As a percent of all crash deaths
2003	13,096	31%
2004	13,099	31
2005	13,582	31
2006	13,491	32
2007	13,041	32
2008	11,711	31
2009	10,759	32
2010	10,136	31
2011	9,865	30
2012	10,322	31

[1]Alcohol-impaired driving crashes are crashes that involve at least one driver or a motorcycle operator with a blood alcohol concentration of 0.08 percent or above, the legal definition of drunk driving.

Source: U.S. Department of Transportation, National Highway Traffic Safety Administration.

PERCENT OF ALCOHOL-IMPAIRED DRIVERS INVOLVED IN FATAL CRASHES BY AGE, 2003 AND 2012[1]

- In 2012 the percentage of drivers involved in fatal crashes who were alcohol-impaired was highest in the 21 to 24 and the 25 to 34 age groups, the same as in 2003.

Age	2003	2012	Point change
16 to 20	19%	18%	-1 pt.
21 to 24	32	32	0
25 to 34	27	29	2
35 to 44	24	25	1
45 to 54	19	21	2
55 to 64	11	14	3
65 to 74	8	9	1
Over 74	5	5	0

[1]Alcohol-impaired driving crashes are crashes that involve at least one driver or a motorcycle operator with a blood alcohol concentration of 0.08 percent or above, the legal definition of drunk driving.

Source: U.S. Department of Transportation, National Highway Traffic Safety Administration.

PERSONS KILLED IN TOTAL AND ALCOHOL-IMPAIRED CRASHES BY PERSON TYPE, 2012

Person type	Total killed	Alcohol-impaired driving fatalities[1]	
		Number	Percent of total killed
Vehicle occupants			
Driver	16,769	5,993	36%
Passenger	6,061	1,917	32
Unknown occupant	82	6	7
Total	**22,912**	**7,916**	**35%**
Motorcyclists	**4,957**	**1,596**	**32%**
Nonoccupants			
Pedestrian	4,743	688	14
Pedalcyclist	726	89	12
Other/unknown	223	33	15
Total	**5,692**	**810**	**14%**
Total	**33,561**	**10,322**	**31%**

[1]Alcohol-impaired driving crashes are crashes that involve at least one driver or a motorcycle operator with a blood alcohol concentration of 0.08 percent or above, the legal definition of drunk driving.

Source: U.S. Department of Transportation, National Highway Traffic Safety Administration.

MOTORCYCLE HELMET USE, 1994-2013[1]

Year	Percent	Year	Percent
1994	63%	2007	58%
1996	64	2008	63
1998	67	2009	67
2000	71	2010	54
2002	58	2011	66
2004	58	2012	60
2005	48	2013	60
2006	51		

[1]Based on surveys of motorcyclists using helmets meeting Department of Transportation standards. Surveys conducted in October for 1994-2000 and in June thereafter.

Source: U.S. Department of Transportation, National Occupant Protection Use Survey, National Highway Traffic Safety Administration's National Center for Statistics and Analysis.

- Motorcycle helmet usage remained at 60 percent in June 2013, unchanged from 2012. It fell from 66 percent in June 2011.

- Helmet use was highest in the West, at 92 percent, up from 82 percent in 2012. In the South, helmet use rose to 65 percent from 61 percent in 2012. Helmet use was 52 percent in the Northeast, down from 60 percent in 2012, and 42 percent in the Midwest, the lowest of all the regions, down from 49 percent in 2012.

Collision Losses

The chart below shows the claim frequency and average loss payment per claim and average loss payment per insured vehicle year under collision coverage for recent model vehicles. The claim frequency is expressed as a rate per 100 insured vehicle years. A vehicle year is equal to 365 days of insurance coverage for a single vehicle.

PASSENGER VEHICLE COLLISION COVERAGE INSURANCE LOSSES, 2011-2013 MODEL YEARS

	Claim frequency[1]	Claim severity
Passenger cars and minivans	7.5	$4,486
Pickups	6.1	4,349
SUVs	6.1	4,369
All passenger vehicles	**6.9**	**$4,439**

[1]Per 100 insured vehicle years.

Source: Highway Loss Data Institute.

Aggressive Driving

Aggressive driving is a major factor in U.S. traffic accidents, playing a role not just in well-publicized incidents of road rage, but in a large number of fatal highway collisions each year. The National Highway Traffic Safety Administration (NTHSA) defines aggressive driving as occurring when "an individual commits a combination of moving traffic offenses so as to endanger other persons or property." While aggressive driving is difficult to quantify, a 2009 study by the American Automobile Association reported that, based on data tracked by NHTSA's Fatal Accident Report System, aggressive driving played a role in 56 percent of fatal crashes from 2003 through 2007, with excessive speed being the number one factor. Speeding was also the leading driving behavior associated with fatal crashes in 2012 (20.6 percent), followed by driving under the influence (13.7 percent), according to NHTSA. (See chart, page 177.)

Distracted Driving

Activities that take a driver's attention off the road, including talking or texting on cellphones, eating, conversing with passengers and other distractions, are a major safety threat. Beginning with 2010 data, the National Highway Traffic Safety Administration (NHTSA) revised the way it gauged distracted driving, introducing a narrower measure called "distraction-affected crashes," which focuses on distractions that are most likely to affect crash involvement such as dialing a cellphone or texting and being distracted by another person or outside event. There were 3,050 distraction-affected fatal crashes in 2012, according to the latest estimate from NHTSA. In 2012, 3,328 people were killed in such crashes, compared with 3,360 in 2011. An estimated 421,000 people were injured in distraction-affected crashes in 2012, up 9 percent from 387,000 in 2011.

DRIVER HAND-HELD CELLPHONE USE BY AGE, 2004-2012

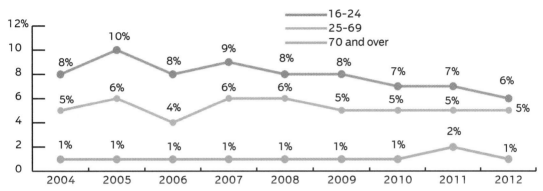

Source: U.S. Department of Transportation, National Highway Traffic Safety Administration.

FATAL CRASHES AFFECTED BY DISTRACTED DRIVERS, 2012

	Crashes	Drivers	Fatalities
Total fatal crashes	**30,800**	**45,337**	**33,561**
Distracted-affected fatal crashes			
Number	3,050	3,119	3,328
Percent of total fatal crashes	10%	7%	10%
Cellphone in use in distracted-affected fatal crashes			
Number	378	394	415
Percent of fatal distracted-affected crashes	12%	13%	12%

Source: U.S. Department of Transportation, National Highway Traffic Safety Administration.

- Cellphone use was a factor in 1 percent of the 30,800 fatal crashes reported in 2012.

- Distraction was a factor in 10 percent of fatal crashes reported in 2012.

The FBI includes the theft or attempted theft of automobiles, trucks, buses, motorcycles, scooters, snowmobiles and other vehicles in its definition of motor vehicle theft. A motor vehicle is stolen on average every 44 seconds in the U.S.

MOTOR VEHICLE THEFT IN THE UNITED STATES, 2003-2012

- Motor vehicles were stolen at a rate of 229.6 per 100,000 people in 2011, down 4.0 percent from 2010, down 37.1 percent from 2007 and down 47.0 percent from 2002.

- More than $4.3 billion was lost to motor vehicle theft in 2011. The average dollar loss per theft was $6,089.

Year	Vehicles stolen	Percent change
2003	1,261,226	1.2%
2004	1,237,851	-1.9
2005	1,235,859	-0.2
2006	1,198,245	-3.0
2007	1,100,472	-8.2
2008	959,059	-12.9
2009	795,652	-17.0
2010	739,565	-7.0
2011	716,508	-3.1
2012	721,053	0.6

Source: U.S. Department of Justice, Federal Bureau of Investigation, *Uniform Crime Reports.*

TOP TEN U.S. METROPOLITAN STATISTICAL AREAS BY MOTOR VEHICLE THEFT RATE, 2013

- All but one of the top 10 U.S. Metropolitan Statistical Areas for motor vehicle theft were in California in 2013. The remaining area is in Washington state.

Rank	Metropolitan Statistical Area[1]	Vehicles stolen	Rate[2]
1	Bakersfield, CA	6,267	725.24
2	Fresno, CA	6,750	706.61
3	Modesto, CA	3,565	678.41
4	San Francisco-Oakland-Hayward, CA	29,326	649.34
5	Stockton-Lodi, CA	4,463	633.61
6	Redding, CA	1,120	625.77
7	Spokane-Spokane Valley, WA	3,205	598.26
8	Vallejo-Fairfield, CA	2,540	597.95
9	San Jose-Sunnyvale-Santa Clara, CA	10,925	569.12
10	Yuba City, CA	930	551.31

[1]Metropolitan statistical areas are designated by the federal Office of Management and Budget and usually include areas much larger than the cities for which they are named.
[2]Ranked by the rate of vehicle thefts reported per 100,000 people based on the 2013 U.S. Census population estimates.

Source: National Insurance Crime Bureau.

TOP TEN STATES WITH THE MOST AND THE FEWEST
MOTOR VEHICLE THEFTS, 2012

	Most motor vehicle thefts			Fewest motor vehicle thefts	
Rank	State	Vehicles stolen	Rank	State	Vehicles stolen
1	California	168,608	1	Vermont	435
2	Texas	64,996	2	Wyoming	584
3	Florida	37,330	3	Maine	995
4	Georgia	28,536	4	New Hampshire	1,023
5	Washington	26,402	5	South Dakota	1,065
6	Illinois	25,690	6	North Dakota	1,151
7	Michigan	25,115	7	Idaho	1,364
8	Ohio	19,512	8	Delaware	1,436
9	Arizona	19,158	9	Alaska	1,522
10	New York	17,348	10	Montana	1,689

Source: U.S. Department of Justice, Federal Bureau of Investigation, *Uniform Crime Reports.*

TOP TEN MOST FREQUENTLY STOLEN PASSENGER VEHICLES, 2013

Rank	Model[1]	Thefts
1	Honda Accord	53,995
2	Honda Civic	45,001
3	Chevrolet Pickup (Full Size)	27,809
4	Ford Pickup (Full Size)	26,494
5	Toyota Camry	14,420
6	Dodge Pickup (Full Size)	11,347
7	Dodge Caravan	10,911
8	Jeep Cherokee/Grand Cherokee	9,272
9	Toyota Corolla	9,010
10	Nissan Altima	8,892

[1]Includes all model years for each vehicle.

Source: National Insurance Crime Bureau.

TOP TEN MOST FREQUENTLY STOLEN PASSENGER VEHICLES, 2013 MODEL YEAR

Rank	Model	Thefts
1	Nissan Altima	810
2	Ford Fusion	793
3	Ford Pickup (Full Size)	775
4	Toyota Corolla	669
5	Chevrolet Impala	654
6	Hyundai Elantra	541
7	Dodge Charger	536
8	Chevrolet Malibu	529
9	Chevrolet Cruze	499
10	Ford Focus	483

Source: National Insurance Crime Bureau.

Recreation

Watercraft Accidents

Federal law requires owners of recreational boats and other watercraft to register them. In 2013 there were 12.0 million registered recreational boats, down from 12.7 million in 2009. Recreational boating accidents must be reported to the Coast Guard if a person dies or is injured and requires medical treatment beyond first aid, if damage to the boat or other property exceeds $2,000, if the boat is lost or if a person disappears from the boat. Out of the 4,062 accidents reported in 2013, 685 occurred in Florida, accounting for 16.9 percent of all incidents. Other states with a high number of boating accidents were California (426), New York (180), Texas (146) and North Carolina (139).

Boating fatalities fell 14.0 percent to 560 in 2013 from 651 in 2012. The rate per 100,000 registered recreational boats was 4.7, down from 5.4 in 2012. The number of accidents fell 10.0 percent to 4,062 in 2013 from 4,515 in 2012. Injuries also fell, to 2,620 in 2013 from 3,000 in 2012, or 12.7 percent. Property damage totaled $39 million in 2013, up 2.6 percent from 2012.

Research has shown that alcohol, combined with typical boating conditions such as motion, vibration, engine noise, sun, wind and spray can impair a person's abilities much faster than alcohol consumption on land. Boat operators with a blood alcohol concentration (BAC) above 0.10 percent are estimated to be more than 10 times more likely to be killed in a boating accident than boat operators with zero BAC. Alcohol was the largest human factor in boating deaths in 2013 (16 percent of boating fatalities), causing 94 deaths in 305 accidents and resulting in 251 injuries. Other primary contributing factors were operator inattention, accounting for 57 deaths, and operator inexperience, resulting in 34 deaths.

RECREATIONAL WATERCRAFT ACCIDENTS, 2009-2013[1]

Year	Accidents Total	Accidents Involving alcohol use[2]	Fatalities Total	Fatalities Involving alcohol use[2]	Injuries	Property damage ($ millions)
2009	4,730	397	736	165	3,358	$36
2010	4,604	395	672	154	3,153	36
2011	4,588	361	758	149	3,081	52
2012	4,515	368	651	140	3,000	38
2013	4,062	305	560	94	2,620	39

[1]Includes accidents involving $2,000 or more in property damage. Includes watercraft such as motorboats and sailboats and other vessels such as jet skis.
[2]The use of alcohol by a boat's occupants was a direct or indirect cause of the accident.
Source: U.S. Department of Transportation, U.S. Coast Guard.

- 77 percent of fatal boating accident victims died by drowning in 2013 and, of those, 84 percent were not wearing life jackets.

- The most common types of boats involved in reported accidents in 2013 were open motorboats (46 percent), personal watercraft (18 percent) and cabin motorboats (17 percent).

TOP TEN STATES BY RECREATIONAL WATERCRAFT ACCIDENTS, 2013[1]

Rank	State	Accidents	Deaths	People injured	Property damage ($000)
1	Florida	685	58	406	$9,490
2	California	426	37	277	2,244
3	New York	180	18	113	2,699
4	Texas	146	31	106	977
5	North Carolina	139	16	90	754
6	New Jersey	123	8	60	152
7	Tennessee	119	20	75	2,373
8	Missouri	111	16	86	1,037
9	Maryland	110	14	77	713
10	Ohio	108	13	41	1,412

[1]Includes accidents involving $2,000 or more in property damage. Includes watercraft such as motorboats and sailboats and other vessels such as jet skis.
Source: U.S. Department of Transportation, U.S. Coast Guard.

Watercraft Thefts

There were 5,537 watercraft thefts in the United States in 2013, down 6 percent from 2012, according to an analysis of federal government data by the National Insurance Crime Bureau. Watercraft include motor boats, sail boats and other vessels such as jet skis. Of these thefts, 2,195, or 40 percent, were recovered by April 30, 2014. Jet skis were the most frequently stolen watercraft, with 1,215 thefts, followed by runabouts (871), utility boats (363), cruisers (214) and sail boats (44). July saw the highest number of reported thefts (691), and February had the fewest (260).

TOP TEN STATES BY WATERCRAFT THEFT, 2013[1]

Rank	State	Thefts	Rank	State	Thefts
1	Florida	1,310	6	North Carolina	178
2	Californa	628	7	Tennessee	167
3	Texas	382	8	Alabama	165
4	Washington	208	9	Arkansas	157
5	Georgia	182	10	South Carolina	151

[1]Includes watercraft such as motorboats and sailboats and other vessels such as jet skis.
Source: National Insurance Crime Bureau.

SPORTS INJURIES IN THE UNITED STATES, 2012

Sport or activity	Injuries[1]	Percent of injuries by age				
		0-4	5-14	15-24	25-64	65 and over
Archery	6,055	3.6%	10.1%	22.9%	49.1%	14.3%
Baseball	159,220	3.3	50.0	28.0	18.0	0.7
Basketball	569,746	0.4	33.3	48.4	17.8	0.2
Bicycle riding[2]	547,499	5.1	35.0	18.6	37.1	4.1
Billiards, pool	4,983	6.6	17.2	21.5	49.4	5.3
Bowling	18,685	8.5	10.5	11.3	57.7	12.0
Boxing	20,203	1.2	8.4	48.4	42.0	[3]
Cheerleading	39,153	0.1	52.9	46.1	0.9	[3]
Exercise	364,137[4]	2.1	11.8	20.1	55.0	11.0
Fishing	72,629	2.8	17.7	12.9	55.9	10.6
Football	466,492	0.2	51.6	38.9	9.2	0.1
Golf	36,308[5]	3.7	16.3	9.5	36.5	34.0
Gymnastics	30,600[6]	3.1	71.0	21.1	4.5	0.3
Hockey (street, roller, and field)	8,243	0.1	36.3	51.0	12.7	[3]

(table continues)

SPORTS INJURIES IN THE UNITED STATES, 2012 (Cont'd)

Sport or activity	Injuries[1]	Percent of injuries by age				
		0-4	5-14	15-24	25-64	65 and over
Horseback riding	66,543	1.8%	17.5%	22.4%	53.5%	4.8%
Horseshoe pitching	1,898	8.9	31.6	7.9	42.9	8.7
Ice hockey	18,962	[3]	33.7	44.8	21.3	0.2
Ice skating	20,873[7]	1.6	49.0	18.2	30.2	1.1
Martial arts	36,065	0.6	25.8	31.2	42.2	0.2
Mountain biking	9,176	0.9	7.0	22.2	68.3	1.7
Mountain climbing	4,446	0.1	14.6	37.4	43.8	4.1
Racquetball, squash, and paddleball	5,601	[3]	12.5	25.1	53.7	8.7
Roller skating	62,906[8]	0.8	53.2	14.2	30.9	0.9
Rugby	15,270	[3]	2.8	79.3	17.8	[3]
Scuba diving	1,437	5.0	10.3	22.6	55.2	6.9
Skateboarding	114,120	1.2	34.3	51.1	13.4	[3]
Snowboarding	38,805	0.2	23.6	53.9	22.2	[3]
Snowmobiling	5,633	1.2	13.0	24.5	56.7	4.6
Soccer	231,447	0.7	42.8	39.2	17.1	0.2
Softball	106,490	0.5	31.0	30.4	37.4	0.7
Swimming	213,464[9]	9.6	41.7	17.4	27.6	3.6
Tennis	24,224	0.4	17.7	18.4	39.7	23.6
Track and field	29,679	[3]	41.0	47.5	11.2	0.2
Volleyball	61,495	[3]	33.1	45.1	21.3	0.5
Waterskiing	7,577	[3]	8.4	38.0	51.7	1.9
Weight lifting	100,300	3.0	8.7	36.6	49.2	2.5
Wrestling	45,646	[3]	37.2	56.5	6.2	[3]

[1]Treated in hospital emergency departments. [2]Excludes mountain biking. [3]Less than 0.1 percent. [4]Includes exercise equipment (65,934 injuries) and exercise activity (298,203 injuries). [5]Excludes golf carts (17,266 injuries). [6]Excludes trampolines (94,945 injuries). [7]Excludes 6,684 injuries in skating, unspecified. [8]Includes roller skating (50,078 injuries) and in-line skating (12,828 injuries). [9]Includes injuries associated with swimming, swimming pools, pool slides, diving or diving boards and swimming pool equipment.

Source: National Safety Council. (2014). Injury Facts®, 2014 Edition. Itasca, IL.

ATV Accidents

One in four people (25 percent) injured in accidents involving all-terrain vehicles (ATVs) in 2012 were children under the age of sixteen, according to the Consumer Product Safety Commission. ATVs are open-air vehicles with three, four or six wheels designed for off-road use. Many states require ATV insurance for vehicles operated on state-owned land.

ATV-RELATED DEATHS AND INJURIES, 2007-2012[1]

| Year | Estimated number of deaths | | | Estimated number of injuries[2] | | |
| | | Younger than 16 years | | | Younger than 16 years | |
	Total	Number	Percent of total	Total	Number	Percent of total
2007	831	136	16%	150,900	40,000	27%
2008	755	109	14	135,100	37,700	28
2009	718	95	13	131,900	32,400	25
2010	657	88	13	115,000	28,300	25
2011	554	73	13	107,500	29,000	27
2012	353	54	15	107,900	26,500	25

[1]ATVs with 3, 4 or unknown number of wheels.
[2]Emergency room-treated.
Source: U.S. Consumer Product Safety Commission.

Aviation

- There were 1,297 civil aviation accidents in 2013, down from 1,539 in 2012. Total fatalities fell to 429 from 447.

- There were two fatalities on large scheduled commercial airlines in 2013, following three years with no fatalities. There were seven fatalities on large nonscheduled airlines (charter airlines) in 2013. There were no fatalities in the prior two years.

United States

In the United States the National Transportation Safety Board compiles data on aviation flight hours, accidents and fatalities for commercial and general aviation.

Commercial airlines are divided into two categories according to the type of aircraft used: aircraft with 10 or more seats and aircraft with fewer than 10 seats. The nonscheduled commercial aircraft with more than 10 seats are also called charter airlines. Commercial airlines flying aircraft with fewer than 10 seats include commuter (scheduled) airlines, and on-demand air taxis. General aviation includes all U.S. noncommercial or privately owned aircraft.

In 2013, 744 million people flew on commercial airlines in the United States, compared with 739 million in 2012 and 734 million in 2011. The Federal Aviation Administration projects that more than 1 billion people will fly on scheduled commercial airlines in the United States annually by 2028.

AIRCRAFT ACCIDENTS IN THE UNITED STATES, 2013[1]

	Flight hours (000)	Number of accidents		Number of fatalities[2]	Accidents per 100,000 flight hours
		Total	Fatal		
Commercial airlines					
10 or more seats					
Scheduled	17,150	20	1	2	0.117
Nonscheduled	478	3	1	7	0.628
Less than 10 seats					
Commuter	322	8	3	6	2.481
On-demand	3,562	44	10	27	1.240
General aviation	20,887	1,222	221	387	5.850
Total civil aviation	**NA**	**1,297**	**236**	**429**	**NA**

[1]Preliminary data. Totals do not add because of collisions involving aircraft in different categories.
[2]Includes nonpassenger deaths.
NA=Data not available.
Source: National Transportation Safety Board.

- Small commuter airlines had eight accidents 2013 compared with four in 2012. There were six fatalities in 2013 after six years with no fatalities.

- The number of small on-demand airline (air taxi) accidents grew to 44 in 2013 from 37 in 2012.

- There were 1,222 general aviation (noncommercial) accidents in 2013, down 17 percent from 1,471 in 2012. 2013 accidents resulted in 387 deaths, down from 432 in 2012.

LARGE AIRLINE ACCIDENTS IN THE UNITED STATES, 2004-2013[1]

Year	Flight hours	Total accidents	Fatal accidents	Total fatalities[2]	Total accidents per 100,000 flight hours
2004	18,882,503	30	2	14	0.159
2005	19,390,029	40	3	22	0.206
2006	19,263,209	33	2	50	0.171
2007	19,637,322	28	1	1	0.143
2008	19,126,766	28	2	3	0.146
2009	17,626,832	30	2	52	0.170
2010	17,750,986	29	1	2	0.163
2011	17,962,965	31	0	0	0.173
2012	17,722,235	27	0	0	0.152
2013[3]	17,627,600	23	2	9	0.130

[1]Scheduled and unscheduled planes with more than 10 seats.
[2]Includes nonpassenger deaths.
[3]Preliminary.
Source: National Transportation Safety Board.

World Aviation Losses

In 2013 more than 3 billion people flew safely on 36.4 million flights, according to the International Air Transport Association. The global accident rate (as measured by the rate of hull losses on western-built jets) was 0.41 in 2013, or about one accident for every 2.4 million flights. This was a deterioration from 2012, at 0.21, which was the lowest in aviation history. (A hull loss is an accident in which the aircraft is destroyed or substantially damaged and is not subsequently repaired.) There were 81 accidents in 2013 (on eastern- and western-built aircraft), up from 75 in 2012. A Malaysia Airlines jet shot down on July 17, 2014, over the Ukraine became the seventh deadliest crash in history, with 298 fatalities. Malaysia Airlines Flight 370 en route to Beijing disappeared on March 8, 2014, with 239 on board.

FATAL WORLD AVIATION ACCIDENTS, 2009-2013

Year	Fatal accidents[1]	Fatalities[1]	Accident rate[2]
2009	18	685	0.75
2010	23	786	0.65
2011	22	490	0.40
2012	15	414	0.21
2013	16	210	0.41

[1]On eastern- and western-built jet aircraft.
[2]Measured in hull losses per million flights of western-built jet aircraft. A hull loss is an accident in which the aircraft is destroyed or substantially damaged and is not subsequently repaired.
Source: International Air Transport Association.

THE TEN DEADLIEST AVIATION CRASHES

Rank	Date	Location	Country	Operator	Fatalities
1	Mar. 27, 1977	Tenerife	Spain	Pan Am, KLM	583
2	Aug. 12, 1985	Yokota AFB	Japan	JAL	520
3	Nov. 12, 1996	New Delhi	India	Saudi Arabian Airlines, Kazakhstan Airlines	349
4	Mar. 3, 1974	Ermenonville	France	Turkish Airlines	346
5	Jun. 23, 1985	Atlantic Ocean		Air India	329
6	Aug. 19, 1980	Jedda	Saudi Arabia	Saudi Arabian Airlines	301
7	Jul. 17, 2014	Grabovo	Ukraine	Malaysia Airlines	298
8	Jul. 3, 1988	Persian Gulf		Iran Air	290
9	Feb. 19, 2003	Kerman	Iran	Islamic Republic of Iran Air Force	275
10	May 25, 1979	Chicago	U.S.	American Airlines	273

Source: Aircraft Crashes Record Office, Geneva (baaa-acro.com/Statistics.html).

Workplace Losses

According to the National Safety Council (NSC), the total cost of unintentional workplace deaths and injuries in 2012 was an estimated $198.2 billion. This figure includes wage and productivity losses of injured workers of $89.6 billion, medical costs of $55.7 billion and administrative expenses of $36.5 billion. Other employers' costs include the value of time lost by workers dealing with injured employees and the time required to investigate injuries and write up injury reports. These factors add another $11.0 billion. Also included are fire losses of $3.2 billion and $2.2 billion in motor vehicle damage. Economic losses from work injuries are not comparable from year to year; as additional or more precise data become available to the NSC, they are used from that year forward. Previously estimated figures are not revised.

WORKPLACE LOSSES AND DEATHS, 2003-2012

| Year | Workers[3] | Economic loss[1] ($ millions) | | Loss per worker (In 2012 dollars)[4] | Fatalities[2] | |
		Dollars when occurred	In 2012 dollars[4]		Number	Per 100,000 workers
2003	138,988	$156,200	$194,905	$1,402	4,725	3.4
2004	140,504	142,200	172,834	1,230	4,995	3.6
2005	142,946	160,400	188,566	1,319	4,984	3.5
2006	145,607	164,700	187,570	1,288	5,088	3.5
2007	147,203	175,300	194,113	1,319	4,829	3.3
2008	146,535	183,000	195,147	1,332	4,423	3.3
2009	141,102	168,900	180,754	1,281	3,744	2.9
2010	140,298	176,900	186,260	1,328	3,896	3.0
2011	140,298	188,900	192,809	1,374	3,901	3.0
2012	143,709	198,200	198,200	1,379	3,613	2.7

[1]Economic loss from unintentional injuries. These estimates are not comparable from year to year.
[2]From unintentional injuries.
[3]Age 16 and over, gainfully employed, includes owners, managers and other paid employees, the self-employed, unpaid family workers and active duty resident military personnel.
[4]Adjusted to 2012 dollars by the Insurance Information Institute using the Bureau of Labor Statistics' Inflation Calculator.

Source: National Safety Council. (2014). Injury Facts®, 2014 Edition. Itasca, IL; U.S. Department of Labor, Bureau of Labor Statistics.

PRIVATE INDUSTRIES WITH THE LARGEST NUMBER OF NONFATAL OCCUPATIONAL INJURIES AND ILLNESSES, 2012[1]

Rank	Industry	Number (000)	Incidence rate[2]
1	General medical and surgical hospitals	230.2	6.5
2	Food services and drinking places	208.4	3.4
3	Ambulatory health care services	123.5	2.6
4	Specialty trade contractors	119.2	3.9
5	General merchandise stores	118.5	5.3
6	Administrative and support services	108.8	2.6
7	Nursing care facilities	100.2	7.9
	Total, private industry	**2,976.4**	**3.4**

[1]Based on industries with 100,000 or more cases in 2012. Excludes farms with fewer than 11 employees.
[2]The incidence rates represent the number of injuries and illnesses per 100 full-time workers.

Source: U.S. Department of Labor, Bureau of Labor Statistics.

THE TEN OCCUPATIONS WITH THE LARGEST NUMBER OF INJURIES AND ILLNESSES, 2012[1]

Rank	Occupation	Number	Percent of total
1	Laborers (nonconstruction)	60,640	6.7%
2	Truck drivers, heavy	40,440	4.5
3	Nursing assistants	38,010	4.2
4	Production workers	28,090	3.1
5	Truck drivers, light	24,620	2.7
6	Retail salespersons	24,520	2.7
7	Maintenance, general	23,470	2.6
8	Janitors and cleaners	21,970	2.4
9	Stock clerks and order fillers	20,940	2.3
10	Registered nurses	20,930	2.3
	Total, top ten	**303,630**	**33.5%**
	Total, all occupations	**905,690**	**100.0%**

[1]Nonfatal injuries and illnesses involving days off from work for private industries; excludes farms with fewer than 11 employees.

Source: U.S. Department of Labor, Bureau of Labor Statistics.

Causes of Workplace Deaths

According to the U.S. Department of Labor, the highest rate of workplace fatalities in 2013 was among logging workers, with 91.3 deaths per 100,000 full-time employees, followed by fishing workers, aircraft pilots and flight engineers, and roofers. The all-industry average was 3.2 deaths per 100,000 workers.

WORKPLACE DEATHS BY CAUSE, 2012-2013[1]

Cause	2012 Number	2013 Number	2013 Percent of total
All transportation (includes vehicle crashes)	1,923	1,740	40%
Vehicle crashes[2]	1,153	991	22
Assaults and violence (includes homicides)	803	753	17
Homicides	475	397	9
Contact with objects and equipment	723	717	16
Falls	704	699	16
Exposure to harmful substances or environments	340	330	7
Fires and explosions	122	148	3
Total workplace fatalities	**4,628**	**4,405**	**100%**

[1]From intentional and unintentional sources. [2]Roadway incidents involving motorized land vehicles.

Source: U.S. Department of Labor, Bureau of Labor Statistics, Census of Fatal Occupational Injuries.

Occupational Disease

According to the U.S. Department of Labor's Bureau of Labor Statistics, an occupational disease is any new abnormal condition or disorder, other than one resulting from an occupational injury, caused by exposure to factors associated with employment. Included are acute and chronic diseases which may be caused by inhalation, absorption, ingestion or direct contact in the workplace.

The overwhelming majority of reported new illnesses are those that directly relate to workplace activity (e.g., contact dermatitis or carpal tunnel syndrome) and are easy to identify. However, some conditions, such as long-term latent illnesses caused by exposure to carcinogens, often are difficult to relate to the workplace and may be understated.

Asbestos-Related Illness

Exposure to asbestos can cause lung cancer and other respiratory diseases. The first asbestos-related lawsuit was filed in 1966. A large number of workers who may have physical signs of exposure but not a debilitating disease are filing claims now out of concern that if they later develop an illness, the company responsible may be bankrupt, due to other asbestos claims. It can take as long as 40 years after exposure for someone to be diagnosed with an asbestos-related illness.

ESTIMATED ASBESTOS LOSSES, 2004-2013[1]

($ billions)

- Incurred asbestos losses grew 5.3 percent to $2.0 billion in 2013 from $1.9 billion in 2012.

Year	Beginning reserve	Losses		Ending reserve[3]
		Incurred[2]	Paid	
2004	$22.4	$3.6	$2.9	$24.0
2005	24.0	3.8	2.4	26.6
2006	25.2	1.7	2.6	24.1
2007	23.2	2.5	2.5	23.5
2008	23.5	1.1	3.7	20.5
2009	20.6	1.9	2.0	20.4
2010	20.5	2.4	2.3	20.6
2011	20.6	1.8	1.8	20.6
2012	20.4	1.9	2.0	20.3
2013	20.4	2.0	2.1	20.3

[1]All amounts are net of reinsurance recoveries.
[2]Incurred losses are losses related to events that have occurred, regardless of whether or not the claims have been paid, net of reinsurance. Includes loss adjustment expenses.
[3]Because of changes in the population of insurers reporting data each year, the beginning reserve may not equal the ending reserve of the prior year.

Source: SNL Financial LC.

Home

In 2012, 19.3 million Americans, or one in 16 people, experienced an unintentional injury in the home that required aid from a medical professional, according to an analysis by the National Safety Council (NSC). Injuries requiring medical attention occur more often at home than in public places, the workplace and motor vehicle crashes combined, according to the NSC. There were 63,000 deaths from unintentional home injuries in 2012. Despite population growth and a corresponding rise in the number of fatal injuries, the rate of fatal home injuries has declined dramatically over the past 100 years, falling by 28 percent to 20.1 deaths per 100,000 people in 2012 from 28 deaths per 100,000 people in 1912. However, the number and rate of unintentional home injury deaths has been steadily rising since 2000, largely due to increases in unintentional poisonings and falls.

UNINTENTIONAL HOME DEATHS AND INJURIES, 2012

Deaths	63,000
Medically consulted injuries	19,300,000
Death rate per 100,000 population	20.1
Costs	$220.3 billion

Source: National Safety Council. (2014). Injury Facts®, 2014 Edition. Itasca, IL.

PRINCIPAL TYPES OF HOME UNINTENTIONAL INJURY DEATHS, 2012

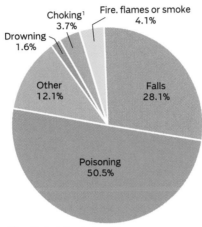

Choking[1]
3.7%

Fire. flames or smoke
4.1%

Drowning
1.6%

Other
12.1%

Falls
28.1%

Poisoning
50.5%

[1]Inhalation and ingestion of food or other object that obstructs breathing.

Source: National Safety Council. (2014). Injury Facts®, 2014 Edition. Itasca, IL.

Causes of Death

Mortality Risks

Heart disease is the leading cause of death in the U.S., accounting for nearly 600,000 fatalities in 2011, according to the Centers for Disease Control and Prevention. Influenza and pneumonia ranked eighth in 2011, accounting for some 54,000 fatalities. However, pandemic influenza viruses have the potential to be far more deadly. An estimated 675,000 Americans died during the 1918 Spanish influenza pandemic, the deadliest and most infectious known influenza strain to date.

DEATH RATES FROM MAJOR CAUSES IN THE UNITED STATES, 2010-2011

Cause of death	Number of deaths, 2011	Age-adjusted death rate[1]		
		2010	2011[2]	Percent change
Heart disease	596,339	179.1	173.7	-3.0%
Malignant neoplasms (tumors)	575,313	172.8	168.6	-2.4
Chronic lower respiratory diseases	143,382	42.2	42.7	1.2
Cerebrovascular diseases (stroke)	128,931	39.1	37.9	-3.1
Accidents (unintentional injuries)	122,777	38.0	38.0	[3]
Alzheimer's disease	84,691	25.1	24.6	-2.0
Diabetes	73,282	20.8	21.5	3.4
Influenza and pneunonia	53,667	15.1	15.7	4.0

(table continues)

DEATH RATES FROM MAJOR CAUSES IN THE UNITED STATES, 2010-2011 (Cont'd)

Cause of death	Number of deaths, 2011	Age-adjusted death rate[1] 2010	2011[2]	Percent change
Kidney disease	45,731	15.3	13.4	-12.4%
Intentional self-harm (suicide)	38,285	12.1	12.0	-0.8
Septicemia	35,539	10.6	10.5	-0.9
Chronic liver disease and cirrhosis	33,539	9.4	9.7	3.2
Hypertension[4]	27,477	8.0	8.0	[3]
Parkinson's disease	23,107	6.8	7.0	2.9
Pneumonitis due to solids and liquids	18,090	5.1	5.3	3.9
All other causes	512,723	NA	NA	NA
Total deaths	**2,512,873**	**747.0**	**740.6**	**-0.9%**

[1]Per 100,000 population; factors out differences based on age.
[2]Preliminary.
[3]Less than 0.1 percent.
[4]Essential (primary) hypertension and hypertensive renal disease.
NA=Not applicable.

Source: National Center for Health Statistics.

Gun Deaths and Injuries

The societal cost of U.S. injuries from firearms, including lost work time, medical care, insurance, criminal-justice expenses, pain and suffering and lost quality of life, amounted to about $174 billion in 2010, according to an analysis of Centers for Disease Control and Prevention data by the Pacific Institute for Research and Evaluation. Fatal injuries accounted for $153.3 billion, or nearly 90 percent of the costs. Assaults and homicides accounted for 65 percent of the costs, followed by suicides, accounting for 31 percent of all injuries caused by firearms. Unintentional acts, legal intervention and acts of undetermined intent account for the remainder.

DEATHS IN THE UNITED STATES BY FIREARM, 2010 AND 2011

Deaths caused by firearms	Number 2010	2011[1]	Percent of total 2010	2011[1]
Accidental discharge of firearms	606	851	1.9%	2.6%
Suicide by firearm	19,392	19,766	61.9	61.5
Assault (homicide) by firearm	11,078	11,101	35.4	34.5
Undetermined intent	252	222	0.8	0.7
Total[2]	**31,328**	**32,163**	**100.0%**	**100.0%**

[1]Preliminary.
[2]Does not include deaths resulting from legal intervention.

Source: Centers for Disease Control and Prevention, National Vital Statistics Report.

Cost of Goods and Services

The Bureau of Labor Statistics' Consumer Expenditures Survey describes the buying habits of American consumers, using household expenditure records and surveys. Expenditures include goods and services purchased, whether or not payment was made at the time of purchase, and all sales and excise taxes.

Income, age of family members, geographic location, taste and personal preference influence expenditures. Location often affects the cost of auto and homeowners insurance. Rural households spend less than urban households on auto insurance; regional variations in residential building costs affect spending on homeowners insurance. In addition to the number and type of cars, where they are driven and by whom, auto insurance prices are influenced by such factors as the degree of competition in the marketplace and how claimants are compensated (through the no-fault or traditional tort systems).

INSURANCE AND OTHER CONSUMER EXPENDITURES AS A PERCENT OF TOTAL HOUSEHOLD SPENDING, 1990-2013[1]

	1990	1995	2000	2005	2010	2011	2012	2013
Housing	30.0%	31.7%	31.7%	31.9%	33.7%	33.1%	32.1%	32.8%
Transportation	15.9	16.4	17.5	16.0	13.9	14.7	15.5	15.6
Food	15.0	14.0	13.6	12.8	12.7	13.0	12.8	12.9
Retirement[2]	8.8	8.0	7.8	10.4	10.5	10.3	10.2	10.2
Other	10.6	10.2	10.5	10.4	10.4	10.3	10.6	10.0
Total insurance	5.8	6.8	6.3	6.5	7.3	7.2	7.4	7.7
Health	2.0	2.7	2.6	2.9	3.8	3.9	3.9	4.4
Vehicle	2.0	2.2	2.0	2.0	2.1	2.0	2.0	2.0
Homeowners	0.5	0.7	0.7	0.7	0.8	0.8	0.8	0.7
Life	1.2	1.1	1.0	0.8	0.6	0.6	0.6	0.6
Other	0.1	0.1	0.1	0.1	[3]	[3]	[3]	[3]
Entertainment	5.0	5.0	4.9	5.1	5.2	5.2	5.1	4.9
Clothing	5.7	5.3	4.9	4.1	3.5	3.5	3.4	3.1
Healthcare	3.1	2.7	2.8	2.8	2.8	2.8	2.9	2.7

[1]Ranked by 2013 data.
[2]Mostly payroll deductions for retirement purposes such as Social Security (78% of retirement expenditures), government and private pension plans (13%) and nonpayroll deposits such as IRAs (9%) in 2013.
[3]Less than 0.1 percent.
Note: Percentages may not add due to rounding.
Source: U.S. Department of Labor, Bureau of Labor Statistics.

INSURANCE EXPENDITURES AS A PERCENTAGE OF TOTAL HOUSEHOLD SPENDING, 2013

- Insurance accounted for 7.7 percent of household spending in 2013, up 0.3 percentage points from 2012. The share spent on homeowners, life and vehicle insurance basically remained the same, while the healthcare insurance share grew 0.5 percentage points.

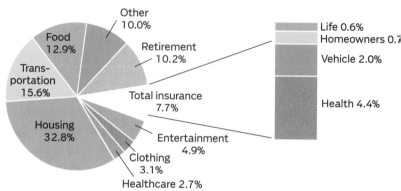

Other 10.0%
Food 12.9%
Retirement 10.2%
Transportation 15.6%
Total insurance 7.7%
Housing 32.8%
Entertainment 4.9%
Clothing 3.1%
Healthcare 2.7%

Life 0.6%
Homeowners 0.7
Vehicle 2.0%
Health 4.4%

Source: U.S. Department of Labor, Bureau of Labor Statistics.

Consumer Prices

The Bureau of Labor Statistics' consumer price index (CPI) tracks changes in the prices paid by consumers for a representative basket of goods and services. The cost of living (all items) rose 1.5 percent in 2013. The rise in the cost of auto insurance was steeper (4.2 percent). The cost of legal services rose 2.8 percent, and doctors' services rose 2.0 percent.

CONSUMER PRICE INDICES FOR INSURANCE AND RELATED ITEMS AND ANNUAL RATES OF CHANGE, 2004-2013
(Base: 1982-84=100)

Year	Cost of living (all items)		Motor vehicle insurance		Medical care items		Physicians' services		Hospital services[1]	
	Index	Percent change	Index	Percent change	Index	Percent change	Index	Percent change	Index	Percent change
2004	188.9	2.7%	323.2	2.8%	310.1	4.4%	278.3	4.0%	153.4	6.0%
2005	195.3	3.4	329.9	2.1	323.2	4.2	287.5	3.3	161.6	5.3
2006	201.6	3.2	331.8	0.6	336.2	4.0	291.9	1.5	172.1	6.5
2007	207.3	2.8	333.1	0.4	351.1	4.4	303.2	3.9	183.6	6.7
2008	215.3	3.8	341.5	2.5	364.1	3.7	311.3	2.7	197.2	7.4
2009	214.5	-0.4	357.0	4.5	375.6	3.2	320.8	3.0	210.7	6.9
2010	218.1	1.6	375.2	5.1	388.4	3.4	331.3	3.3	227.2	7.8
2011	224.9	3.2	388.7	3.6	400.3	3.0	340.3	2.7	241.2	6.2
2012	229.6	2.1	402.5	3.6	414.9	3.7	347.3	2.1	253.6	5.1
2013	233.0	1.5	419.4	4.2	425.1	2.5	354.2	2.0	265.4	4.7
Percent change 2004-2013		**23.3%**		**29.8%**		**37.1%**		**27.3%**		**73.0%**

(table continues)

CONSUMER PRICE INDICES FOR INSURANCE AND
RELATED ITEMS AND ANNUAL RATES OF CHANGE, 2004-2013 (Cont'd)
(Base: 1982-84=100)

Year	Motor vehicle body work Index	Percent change	New vehicles Index	Percent change	New cars Index	Percent change	New trucks[2] Index	Percent change
2004	208.2	2.6%	137.1	-0.6%	133.9	-0.6%	145.0	-0.8%
2005	215.0	3.3	137.9	0.6	135.2	1.0	145.3	0.2
2006	224.8	4.6	137.6	-0.2	136.4	0.9	142.9	-1.7
2007	232.2	3.3	136.3	-1.0	135.9	-0.4	140.7	-1.5
2008	239.7	3.2	134.2	-1.5	135.4	-0.3	137.1	-2.6
2009	248.5	3.7	135.6	1.1	136.7	0.9	138.8	1.3
2010	254.4	2.4	138.0	1.8	138.1	1.0	142.7	2.8
2011	259.9	2.2	141.9	2.8	142.2	3.0	146.5	2.7
2012	264.9	1.9	144.2	1.7	144.2	1.4	149.4	1.9
2013	271.0	2.3	145.8	1.1	144.9	0.5	151.8	1.6
Percent change 2004-2013		**30.2%**		**6.3%**		**8.2%**		**4.7%**

Year	Used cars and trucks Index	Percent change	Tenants and household insurance[3,4] Index	Percent change	Repair of household items[3,5] Index	Percent change	Legal services Index	Percent change	Existing single-family homes Median price ($000)	Percent change
2004	133.3	-6.7%	116.2	1.2%	139.4	6.4%	232.3	4.8%	$195	9.3%
2005	139.4	4.6	117.6	1.2	147.4	5.7	241.8	4.1	220	12.4
2006	140.0	0.4	116.5	-0.9	154.7	5.0	250.0	3.4	222	1.0
2007	135.7	-3.0	117.0	0.4	161.2	4.2	260.3	4.1	219	-1.3
2008	134.0	-1.3	118.8	1.6	170.0	5.5	270.7	4.0	198	-9.5
2009	127.0	-5.2	121.5	2.2	176.0	3.5	278.1	2.7	173	-12.9
2010	143.1	12.7	125.7	3.5	181.7	3.2	288.1	3.6	173	0.3
2011	149.0	4.1	127.4	1.4	NA	NA	297.4	3.2	166	-4.0
2012	150.3	0.9	131.3	3.1	198.7	NA	303.5	2.0	177	6.6
2013	149.9	-0.3	135.4	3.1	206.7	4.0	311.8	2.8	197	11.4
Percent change 2004-2013		**12.4%**		**16.5%**		**48.2%**		**34.2%**		**1.0%**

[1]December 1996=100. [2]December 1983=100. [3]December 1997=100. [4]Only includes insurance covering rental properties. [5]Includes appliances, reupholstery and inside home maintenance. NA=Data not available. Note: Percent changes after 2007 for consumer price indices and all years for the median price of existing single-family homes calculated from unrounded data.

Source: U.S. Department of Labor, Bureau of Labor Statistics; National Association of Realtors.

Insurance Fraud

Insurance fraud is a deliberate deception perpetrated against or by an insurance company or agent for the purpose of financial gain. Fraud may be committed at different points in the insurance transaction by applicants for insurance, policyholders, third-party claimants or professionals who provide services to claimants. Insurance agents and company employees may also commit insurance fraud. Common frauds include padding, or inflating actual claims, misrepresenting facts on an insurance application, submitting claims for injuries or damage that never occurred and staging accidents.

The exact amount of fraud committed is difficult to determine. The proportion of fraud varies among different lines of insurance, with healthcare, workers compensation and auto insurance believed to be the most vulnerable lines. The nature of fraud is constantly evolving.

- Insurance industry estimates generally put fraud at about 10 percent of the property/casualty insurance industry's incurred losses and loss adjustment expenses each year, although the figure can fluctuate based on the line of business, economic conditions and other factors.

TOP TEN QUESTIONABLE CLAIMS BY INSURANCE TYPE, 2011-2012[1]

Rank	Type of insurance	2011	2012	Percent change, 2011-2012
1	Personal automobile	69,219	78,024	12.7%
2	Personal property: homeowners	11,887	17,183	44.6
3	Workers compensation[2]	3,470	4,459	28.5
4	Commercial automobile	3,092	3,554	14.9
5	Commercial and general liability	2,571	2,650	3.1
6	Personal property: other	1,090	2,621	140.5
7	Commercial property: commercial multiple peril	698	941	34.8
8	Commercial liability: business owners	387	464	19.9
9	Personal property: fire	488	411	-15.8
10	Commercial property: business owners	325	406	24.9
	All questionable claims[3]	**100,201**	**116,171**	**15.9%**

[1]Based on claims insurance companies refer to the National Insurance Crime Bureau to be reviewed and investigated.
[2]Includes employers' liability.
[3]Includes all policy types, not just top 10.

Source: National Insurance Crime Bureau.

KEY STATE LAWS AGAINST INSURANCE FRAUD

State	Insurance fraud classified as a crime	Immunity statutes	Fraud bureau	Mandatory insurer fraud plan	Mandatory auto photo inspection
Alabama	X[1,2]	X	X		
Alaska	X	X	X		
Arizona	X	X	X		
Arkansas	X	X	X	X	
California	X	X	X	X	
Colorado	X	X	X[4]	X	
Connecticut	X	X	X[1,5]		
Delaware	X	X	X		
D.C.	X	X	X[6]	X	
Florida	X	X	X	X	X
Georgia	X	X	X		
Hawaii	X[1,2]	X	X		
Idaho	X	X	X		
Illinois	X	X	X[1]		
Indiana	X	X			
Iowa	X	X	X		
Kansas	X	X	X	X	
Kentucky	X	X	X	X	
Louisiana	X	X	X	X	
Maine	X	X	X[1]	X	
Maryland	X	X	X	X	
Massachusetts	X	X	X		X
Michigan	X	X			
Minnesota	X	X	X	X	
Mississippi	X	X[3]	X[5]		
Missouri	X	X	X		
Montana	X	X	X		
Nebraska	X	X	X		
Nevada	X	X	X[5]		
New Hampshire	X	X	X	X	

- Immunity statutes protect the person or insurance company that reports insurance fraud from criminal and civil prosecution.

- Fraud bureaus are state law enforcement agencies, mostly set up in insurance departments, where investigators review fraud reports and begin the prosecution process.

(table continues)

State mandated insurer fraud plans require insurance companies to formulate a program for fighting fraud and sometimes to establish special investigation units to identify fraud patterns.

KEY STATE LAWS AGAINST INSURANCE FRAUD (Cont'd)

State	Insurance fraud classified as a crime	Immunity statutes	Fraud bureau	Mandatory insurer fraud plan	Mandatory auto photo inspection
New Jersey	X	X	X[5]	X	X
New Mexico	X	X	X	X	
New York	X	X	X	X	X
North Carolina	X	X	X		
North Dakota	X	X	X		
Ohio	X	X	X	X	
Oklahoma	X	X	X		
Oregon	X[1]	X			
Pennsylvania	X	X	X[5]	X	
Rhode Island	X	X[1,3,7]	X[5,8]	X	X
South Carolina	X	X	X[5]		
South Dakota	X	X	X[5]		
Tennessee	X	X		X	
Texas	X	X	X	X	
Utah	X	X	X		
Vermont	X	X		X	
Virginia	X	X	X[8]		
Washington	X	X	X	X	
West Virginia	X	X	X		
Wisconsin	X	X	X[5]		
Wyoming	X	X[3]			

[1]Workers compensation insurance only.
[2]Healthcare insurance only.
[3]Arson only.
[4]No fraud bureau. Industry assessment payable to the Insurance Cash Fund. Attorney General's Office conducts fraud prosecution.
[5]Fraud bureau set up in the state Attorney General's office.
[6]In the District of Columbia fraud is investigated by the Enforcement and Consumer Protection Bureau in the Department of Insurance, Securities and Banking which investigates fraud in all three financial sectors.
[7]Auto insurance only.
[8]Fraud bureau set up in the state police office.

Source: Property Casualty Insurers Association of America; Coalition Against Insurance Fraud.

Insurers' Legal Defense Costs

Lawsuits against businesses affect the cost of insurance and the products and services of the industries sued. According to Towers Watson, an actuarial consulting firm, the American civil liability (tort) system cost about $265 billion in 2010 in direct costs, up from $180 billion in 2000. Tort costs rose 5.1 percent in 2010 after dropping 1.2 percent in 2009. Absent payouts from the April 2010 Deepwater Horizon drilling rig explosion, tort costs would have shown an overall decrease of 2.4 percent in 2010, according to Towers Watson. The U.S. tort system cost $857 per person in 2010, up from $820 per person in 2009.

Most lawsuits are settled out of court. Of those that are tried and proceed to verdict, Jury Verdict Research data show that in 2012 the median, or midpoint, plaintiff award in personal injury cases was $75,000, up 87.5 percent from $40,000 in 2008.

Insurers are required to defend their policyholders against lawsuits. The costs of settling a claim are reported on insurers' financial statements as "defense and cost containment expenses incurred." These expenses include defense, litigation and medical cost containment. Expenditures for surveillance, litigation management and fees for appraisers, private investigators, hearing representatives and fraud investigators are included. In addition, attorney legal fees may be incurred owing to a duty to defend, even when coverage does not exist, because attorneys must be hired to issue opinions about coverage. Insurers' defense costs as a percentage of incurred losses are relatively high in some lines such as products liability and medical malpractice, reflecting the high cost of defending certain types of lawsuits, such as medical injury cases and class actions against pharmaceutical companies. For example, in addition to $1.6 billion in products liability incurred losses in 2013, insurers spent $1.2 billion on settlement expenses, equivalent to 75.1 percent of the losses.

**DEFENSE COSTS AND COST CONTAINMENT EXPENSES
AS A PERCENT OF INCURRED LOSSES, 2011-2013[1]**

($000)

	2011		2012		2013	
	Amount	As a percent of incurred losses	Amount	As a percent of incurred losses	Amount	As a percent of incurred losses
Products liability	$1,140,230	72.0%	$873,860	114.7%	$1,166,236	75.1%
Medical malpractice	1,793,296	57.5	1,686,009	45.7	1,656,049	53.3
Commercial multiple peril[2]	1,896,935	37.6	2,022,739	46.0	2,096,543	37.7
Other liability	4,464,140	25.0	4,959,838	24.8	4,914,106	25.4
Workers compensation	3,087,836	12.6	3,071,093	12.3	3,012,719	12.3
Commercial auto liability	960,961	10.3	1,091,434	10.4	1,207,596	10.7
Private passenger auto liability	3,960,967	6.2	4,353,427	6.7	4,600,395	6.8
All liability lines	**$17,304,365**	**13.8%**	**$18,058,400**	**13.9%**	**$18,653,644**	**14.0%**

[1]Net of reinsurance, excludes state funds.
[2]Liability portion only.

Source: SNL Financial LC.

Personal Injury Awards

In 2012 the median (or midpoint) award in personal injury cases was $75,000, up from $60,000 the previous year, according to Thomson Reuters' Jury Verdict Research Series. The average award rose to $989,580 from $775,735 during the same period. Thomson Reuters notes that average awards can be skewed by a few very high awards and that medians are more representative. In cases of products liability, the highest median award was in transportation products cases ($2,643,000). In disputes concerning medical malpractice, the highest median award was in childbirth cases ($2,452,214). In cases involving business negligence, the highest median award was against transportation industries ($588,500).

Awards of $1 million or more accounted for 17 percent of all personal injury awards in 2011 and 2012, up from 13 percent in the prior two-year period. In 2011 and 2012 half of medical malpractice awards and 57 percent of products liability awards amounted to $1 million or more, the highest proportion of awards. Vehicular liability and premises liability cases had the lowest proportion of awards of $1 million or more, at 7 percent and 14 percent, respectively.

TRENDS IN PERSONAL INJURY LAWSUITS, 2008-2012[1]

Year	Award median	Probabiity range[2]	Award range	Award mean
2008	$40,000	$10,000 - $225,390	$1 - $188,000,000	$836,798
2009	39,864	9,880 - 207,451	1 - 77,418,670	752,525
2010	39,183	10,000 - 200,000	1 - 71,000,000	653,647
2011	60,000	12,075 - 335,670	1 - 58,619,989	775,735
2012	75,000	18,949 - 350,000	1 - 140,000,000	989,580
Overall	**$41,444**	**$10,000 - $249,071**	**$1 - $188,000,000**	**$789,784**

[1]Excludes punitive damages.
[2]25 percent above and below the median award. The median represents the midpoint jury award. Half of the awards are above the median and half are below. This helps establish where awards tend to cluster.

Source: Reprinted with permission of Thomson Reuters, *Current Award Trends in Personal Injury*, 53rd edition.

AVERAGE PERSONAL INJURY JURY AWARDS, 2008-2012

Source: Reprinted with permission of Thomson Reuters, *Current Award Trends in Personal Injury*, 53rd edition.

MEDIAN AND AVERAGE PERSONAL INJURY JURY AWARDS BY TYPE OF LIABILITY, 2012

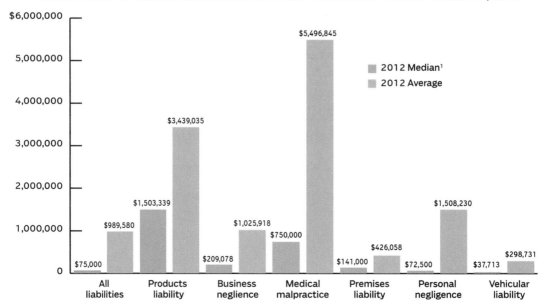

■ 2012 Median[1]
■ 2012 Average

[1]Represents the midpoint jury award. Half of awards are above the median and half are below.

Source: Reprinted with permission of Thomson Reuters, *Current Award Trends in Personal Injury*, 53rd edition.

PERCENT OF PERSONAL INJURY JURY AWARDS OVER $1 MILLION, 2003-2012

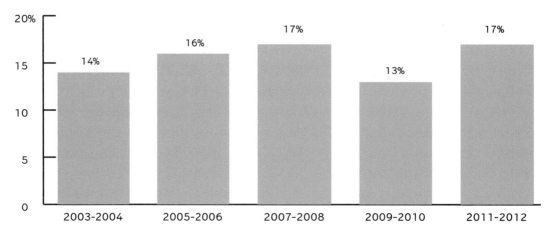

Source: Reprinted with permission of Thomson Reuters, *Current Award Trends in Personal Injury*, 53rd edition and earlier editions.

Directors and Officers Liability Insurance

Directors and officers liability insurance (D&O) covers directors and officers of a company for negligent acts or omissions and for misleading statements that result in suits against the company. There are various forms of D&O coverage. Corporate reimbursement coverage indemnifies directors and officers of the organization. Side-A coverage provides D&O coverage for personal liability when directors and officers are not indemnified by the firm. Entity coverage for claims made specifically against the company is also available. D&O policies may be broadened to include coverage for employment practices liability (EPL). EPL coverage may also be purchased as a stand-alone policy.

Sixty-five percent of corporations purchased D&O coverage in 2013, according to the Cost of Risk survey from the Risk and Insurance Management Society, based on a survey of 1,441 corporations. Banks were the most likely to purchase D&O coverage, with 82 percent of industry respondents purchasing the coverage, followed by 78 percent of respondents in telecommunication services. The 2013 Director and Officers Liability Survey of 171 U.S. organizations that purchase D&O liability insurance found that the group's average D&O limits purchased was $111.9 million and the median limit purchased was $90 million. For public companies, the average limit was $145.4 million. For private companies, the average was $50.7 million. Nineteen percent of public companies and 18 percent of private companies increased their D&O limits from their previous purchase. According to the 2013 survey, 30 percent of respondents reported having had a claim in the past 10 years, with nonprofits reporting the highest proportion of claims (61 percent).

TYPES OF DIRECTORS AND OFFICERS LIABILITY CLAIMS BY OWNERSHIP, 2004-2013[1]

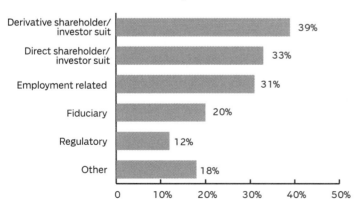

- The percentage of respondents reporting derivative shareholder/investor lawsuits, the most widespread claim, dropped from 40 percent in 2012 to 39 percent in 2013.

- Regulatory claims fell fastest, dropping to 12 percent in 2013 from 23 percent in 2012.

[1]Based on participants in the survey that reported one or more claims over the 10-year period.
Source: *2013 Directors and Officers Liability Survey*, JLT PARK Ltd.

TOP TEN WRITERS OF DIRECTORS AND OFFICERS INSURANCE BY DIRECT PREMIUMS WRITTEN, 2013[1]

($000)

- Directors and officers liability insurance direct premiums written totaled $6.0 billion in 2013, according to SNL Financial.

Rank	Group/company	Direct premiums written	Market share
1	American International Group	$909,515	15.1%
2	XL Group plc	619,371	10.3
3	Chubb Corporation	581,290	9.7
4	HCC Insurance Holdings Inc.	336,353	5.6
5	Travelers Companies Inc.	334,446	5.6
6	ACE Ltd.	311,822	5.2
7	CNA Financial Corp.	286,609	4.8
8	Zurich Insurance Group	233,838	3.9
9	Tokio Marine Group	216,946	3.6
10	AXIS Capital Holdings Ltd.	215,201	3.6

[1]Includes property/casualty insurers that provided monoline directors and officers policies. The coverage may also be purchased as part of a package commercial multiperil policy. Includes some state funds.

Source: SNL Financial LC.

DIRECTORS AND OFFICERS LIABILITY CLAIMS BY TYPE OF CLAIMANT IN THE UNITED STATES, 2004-2013[1]

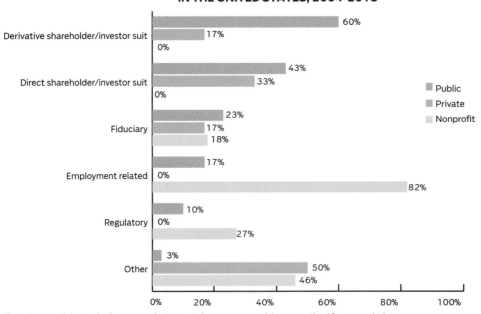

[1]Based on participants in the survey that reported one or more claims over the 10-year period.

Source: *2013 Directors and Officers Liability Survey*, JLT PARK Ltd.

Employment Practices Liability

Employment practices are a frequent source of claims against directors, officers and their organizations. Organizations that purchase insurance for employment practices liability (EPL) claims typically either buy a stand-alone EPL insurance policy or endorse their directors and officers liability (D&O) policy to cover employment practices liability. In 2011, 14 percent of public companies responding to a Towers Watson survey shared or blended their D&O limits with another coverage such as EPL or fiduciary liability, compared with 44 percent of private companies and nonprofits.

In 2012, 34 percent of the respondents to a survey of risk managers by the Risk and Insurance Management Society said they bought EPL policies. The pickup rate was greatest for the banking industry, with 50 percent of respondents purchasing the coverage, followed by consumer staples (49 percent), telecommunications (46 percent) and information technology (43 percent). Chartis was the leading writer, based on EPL premiums written, with a 38.1 percent market share in 2012, followed by Chubb (10.6 percent), ACE (10.5 percent), Zurich (9.5 percent) and Alterra Capital Holdings (8.0 percent).

TRENDS IN EMPLOYMENT PRACTICES LIABILITY, 2009-2013

Year	Median (midpoint) award	Probability range[1]
2009	$207,235	$60,000 - $600,281
2010	172,000	50,000 - 385,000
2011	271,000	82,121 - 555,000
2012	65,460	11,000 - 249,081
2013	109,300	25,000 - 258,564

[1]The middle 50 percent of all awards arranged in ascending order in a sampling, 25 percent above and below the median award.

Source: Reprinted with permission of Thomson Reuters, *Employment Practice Liability: Jury Award Trends And Statistics*, 2014 edition.

EMPLOYMENT PRACTICES LIABILITY, BY DEFENDANT TYPE, 2007-2013[1]

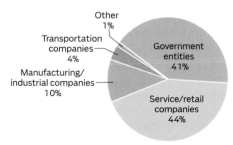

Other 1%
Transportation companies 4%
Manufacturing/ industrial companies 10%
Government entities 41%
Service/retail companies 44%

[1]Based on plaintiff and defendant verdicts rendered.

Source: Reprinted with permission of Thomson Reuters, *Employment Practice Liability: Jury Award Trends And Statistics*, 2014 edition.

Shareholder Lawsuits

Cornerstone Research has conducted annual studies of securities class-action lawsuit settlements and filings each year since the passage of the 1995 Private Securities Litigation Reform Act, enacted to curb frivolous shareholder lawsuits.

Filings

The number of securities class-action lawsuits filed rose 9.2 percent to 166 in 2013 from 152 in 2012, according to Cornerstone's 2013 study. The 166 filings in 2013 compare with an annual average of 191 recorded between 1997 and 2012. In 2013 healthcare, biotechnology and pharmaceutical companies accounted for 21 percent of total filings. Filings related to the financial crisis as well as mergers and acquisitions and Chinese reverse merger filings have continued to subside. Reverse mergers involve the acquisition of a private company by a public "shell" company, giving it access to capital markets.

Settlements

The number of court-approved securities class-action settlements rose 17.5 percent to 67 in 2013 from 57 in 2012, according to Cornerstone Research. The 2013 increase was the first year-to-year increase since 2009. Driven by mega-settlements, total settlement amounts rose 45.5 percent to $4.8 billion in 2013 from $3.3 billion in 2012. These mega-settlements (i.e., those in excess of $100 million) accounted for 84 percent of all 2013 settlement dollars, the second-highest proportion in the last decade. The median settlement amount fell by 47.9 percent to $358 million in 2013 and was 17.5 percent lower than the median settlement amount in the prior five years.

POST-REFORM ACT SETTLEMENTS OF SECURITIES LAWSUITS, 1996-2013[1]
(2013 dollars)

	1996-2012	2013
Minimum	$0.1 million	$0.7 million
Median	8.3 million	6.5 million
Average	55.5 million	71.3 million
Maximum	8.4 billion	2.4 billion
Total settlements	**$73.7 billion**	**$4.8 billion**

[1]Private Securities Litigation Reform Act of 1995; adjusted for inflation by Cornerstone Research.

Source: Cornerstone Research.

I.I.I. Store

The I.I.I. Store is your gateway to a wide array of books and brochures from the Insurance Information Institute.

Print, PDF and ebook formats. Quantity discounts are available for many products. Order online at www.iii.org/publications, call 212-346-5500 or email publications@iii.org.

I.I.I. Insurance Fact Book

Thousands of insurance facts, figures, tables and graphs designed for quick and easy reference.

Insurance Handbook

A guide to the insurance industry for reporters, public policymakers, students, insurance company employees, regulators and others.

Online version available at www.iii.org/insurancehandbook

Insuring Your Business: A Small Businessowners' Guide to Insurance

A comprehensive insurance guide for small businessowners.

Online version available at www.iii.org/smallbusiness

A Firm Foundation Online: How Insurance Supports the Economy

Shows the myriad ways in which insurance provides economic support—from offering employment and fueling the capital markets, to providing financial security and income to individuals and businesses. Provides national and state data. Selected state versions are also available.

Available at www.iii.org/economics

International Insurance Fact Book Online

Facts and statistics on the property/casualty and life insurance industries of dozens of countries.

Available at www.iii.org/international

Commercial Insurance Online

A guide to the commercial insurance market—what it does, how it functions and its key players.

Available at www.iii.org/commerciallines

I.I.I. Insurance Daily

Keeps thousands of readers up-to-date on important events, issues and trends in the insurance industry. Transmitted early each business day via email.

Contact: daily@iii.org

Consumer Brochures

Renters Insurance

Your Home Inventory

Nine Ways to Lower Your Auto Insurance Costs

Settling Insurance Claims After a Disaster

Twelve Ways to Lower Your Homeowners Insurance Costs   ...and many others

Digital, Social and Mobile

Apps and Software

   The I.I.I. Toolkit is a handy, free app suite that puts everything you need to plan, prepare, respond and restore in the palm of your hand. It includes three indispensable apps: Know Your Plan™, the award-winning disaster preparedness app that helps you, your family and even your pets be ready to safely get out of harm's way before trouble starts; Know Your Coverage™ to help you work out an insurance plan for your needs and budget through fun, interactive quizzes; and Know Your Stuff® – Home Inventory app, which ensures you'll always have an up-to-date record of your belongings. (Available in the Apple App Store and Google Play.)

 Know Your Stuff® – Home Inventory is also accessible on the Web. Visit www.KnowYourStuff.org to start your home inventory today.

Social

Find us on:

 facebook.com/InsuranceInformationInstitute

 @iiiorg   @IIIindustryblog
@III_Research   @InsuringFlorida

 youtube.com/user/iiivideo

 linkedin.com/company/insurance-information-institute

 pinterest.com/iiiorg

Blogs

Terms + Conditions: An insider look at the insurance industry and current issues.

Straight Talk: The Insuring Florida (InsuringFlorida.org) blog, helping Florida residents understand insurance coverage and related issues in the Sunshine State.

YEAR	EVENT
1601	First insurance legislation in the United Kingdom was enacted. Modern insurance has its roots in this law which concerned coverage for merchandise and ships.
1666	Great Fire of London demonstrated destructive power of fire in an urban environment, leading entrepreneur Nicholas Barbon to form a business to repair houses damaged by fire.
1684	Participants in the Friendly Society in England formed a mutual insurance company to cover fire losses.
1688	Edward Lloyd's coffee house, the precursor of Lloyd's of London, became the central meeting place for ship owners seeking insurance for a voyage.
1696	Hand in Hand Mutual Fire Company was formed in London. Aviva, the world's oldest continuously operating insurance company traces its origins to this company.
1710	Charles Povey formed the Sun in London, the oldest insurance company in existence which still conducts business in its own name. It is the forerunner of the Royal & Sun Alliance Group.
1735	The Friendly Society, the first insurance company in the United States, was established in Charleston, South Carolina. This mutual insurance company went out of business in 1740.
1752	The Philadelphia Contributionship for the Insurance of Houses from Loss by Fire, the oldest insurance carrier in continuous operation in the United States, was established in Philadelphia.
1759	Presbyterian Ministers Fund, the first life insurance company in the United States was founded in Philadelphia.
1762	Equitable Life Assurance Society, the world's oldest mutual life insurer, was formed in England.
1776	Charleston Insurance Company and the South Carolina Insurance Company, the first two United States marine insurance companies, were formed in South Carolina.
1779	Lloyd's of London introduced the first uniform ocean marine policy.
1792	Insurance Company of North America, the first stock insurance company in the United States, was established in Philadelphia.
1813	Eagle Fire Insurance Company of New York assumed all outstanding risks of the Union Insurance Company, in the first recorded fire reinsurance agreement in the United States.
1849	New York passed the first general insurance law in the United States.
1850	Franklin Health Assurance Company of Massachusetts offered the first accident and health insurance.
1851	New Hampshire created the first formal agency to regulate insurance in the United States.
1861	First war-risk insurance policies were issued, written by life insurance companies during the Civil War.
1866	National Board of Fire Underwriters was formed in New York City, marking the beginning of insurance rate standardization.
	Hartford Steam Boiler Inspection and Insurance Company, the first boiler insurance company, was established in Hartford, Connecticut.
1873	The Massachusetts Legislature adopted the first standard fire insurance policy.
1878	Fidelity and Casualty Company of New York began providing fidelity and surety bonds.

Appendices

Brief History

YEAR	EVENT
1885	Liability protection was first offered with the introduction of employers liability policies.
1890	First policies providing benefits for disabilities from specific diseases were offered.
1894	National Board of Fire Underwriters established Underwriters' Laboratories to investigate and test electrical materials to ensure they meet fire safety standards.
1898	Travelers Insurance Company issued the first automobile insurance policy in the United States.
1899	First pedestrian killed by an automobile, in New York City.
1910	New York passed the first United States workers compensation law. It was later found to be unconstitutional.
1911	Wisconsin enacted the first permanent workers compensation law in the United States.
1912	Lloyd's of London introduced aviation insurance coverage.
1925	Massachusetts passed the first compulsory automobile insurance legislation.
	Connecticut passed the first financial responsibility law for motorists.
1938	Federal Crop Insurance Act created the first federal crop insurance program.
1945	McCarran-Ferguson Act (Public Law 15) was enacted. It provided the insurance industry with a limited exemption to federal antitrust law, assuring the pre-eminence of state regulation of the industry.
1947	New York established the Motor Vehicle Liability Security Fund to cover auto insurance company insolvencies. This organization was a precursor of the state guaranty funds established by insurers in all states to absorb the claims of insolvent insurers.
1950	First package insurance policies for homeowners coverage were introduced.
1960	Boston Plan was established to address insurance availability problems in urban areas in Boston.
1968	First state-run Fair Access to Insurance Requirements (FAIR) Plans were set up to ensure property insurance availability in high-risk areas.
	The federal flood insurance program was established with the passage of the National Flood Insurance Act. It enabled property owners in communities that participate in flood reduction programs to purchase insurance against flood losses.
1971	Massachusetts became the first state to establish a true no-fault automobile insurance plan.
1974	Hawaii became first U.S. state to enact a law creating a near universal healthcare coverage system.
1981	Federal Risk Retention Act of 1981 was enacted. The law fostered the growth of risk retention groups and other nontraditional insurance mechanisms.
	The Illinois Legislature created the Illinois Insurance Exchange, a cooperative effort of individual brokers and risk bearers operating as a single market, similar to Lloyd's of London.
1985	Mission Insurance Group failed. The insolvency incurred the largest payout by state guaranty funds for a single property/casualty insurance company failure at that time. This and other insolvencies in the 1980s led to stricter state regulation of insurer solvency.
	Montana became the first state to forbid discrimination by sex in the setting of insurance rates.

YEAR	EVENT
1992	European Union's Third Nonlife Insurance Directive became effective, establishing a single European market for insurance.
1996	Florida enacted rules requiring insurers to offer separate deductibles for hurricane losses, marking a shift to hurricane deductibles based on a percentage of insured property value rather than a set dollar figure.
	Catastrophe bonds, vehicles for covering disaster risk in the capital markets, were introduced.
1997	World Trade Organization agreement to dismantle barriers to trade in financial services, including insurance, banking and securities, was signed by the United States and some 100 other countries.
1998	Travelers became first insurer to sell auto insurance on the Internet.
1999	Financial Services Modernization Act (Gramm-Leach-Bliley) enacted, allowing insurers, banks and securities firms to affiliate under a financial holding company structure.
2001	Terrorist attacks upon the World Trade Center in New York City and the Pentagon in Washington, D.C. caused about $40 billion in insured losses.
	New York became the first state to ban the use of hand-held cellphones while driving.
2002	Terrorism Risk Insurance Act enacted to provide a temporary federal backstop for terrorism insurance losses.
2003	In a landmark ruling, upheld in 2004, the U.S. Supreme Court placed limits on punitive damages, holding in State Farm v. Campbell that punitive damages awards should generally not exceed nine times compensatory awards.
2004	New York Attorney General Eliot Spitzer and a number of state regulators launched investigations into insurance industry sales and accounting practices.
2005	Citigroup sold off its Travelers life insurance unit, following the spin off of its property/casualty business in 2002. This dissolved the arrangement that led to the passage of Gramm-Leach-Bliley in 1999.
	The federal Class Action Fairness Act moved most class-action lawsuits to federal courts, offering the prospect of lower defense costs and fewer and less costly verdicts.
	A string of hurricanes, including Hurricane Katrina, hit the Gulf Coast, making 2005 the most active hurricane season.
2006	Massachusetts passed a mandatory universal health insurance law that established a statewide health insurance exchange.
	Congress passed legislation extending the Terrorism Risk Insurance Act to December 2007. The act, originally passed in 2002, had been set to expire at the end of 2005. Extended again in 2007.
2007	Washington became the first state to ban the practice of texting with a cellphone while driving.
	Congress passes legislation extending the Terrorism Risk Insurance Act through the end of 2014.
2008	The federal government acquired a 79.9 percent share in AIG in exchange for rescue program that eventually cost $182 billion. The funds were fully repaid by the end of 2012, ending the government stake.
	Troubled Asset Relief Program established to stabilize the financial sector. Insurers that own a federally regulated bank or thrift were eligible to participate.

YEAR	EVENT
2010	President Obama signed the Patient Protection and Affordable Care Act, requiring most U.S. citizens to have health insurance.
	The Dodd-Frank Wall Street Reform and Consumer Protection Act, a landmark regulatory overhaul of the financial services industry, was signed into law. While retaining state regulation of insurance, the act established the Federal Insurance Office, an entity that reports to Congress and the President on the insurance industry.
2011	Former Illinois Insurance Department Commissioner Michael McRaith appointed by the Secretary of the Treasury as the first director of the Federal Insurance Office, established under the Dodd-Frank Act. Serves in a nonvoting, advisory capacity to the Financial Stability Oversight Council.
2012	On June 28, 2012 the Supreme Court ruled that the 2010 Patient Protection and Affordable Care Act, requiring most U.S. citizens to have health insurance, is constitutional.
	Biggert-Waters Flood Reform Act, landmark legislation requiring flood insurance rates to better reflect risks, was passed. Many of its key provisions were revoked in 2014.
	Nevada became the first state to approve a license to test driverless cars on public roads.
2013	Health insurance exchanges, established under the 2010 Patient Protection and Affordable Care Act to expand access to insurance, began operations.
	Target discovered a computer breach affecting up to 70 million customers that would cost the retailer $235 million, of which $90 million was insured. The breach and 2014 events at Home Depot and JPMorgan Chase increased interest in and sales of cyberrisk insurance.
2014	Via Medicaid and insurance exchanges, millions of Americans gained health insurance mandated by the Patient Protection and Affordable Care Act. The percentage of uninsured Americans fell to 13.4 percent, from 18.0 percent a year earlier, according to Gallup.
	California and Colorado became the first states to pass laws clarifying the insurance responsibilities of drivers using their own cars to earn money by ferrying passengers using ride-sharing services such as UberX and Lyft.
	Congress was unable to pass a renewal of the Terrorism Risk Insurance Act before the 2014 Congressional lame duck session, setting up the program to expire December 31.

The majority of state commissioners are appointed by state governors and serve at their pleasure. The states designated with an asterisk (*) presently elect insurance commissioners to four-year terms.

Alabama • Jim L. Ridling, Commissioner of Insurance, 201 Monroe St., Suite 502, Montgomery, AL 36104. Tel. 334-269-3550. Fax. 334-241-4192. www.aldoi.gov

Alaska • Lori K. Wing-Heier, Director of Insurance, 550 W. Seventh Ave., Suite 1560, Anchorage, AK 99501-3567. Tel. 907-269-7900. Fax. 907-269-7910. www.commerce.state.ak.us/insurance

American Samoa • Tau Tanuvasa, Commissioner of Insurance, A P Lutali Executive Office Building, Pago Pago, American Samoa 85018-7269. Tel. 684-633-4116. www.americansamoa.gov

Arizona • Germaine L. Marks, Acting Director of Insurance, 2910 N. 44th St., Suite 210, Phoenix, AZ 85018-7269. Tel. 602-364-3100. Fax. 602-364-3470. www.id.state.az.us

Arkansas • Jay Bradford, Insurance Commissioner, 1200 W. Third St., Little Rock, AR 72201-1904. Tel. 501-371-2600. Fax. 501-371-2618. www.insurance.arkansas.gov

*California • Dave Jones, Commissioner of Insurance, 300 Spring St., South Tower, Los Angeles, CA 90013. Tel. 213-897-8921. Fax. 213-897-9051. www.insurance.ca.gov

Colorado • Marguerite Salazar, Commissioner of Insurance, 1560 Broadway, Suite 850, Denver, CO 80202. Tel. 303-894-7499. Fax. 303-894-7455. www.dora.state.co.us/insurance

Connecticut • Thomas B. Leonardi, Commissioner of Insurance, PO Box 816, Hartford, CT 06142-0816. Tel. 860-297-3900. Fax. 860-566-7410. www.ct.gov/cid

*Delaware • Karen Stewart, Insurance Commissioner, The Rodney Bldg., 841 Silver Lake Blvd., Dover, DE 19904. Tel. 302-674-7300. Fax. 302-739-5280. www.delawareinsurance.gov

District of Columbia • Chester A. McPherson, Acting Commissioner of Insurance, 810 First St. NE, Suite 701, Washington, DC 20002. Tel. 202-727-8000. Fax. 202-535-1196. www.disb.dc.gov

Florida • Kevin McCarty, Commissioner Office of Insurance Regulation, The Larsen Building, 200 E. Gaines St., Room 101A, Tallahassee, FL 32399-0301. Tel. 850-413-3140. Fax. 850-488-3334. www.floir.com

*Georgia • Ralph Hudgens, Insurance Commissioner, 2 Martin L. King Jr. Dr., 704 West Tower, Atlanta, GA 30334. Tel. 404-656-2070. Fax. 404-657-8542. www.gainsurance.org

Guam • Artemio B. Llagan, Banking & Insurance Commissioner, 1240 Route 16 Army Drive, Barrigada, Guam 96913. Tel. 671-635-1817. Fax. 671-633-2643. www.guamtax.com

Hawaii • Gordon Ito, Insurance Commissioner, PO Box 3614, Honolulu, HI 96811. Tel. 808-586-2790. Fax. 808-586-2806. www.state.hi.us/dcca/ins

Idaho • William Deal, Director of the Department of Insurance, 700 W. State St., PO Box 83720, Boise, ID 83720-0043. Tel. 208-334-4250. Fax. 208-334-4398. www.doi.idaho.gov

Illinois • Andrew Boron, Director of Insurance, 320 W. Washington St., Springfield, IL 62767-0001. Tel. 217-782-4515. Fax. 217-782-5020. www.insurance.illinois.gov

Indiana • Stephen W. Robertson, Commissioner of Insurance, 311 W. Washington St., Suite 300, Indianapolis, IN 46204-2787. Tel. 317-232-2385. Fax. 317-232-5251. www.in.gov/idoi

Iowa • Nick Gerhart, Commissioner of Insurance, 601 Locust St., Fourth Floor, Des Moines, IA 50309-3438. Tel. 515-281-5705. Fax 515-281-3059. www.iid.state.ia.us

*Kansas • Ken Selzer, Commissioner of Insurance, 420 S. West Ninth St., Topeka, KS 66612-1678. Tel. 785-296-3071. Fax. 785-296-7805. www.ksinsurance.org

Kentucky • Sharon P. Clark, Insurance Commissioner, PO Box 517, Frankfort, KY 40602-0517. Tel. 502-564-3630. Fax. 502-564-1453. http://insurance.ky.gov

*Louisiana • James J. Donelon, Commissioner of Insurance, 1702 N. Third St., Baton Rouge, LA 70802. Tel. 225-342-5423. Fax. 225-342-8622. www.ldi.la.gov

Maine • Eric A. Cioppa, Superintendent of Insurance, 34 State House Station, Augusta, ME 04333-0034. Tel. 207-624-8475. Fax. 207-624-8599. www.maine.gov/pfr/insurance

Maryland • Therese M. Goldsmith, Insurance Commissioner, 200 St. Paul Place, Suite 2700, Baltimore, MD 21202. Tel. 410-468-2090. Fax. 410-468-2020. www.mdinsurance.state.md.us

Massachusetts • Joseph G. Murphy, Commissioner of Insurance, 1000 Washington St., Eighth Floor, Boston, MA 02118-6200. Tel. 617-521-7794. Fax. 617-753-6830. www.state.ma.us/doi

Michigan • Kevin Clinton, Director of the Department of Insurance and Financial Services, Ottawa Building, 3rd Floor, 611 W. Ottawa, Lansing, MI 48933-1070. Tel. 517-373-0220. Fax. 517-335-4978. www.michigan.gov/difs

Minnesota • Mike Rothman, Commissioner of Commerce, 85 Seventh Place E., Suite 500, St. Paul, MN 55101. Tel. 651-539-1500. Fax. 651-539-1547. www.insurance.mn.gov

*Mississippi • Mike Chaney, Commissioner of Insurance, 1001 Woolfolk State Office Building, 501 N. West St., Jackson, MS 39201. Tel. 601-359-3569. Fax. 601-359-2474. www.mid.state.ms.us

Missouri • John M. Huff, Director of Insurance, 301 W. High St., PO Box 690, Jefferson City, MO 65102-0690. Tel. 573-751-4126. Fax. 573-751-1165. www.insurance.mo.gov

*Montana • Monica Lindeen, Commissioner of Insurance, 840 Helena Ave., Room 270, Helena, MT 59601. Tel. 406-444-2040. Fax. 406-444-3497. www.csi.mt.gov

Nebraska • Bruce R. Ramge, Director of Insurance, Terminal Bldg., 941 O St., Suite 400, Lincoln, NE 68508-3639. Tel. 402-471-2201. Fax. 402-471-4610. www.doi.ne.gov

Nevada • Scott J. Kipper, Commissioner of Insurance, 1818 E. College Parkway, Suite 103, Carson City, NV 89706. Tel. 775-687-0700. Fax. 775-687-0787. www.doi.state.nv.us

New Hampshire • Roger Sevigny, Insurance Commissioner, 21 S. Fruit St., Suite 14, Concord, NH 03301-7317. Tel. 603-271-2261. Fax. 603-271-1406. www.nh.gov/insurance

New Jersey • Kenneth E. Kobylowski, Commissioner of Banking and Insurance, 20 W. State St., PO Box 325, Trenton, NJ 08625. Tel. 609-292-5360. Fax. 609-984-5273. www.dobi.nj.gov

New Mexico • John G. Franchini, Superintendent of Insurance, PERA Building, 1120 Paseo De Peralta, Santa Fe, NM 87501. Tel. 505-827-4601. Fax. 505-476-0326. www.nmprc.state.nm.us/id.htm

New York • Benjamin M. Lawsky, Superintendent of Financial Services, 1 State St., New York, NY 10004-1511. Tel. 212-480-6400. Fax. 212-480-2310. www.dfs.ny.gov

*North Carolina • Wayne Goodwin, Commissioner of Insurance, 1201 Mail Service Center, Raleigh, NC 27699-1201. Tel. 919-807-6750. Fax. 919-733-6495. www.ncdoi.com

*North Dakota • Adam Hamm, Commissioner of Insurance, State Capitol, Fifth Floor, 600 East Boulevard Ave., Bismarck, ND 58505-0320. Tel. 701-328-2440. Fax. 701-328-4880. www.nd.gov/ndins

Ohio • Mary Taylor, Lieutenant Governor/Director of Insurance, 50 W. Town St., Third Floor, Suite 300, Columbus, OH 43215 Tel. 614-644-2658. Fax. 614-644-3743. www.insurance.ohio.gov

*Oklahoma • John Doak, Commissioner of Insurance, Five Corporate Plaza, 3625 NW 56th, Suite 100, Oklahoma City, OK 73112. Tel. 405-521-2828. Fax. 405-521-6635. www.oid.state.ok.us

Oregon • Laura N. Cali, Insurance Commissioner, PO Box 14480, Salem, OR 97309-0405. Tel. 503-947-7980. Fax. 503-378-4351. www.cbs.state.or.us/external/ins

Pennsylvania • Michael F. Consedine, Insurance Commissioner, 1209 Strawberry Square, Harrisburg, PA 17120. Tel. 717-787-2317. Fax. 717-787-8585. www.ins.state.pa.us

Puerto Rico • Angela Weyne, Commissioner of Insurance, B5 Calle Tabonuco, Suite 216, PMB 356, Guaynabo, PR 00968-3029. Tel. 787-304-8686. Fax. 787-273-6365. www.ocs.gobierno.pr

Rhode Island • Joseph Torti III, Superintendent of Insurance, 1511 Pontiac Ave., Cranston, RI 02920. Tel. 401-462-9500. Fax. 401-462-9532. www.dbr.state.ri.us

South Carolina • Raymond Farmer, Director of Insurance, PO Box 100105, Columbia, SC 29202-3105. Tel. 803-737-6160. Fax. 803-737-6205. www.doi.sc.gov

South Dakota • Merle D. Scheiber, Director of Insurance, 445 E. Capitol Ave., Pierre, SD 57501-3185. Tel. 605-773-4104. Fax. 605-773-5369. www.sd.gov/insurance

Tennessee • Julie Mix McPeak, Commissioner of Commerce & Insurance, 500 James Robertson Parkway, Nashville, TN 37243-0565. Tel. 615-741-2241. Fax. 615-532-6934. www.state.tn.us/commerce

Texas • Julia Rathgeber, Commissioner of Insurance, 333 Guadalupe St., Austin, TX 78701. Tel. 512-463-6464. Fax. 512-475-2005. www.tdi.state.tx.us

Utah • Todd E. Kiser, Commissioner of Insurance, 3110 State Office Building, Salt Lake City, UT 84114-6901. Tel. 801-538-3800. Fax. 801-538-3829. www.insurance.utah.gov

Vermont • Susan L. Donegan, Commissioner of the Department of Financial Regulation, 89 Main St., Drawer 20, Montpelier, VT 05620-3101. Tel. 802-828-3301. Fax. 802-828-3306. www.bishca.state.vt.us

Virgin Islands • Gregory R. Francis, Lieutenant Governor/Commissioner, 1131 King St., Third Floor, Suite 101, Christiansted, St. Croix, VI 00820. Tel. 340-773-6459. Fax. 340-774-9458. ltg.gov.vi

Virginia • Jacqueline K. Cunningham, Commissioner of Insurance, PO Box 1157, Richmond, VA 23218. Tel. 804-371-9694. Fax. 804-371-9349. www.scc.virginia.gov/boi

*Washington • Mike Kreidler, Insurance Commissioner, PO Box 40256, Olympia, WA 98504-0256. Tel. 360-725-7100. Fax. 360-586-2018. www.insurance.wa.gov

West Virginia • Michael D. Riley, Insurance Commissioner, 1124 Smith St., Charleston, WV 25301. Tel. 304-558-3354. Fax. 304-558-4965. www.wvinsurance.gov

Wisconsin • Ted Nickel, Commissioner of Insurance, 125 S. Webster St., Madison, WI 53703-3474. Tel. 608-266-3585. Fax. 608-266-9935. www.oci.wi.gov

Wyoming • Tom C. Hirsig, Insurance Commissioner, Herschler Bldg., 106 E. Sixth Ave., Cheyenne, WY 82002. Tel. 307-777-7401. Fax. 307-777-2446. insurance.state.wy.us

The following organizations are supported by insurance companies or have activities closely related to insurance. National and state organizations which subscribe to the services of the Insurance Information Institute are identified by an asterisk (*).

A.M. BEST COMPANY INC. • Ambest Road, Oldwick, NJ 08858, Tel. 908-439-2200. www.ambest.com — Rating organization and publisher of reference books and periodicals relating to the insurance industry.

ACORD • 1 Blue Hill Plaza, 15th Floor, PO Box 1529, Pearl River, NY 10965-8529, Tel. 845-620-1700. www.acord.com — An industry-sponsored institute serving as the focal point for improving the computer processing of insurance transactions through the insurance agency system.

ADVOCATES FOR HIGHWAY AND AUTO SAFETY • 750 First St. NE, Suite 901, Washington, DC 20002, Tel. 202-408-1711. www.saferoads.org — An alliance of consumer, safety and insurance organizations dedicated to highway and auto safety.

AIR WORLDWIDE CORPORATION • 131 Dartmouth St., Boston, MA 02116, Tel. 617-267-6645. www.air-worldwide.com — Risk modeling and technology firm that develops models of global natural hazards, enabling companies to identify, quantify and plan for the financial consequences of catastrophic events.

AMERICA'S HEALTH INSURANCE PLANS (AHIP) • 601 Pennsylvania Ave. NW, South Building, Suite 500, Washington, DC 20004, Tel. 202-778-3200. www.ahip.org — National trade association representing the health insurance industry.

AMERICAN ACADEMY OF ACTUARIES • 1850 M St. NW, Suite 300, Washington, DC 20036, Tel. 202-223-8196. www.actuary.org — Professional association for actuaries. Issues standards of conduct and provides government liaison and advisory opinions.

AMERICAN ASSOCIATION FOR LONG-TERM CARE INSURANCE • 3835 E. Thousand Oaks Blvd., Suite 336, Westlake Village, CA 91362, Tel. 818-597-3227. www.aaltci.org — A national professional organization exclusively dedicated to promoting the importance of planning for long-term care needs.

AMERICAN ASSOCIATION OF CROP INSURERS • 1 Massachusetts Ave. NW, Suite 800, Washington, DC 20001-1401, Tel. 202-789-4100. www.cropinsurers.com — Trade association of insurance companies to promote crop insurance.

AMERICAN ASSOCIATION OF INSURANCE SERVICES • 1745 S. Naperville Road, Wheaton, IL 60189-5898, Tel. 800-564-AAIS. www.aaisonline.com — Rating, statistical and advisory organization, made up principally of small and medium-sized property/casualty companies.

AMERICAN ASSOCIATION OF MANAGING GENERAL AGENTS • 610 Freedom Business Center, Suite 110, King of Prussia, PA 19406, Tel. 610-992-0022. www.aamga.org — Membership association of managing general agents of insurers.

AMERICAN BANKERS INSURANCE ASSOCIATION • 1120 Connecticut Ave. NW, Washington, DC 20036, Tel. 202-663-5172. www.aba.com — A separately chartered affiliate of the American Bankers Association. A full service association for bank insurance interests dedicated to furthering the policy and business objectives of banks in insurance.

AMERICAN COUNCIL OF LIFE INSURERS (ACLI) • 101 Constitution Ave. NW, Suite 700, Washington, DC 20001-2133, Tel. 202-624-2000. www.acli.com — Trade association responsible for the public affairs, government, legislative and research aspects of the life insurance business.

*AMERICAN INSTITUTE OF MARINE UNDERWRITERS • 14 Wall St., New York, NY 10005, Tel. 212-233-0550. www.aimu.org — Provides information of concern to marine underwriters and promotes their interests.

AMERICAN INSURANCE ASSOCIATION (AIA) • 2101 L St. NW, Suite 400, Washington, DC 20037, Tel. 202-828-7139. www.aiadc.org — Trade and service organization for property/casualty insurance companies. Provides a forum for the discussion of problems as well as safety, promotional and legislative services.

AMERICAN LAND TITLE ASSOCIATION • 1828 L St. NW, Suite 705, Washington, DC 20036, Tel. 202-296-3671. www.alta.org — Trade organization for title insurers, abstractors and agents. Performs statistical research and lobbying services.

AMERICAN NUCLEAR INSURERS • 95 Glastonbury Blvd., Suite 300, Glastonbury, CT 06033, Tel. 860-682-1301. www.amnucins.com — A nonprofit unincorporated association through which liability insurance protection is provided against hazards arising out of nuclear reactor installations and their operations.

AMERICAN PREPAID LEGAL SERVICES INSTITUTE • 321 N. Clark St., Chicago, IL 60654, Tel. 312-988-5751. www.aplsi.org — National membership organization providing information and technical assistance to lawyers, insurance companies, administrators, marketers and consumers regarding group and prepaid legal service plans.

AMERICAN RISK AND INSURANCE ASSOCIATION • 716 Providence Road, Malvern, PA 19355-3402, Tel. 610-640-1997. www.aria.org — Association of scholars in the field of risk management and insurance, dedicated to advancing knowledge in the field and enhancing the career development of its members.

AMERICAN TORT REFORM ASSOCIATION • 1101 Connecticut Ave. NW, Suite 400, Washington, DC 20036, Tel. 202-682-1163. www.atra.org — A broad based, bipartisan coalition of more than 300 businesses, corporations, municipalities, associations and professional firms that support civil justice reform.

APIW: A PROFESSIONAL ASSOCIATION OF WOMEN IN INSURANCE • 990 Cedar Bridge Ave., Suite B&PMB 210, Brick, NJ 08723-4157, Tel. 973-941-6024. www.apiw.org — A professional association of women in the insurance and reinsurance industry and related fields. Provides professional education, networking and support services to encourage the development of professional leadership among its members.

ARBITRATION FORUMS, INC. • 3820 Northdale Blvd., Suite 200A, Tampa, FL 33624, Tel. 866-977-3434. www.arbfile.org — Nonprofit provider of interinsurance dispute resolution services for self-insureds, insurers and claim service organizations.

ASSOCIATION OF FINANCIAL GUARANTY INSURERS • Mackin & Company,139 Lancaster St., Albany, NY 12210, Tel. 518-449-4698. www.afgi.org — Trade association of the insurers and reinsurers of municipal bonds and asset-backed securities.

ASSOCIATION OF GOVERNMENTAL RISK POOLS • 9 Cornell Road, Latham, NY 12110, Tel. 518-389-2782. www.agrip.org — Organization for public entity risk and benefits pools in North America.

AUTOMOBILE INSURANCE PLANS SERVICE OFFICE • 302 Central Ave., Johnston, RI 02919, Tel. 800-413-5808. www.aipso.com — Develops and files rates and provides other services for state-mandated automobile insurance plans.

BANK INSURANCE & SECURITIES ASSOCIATION • 2025 M St. NW, Suite 800, Washington, DC 20036, Tel. 202-367-1111. www.bisanet.org — Fosters the full integration of securities and insurance businesses with depository institutions' traditional banking businesses. Participants include executives from the securities, insurance, investment advisory, trust, private banking, retail, capital markets and commercial divisions of depository institutions.

BISRA - BANK INSURANCE & SECURITIES RESEARCH ASSOCIATES • 300 Day Hill Road, Windsor, CT 06095-4761, Tel. 860-298-3935. www.bisra.com — Consultant focusing on the financial services marketplace. Conducts studies of sales penetration, profitability, compensation and compliance. (formerly Kehrer-LIMRA).

CAPTIVE INSURANCE COMPANIES ASSOCIATION • 4248 Park Glen Road, Minneapolis, MN 55416, Tel. 952-928-4655. www.cicaworld.com — Organization that disseminates information useful to firms that utilize the captive insurance company concept to solve corporate insurance problems.

*CASUALTY ACTUARIAL SOCIETY • 4350 N. Fairfax Drive, Suite 250, Arlington, VA 22203, Tel. 703-276-3100. www.casact.org — Promotes actuarial and statistical science in property/casualty insurance fields.

CERTIFIED AUTOMOTIVE PARTS ASSOCIATION • 1000 Vermont Ave. NW, Suite 1010, Washington, DC 20005, Tel. 202-737-2212. www.capacertified.org — Nonprofit organization formed to develop and oversee a test program guaranteeing the suitability and quality of automotive parts.

COALITION AGAINST INSURANCE FRAUD • 1012 14th St. NW, Suite 200, Washington, DC 20005, Tel. 202-393-7330. www.insurancefraud.org — An alliance of consumer, law enforcement and insurance industry groups dedicated to reducing all forms of insurance fraud through public advocacy and education.

CONNING RESEARCH AND CONSULTING, INC. • 1 Financial Plaza, Hartford, CT 06103-2627, Tel. 860-299-2000. www.conningresearch.com — Research and consulting firm that offers an array of specialty information products, insights and analyses of key issues confronting the insurance industry.

CORELOGIC • 40 Pacifica, Suite 900, Irvine, CA 92618, Tel. 800-426-1466. www.corelogic.com — Provides comprehensive data, analytics and services to financial services and real estate professionals.

COUNCIL OF INSURANCE AGENTS AND BROKERS • 701 Pennsylvania Ave. NW, Suite 750, Washington, DC 20004-2608, Tel. 202-783-4400. www.ciab.com — A trade organization representing leading commercial insurance agencies and brokerage firms.

CROP INSURANCE AND REINSURANCE BUREAU • 201 Massachusetts Ave. NE, Suite C5, Washington, DC 20002, Tel. 202-544-0067 . www.cropinsurance.org — Crop insurance trade organization.

DEFENSE RESEARCH INSTITUTE • 55 W. Monroe St., Suite 2000, Chicago, IL 60603, Tel. 312-795-1101. www.dri.org — A national and international membership association of lawyers and others concerned with the defense of civil actions.

EASTBRIDGE CONSULTING GROUP, INC. • 50 Avon Meadow Lane, Avon, CT 06001, Tel. 860-676-9633. www.eastbridge.com — Provides consulting, marketing, training and research services to financial services firms, including those involved in worksite marketing and the distribution of individual and employee benefits products.

EMPLOYEE BENEFIT RESEARCH INSTITUTE • 1100 13th St. NW, Suite 878, Washington, DC 20005-4051, Tel. 202-659-0670. www.ebri.org — The Institute's mission is to advance the public's, the media's and policymakers' knowledge and understanding of employee benefits and their importance to the U.S. economy.

EQECAT • 475 14th St., Suite 550, Oakland, CA 94612-1938, Tel. 510-817-3100. www.eqecat.com — Provider of products and services for managing natural and man-made risks. Provides innovative catastrophe management solutions for property and casualty insurance underwriting, accumulation management and transfer of natural hazard and terrorism risk.

FITCH CREDIT RATING COMPANY • 33 Whitehall St., New York, NY 10004, Tel. 212-908-0500. www.fitchratings.com — Assigns claims-paying ability ratings to insurance companies.

GLOBAL AEROSPACE, INC. • 1 Sylvan Way, Parsippany, NJ 07054, Tel. 973-490-8500. www.global-aero.co.uk — A pool of property/casualty companies engaged in writing all classes of aviation insurance.

GLOBAL ASSOCIATION OF RISK PROFESSIONALS • 111 Town Square Place, 14th Floor, Jersey City, NJ 07310, Tel. 201-719-7210. www.garp.com — International group whose aim is to encourage and enhance communications between risk professionals, practitioners and regulators worldwide.

GRIFFITH INSURANCE EDUCATION FOUNDATION • 720 Providence Road, Suite 100, Malvern, PA 19355, Tel. 855-288-7743. www.griffithfoundation.org — The foundation promotes the teaching and study of risk management and insurance at colleges and universities nationwide and provides education programs for public policymakers on the basic principles of risk management and insurance.

HIGHWAY LOSS DATA INSTITUTE • 1005 N. Glebe Road, Suite 700, Arlington, VA 22201, Tel. 703-247-1600. www.hldi.org — Nonprofit organization to gather, process and provide the public with insurance data concerned with human and economic losses resulting from highway accidents.

INDEPENDENT INSURANCE AGENTS & BROKERS OF AMERICA, INC. • 127 S. Peyton St., Alexandria, VA 22314, Tel. 800-221-7917. www.independentagent.com — Trade association of independent insurance agents.

INLAND MARINE UNDERWRITERS ASSOCIATION • 14 Wall St., Eighth Floor, New York, NY 10005, Tel. 212-233-0550. www.imua.org — Forum for discussion of problems of common concern to inland marine insurers.

INSURANCE ACCOUNTING AND SYSTEMS ASSOCIATION, INC. • PO Box 51340, Durham, NC 27717, Tel. 919-489-0991. www.iasa.org — Promotes the study, research and development of modern techniques in insurance accounting and systems.

INSURANCE COMMITTEE FOR ARSON CONTROL • 3601 Vincennes Road, Indianapolis, IN 46268, Tel. 317-876-6226. www.arsoncontrol.org — All-industry coalition that serves as a catalyst for insurers' anti-arson efforts and a liaison with government agencies and other groups devoted to arson control.

INSURANCE DATA MANAGEMENT ASSOCIATION, INC. • 545 Washington Blvd., Jersey City, NJ 07310-1686, Tel. 201-469-3069. www.idma.org — An independent, nonprofit, professional, learned association dedicated to increasing the level of professionalism, knowledge and visibility of insurance data management.

INSURANCE INDUSTRY CHARITABLE FOUNDATION • 2121 N. California Blvd., Suite 555, Walnut Creek, CA 94596, Tel. 925-280-8009. www.iicf.org — Seeks to help communities and enrich lives by combining the collective strengths of the industry to provide grants, volunteer service and leadership.

INSURANCE INFORMATION INSTITUTE (I.I.I.) • 110 William St., 18th Floor, New York, NY 10038, Tel. 212-346-5500. www.iii.org — A primary source for information, analysis and reference on insurance subjects.

INSURANCE INSTITUTE FOR BUSINESS & HOME SAFETY • 4775 E. Fowler Ave., Tampa, FL 33617, Tel. 813-286-3400. www.DisasterSafety.org — An insurance industry-sponsored nonprofit organization dedicated to reducing losses, deaths, injuries and property damage resulting from natural hazards.

INSURANCE INSTITUTE FOR HIGHWAY SAFETY • 1005 N. Glebe Road, Suite 800, Arlington, VA 22201, Tel. 703-247-1500. www.iihs.org — Research and education organization dedicated to reducing loss, death, injury and property damage on the highways. Fully funded by property/casualty insurers.

INSURANCE LIBRARY ASSOCIATION OF BOSTON • 156 State St., Second Floor, Boston, MA 02109, Tel. 617-227-2087. www.insurancelibrary.org — The Insurance Library Association of Boston founded in 1887, is a nonprofit insurance association that has an extensive insurance library on all lines of insurance.

INSURANCE REGULATORY EXAMINERS SOCIETY • 1821 University Ave. West, Suite S256, St. Paul, MN 55104, Tel. 651-917-6250. www.go-ires.org — Nonprofit professional and educational association for examiners and other professionals working in insurance industry.

INSURANCE RESEARCH COUNCIL (A DIVISION OF THE INSTITUTES) • 718 Providence Road, Malvern, PA 19355-0725, Tel. 610-644-2212. www.insurance-research.org — Provides research relevant to public policy issues affecting risk and insurance.

INSURED RETIREMENT INSTITUTE • 1101 New York Ave. NW, Suite 825, Washington, DC 20005, Tel. 202-469-3000. www.irionline.org — Source of knowledge pertaining to annuities, insured retirement products and retirement planning; provides educational and informational resources. Formerly the National Association for Variable Annuities (NAVA).

INTEGRATED BENEFITS INSTITUTE • 595 Market St., Suite 810, San Francisco, CA 94105, Tel. 415-222-7280. www.ibiweb.org — A private, nonprofit organization that provides research, discussion and analysis, data services and legislative review to measure and improve integrated benefits programs, enhance efficiency in delivery of all employee-based benefits and promote effective return-to-work.

INTERMEDIARIES AND REINSURANCE UNDERWRITERS ASSOCIATION, INC. • c/o The Beaumont Group, Inc., 3626 E. Tremont Ave., Suite 203, Throggs Neck, NY 10465, Tel. 718-892-0228. www.irua.com — Educational association to encourage the exchange of ideas among reinsurers worldwide writing principally treaty reinsurance.

INTERNATIONAL ASSOCIATION OF INSURANCE FRAUD AGENCIES, INC. • PO Box 10018, Kansas City, MO 64171, Tel. 816-204-7360. www.iaifa.org — An international association opening the doors of communication, cooperation and exchange of information in the fight against sophisticated global insurance and related financial insurance fraud.

INTERNATIONAL ASSOCIATION OF INSURANCE PROFESSIONALS • 8023 E. 63rd Place, Suite 540, Tulsa, OK 74133, Tel. 800-766-6249. www.internationalinsuranceprofessionals.org — Provides insurance education, skills enhancement and leadership development to its members.

INTERNATIONAL ASSOCIATION OF SPECIAL INVESTIGATION UNITS • N83 W13410 Leon Road, Menomonee Falls, WI 53051, Tel. 414-375-2992. www.iasiu.org — Group whose goals are to promote a coordinated effort within the industry to combat insurance fraud and to provide education and training for insurance investigators.

*INTERNATIONAL INSURANCE SOCIETY, INC. • 101 Astor Place, New York, NY 10003, Tel. 212-277-5171. www.iisonline.org — A nonprofit membership organization whose mission is to facilitate international understandings, the transfer of ideas and innovations, and the development of personal networks across insurance markets through a joint effort of leading executives and academics throughout the world.

*ISO®, A VERISK ANALYTICS COMPANY® • 545 Washington Blvd., Jersey City, NJ 07310-1686, Tel. 800-888-4476; 201-469-2000. www.iso.com — A leading source of information about property/casualty insurance risk. Provides statistical, actuarial, underwriting and claims information; policy language; information about specific locations; fraud identification tools; and technical services. Products help customers protect people, property and financial assets.

KAREN CLARK & COMPANY • 2 Copley Place Tower 2, First Floor, Boston, MA 02116, Tel. 617-423-2800. www.karenclarkandco.com — Catastrophe risk assessment and modeling firm.

KINETIC ANALYSIS CORPORATION • 8070 Georgia Ave., Suite 413, Silver Spring, MD 20910, Tel. 240-821-1202. www.kinanco.com — Specializes in estimating the impact of natural and man-made hazards on the structures and the economy for clients in engineering, land development and risk management.

LATIN AMERICAN AGENTS ASSOCIATION • PO Box 1239, Montebello, CA 90640, Tel. 323-535-3290. www.latinagents.com — An independent group of Hispanic agents and brokers, whose goal is to educate, influence and inform the insurance community about the specific needs of the Latino community in the United States.

LATIN AMERICAN ASSOCIATION OF INSURANCE AGENCIES • PO Box 520844, Miami, FL 33152-2844, Tel. 305-477-1442. www.laaia.com — An association of insurance professionals whose purpose is to pro-tect the rights of its members, benefit the consumer through education, provide information and net-working services, and promote active participation in the political environment and community service.

LIFE INSURANCE SETTLEMENT ASSOCIATION • 225 S. Eola Drive, Orlando, FL 32801, Tel. 407-894-3797. www.thevoiceoftheindustry.com — Promotes the development, integrity and reputation of the life settlement industry.

*LIGHTNING PROTECTION INSTITUTE • PO Box 99, Maryville, MO 64468, Tel. 800-488-6864. www.lightning.org — Not-for-profit organization dedicated to ensuring that its members' lightning protection systems are the best possible quality in design, materials and installation.

LIMRA • 300 Day Hill Road, Windsor, CT 06095, Tel. 800-235-4672. www.limra.com — Worldwide association providing research, consulting and other services to insurance and financial services companies in more than 60 countries. LIMRA helps its member companies maximize their marketing effectiveness.

LOMA (LIFE OFFICE MANAGEMENT ASSOCIATION) • 2300 Windy Ridge Parkway, Suite 600, Atlanta, GA 30339-8443, Tel. 770-951-1770. www.loma.org — Worldwide association of insurance companies specializing in research and education, with a primary focus on home office management.

LOSS EXECUTIVES ASSOCIATION • PO Box 37, Tenafly, NJ 07670, Tel. 201-569-3346. www.lossexecutives.com — A professional association of property loss executives providing education to the industry.

MARSHALL & SWIFT • 777 S. Figueroa St., 12th Floor, Los Angeles, CA 90017, Tel. 800-421-8042. www.msbinfo.com — Building cost research company providing data and estimating technologies to the property insurance industry.

MIB, INC. • 50 Braintree Hill Park, Suite 400, Braintree, MA 02184-8734, Tel. 781-751-6000. www.mibsolutions.com/lost-life-insurance — Database of individual life insurance applications processed since 1995.

MICHAEL WHITE ASSOCIATES • 823 King of Prussia Road, Radnor, PA 19087, Tel. 610-254-0440. www.bankinsurance.com — Consulting firm that helps clients plan, develop and implement bank insurance sales programs. Conducts research on and benchmarks performance of bank insurance and investment fee income activities.

MOODY'S INVESTORS SERVICE • 7 World Trade Center at 250 Greenwich St., New York, NY 10007, Tel. 212-553-1653. www.moodys.com — Global credit analysis and financial information firm.

MORTGAGE INSURANCE COMPANIES OF AMERICA (MICA) • 1101 17th St. NW, Suite 700, Washington, DC 20036, Tel. 202-280-1820. www.usmi.org — Represents the private mortgage insurance industry. MICA provides information on related legislative and regulatory issues and strives to enhance understanding of the role private mortgage insurance plays in housing Americans.

NATIONAL AFRICAN-AMERICAN INSURANCE ASSOCIATION • PO Box 1110, 1718 M St. NW, Washington, DC 20036, Tel. 866-56-NAAIA. www.naaia.org — NAAIA fosters the nationwide presence, participation and long-term financial success of African-American insurance professionals within the greater insurance community and provides its members and the insurance industry a forum for sharing information and ideas that enhance business and professional development.

NATIONAL ARBITRATION FORUM • PO Box 50191, Minneapolis, MN 55405-0191, Tel. 800-474-2371. www.adrforum.com — A leading neutral administrator of arbitration, mediation and other forms of alternative dispute resolution worldwide.

NATIONAL ASSOCIATION OF HEALTH UNDERWRITERS • 1212 New York Ave. NW, Suite 1100, Washington, DC 20005, Tel. 202-552-5060. www.nahu.org — Professional association of people who sell and service disability income, and hospitalization and major medical health insurance companies.

NATIONAL ASSOCIATION OF INDEPENDENT INSURANCE ADJUSTERS • 1880 Radcliff Court, Tracy, CA 95376, Tel. 209-832-6962. www.naiia.com — Association of claims adjusters and firms operating independently on a fee basis for all insurance companies.

NATIONAL ASSOCIATION OF INSURANCE AND FINANCIAL ADVISORS • 2901 Telestar Court, Falls Church, VA 22042-1205, Tel. 703-770-8100. www.naifa.org — Professional association representing health and life insurance agents.

NATIONAL ASSOCIATION OF INSURANCE COMMISSIONERS • 1100 Walnut St., Suite 1500, Kansas City, MO 64106-2197, Tel. 816-842-3600. www.naic.org — Organization of state insurance commissioners to promote uniformity in state supervision of insurance matters and to recommend legislation in state legislatures.

NATIONAL ASSOCIATION OF MUTUAL INSURANCE COMPANIES (NAMIC) • 3601 Vincennes Road, Indianapolis, IN 46268, Tel. 317-875-5250. www.namic.org — National property/casualty insurance trade and political advocacy association.

NATIONAL ASSOCIATION OF PROFESSIONAL INSURANCE AGENTS • 400 N. Washington St., Alexandria, VA 22314-2353, Tel. 703-836-9340. www.pianet.com — Trade association of independent insurance agents. Operations: Lobbying, Education, Communications, Business Building Tools and Insurance Products.

NATIONAL ASSOCIATION OF PROFESSIONAL SURPLUS LINES OFFICES, LTD. • 4131 N. Mulberry Drive, Suite 200, Kansas City, MO 64116, Tel. 816-741-3910. www.napslo.org — Professional association of wholesale brokers, excess and surplus lines companies, affiliates and supporting members.

NATIONAL ASSOCIATION OF SURETY BOND PRODUCERS (NASBP) • 1140 19th St., Suite 800, Washington, DC 20036-5104, Tel. 202-686-3700. www.nasbp.org — NASBP members are professionals who specialize in providing surety bonds for construction and other commercial purposes.

*NATIONAL CONFERENCE OF INSURANCE GUARANTY FUNDS • 300 N. Meridian St., Suite 1020, Indianapolis, IN 46204, Tel. 317-464-8199. www.ncigf.org — Advisory organization to the state guaranty fund boards; gathers and disseminates information regarding insurer insolvencies.

NATIONAL CONFERENCE OF INSURANCE LEGISLATORS • 385 Jordan Road, Troy, NY 12180, Tel. 518-687-0178. www.ncoil.org — Organization of state legislators whose main area of public policy concern is insurance and insurance regulation.

NATIONAL CROP INSURANCE SERVICES, INC. • 8900 Indian Creek Parkway, Suite 600, Overland Park, KS 66210-1567, Tel. 913-685-2767. www.ag-risk.org — National trade association of insurance companies writing hail insurance, fire insurance and insurance against other weather perils to growing crops, with rating and research services for crop-hail and rain insurers.

NATIONAL FIRE PROTECTION ASSOCIATION • 1 Batterymarch Park, Quincy, MA 02169-7471, Tel. 617-770-3000. www.nfpa.org — Independent, nonprofit source of information on fire protection, prevention and suppression. Develops and publishes consensus fire safety standards; sponsors national Learn Not to Burn campaign.

NATIONAL FLOOD INSURANCE PROGRAM (NFIP) • 500 C St. SW, Washington, DC 20472, Tel. 800-621-FEMA. www.floodsmart.gov/floodsmart — The NFIP offers flood insurance to homeowners, renters and business owners if their community participates in the program. Participating communities agree to adopt and enforce ordinances that meet or exceed FEMA requirements to reduce the risk of flooding.

NATIONAL HIGHWAY TRAFFIC SAFETY ADMINISTRATION (NHTSA) • 1200 New Jersey Ave. SE, West Building, Washington, DC 20590, Tel. 888-327-4236. www.nhtsa.dot.gov — Carries out programs and studies aimed at reducing economic losses in motor vehicle crashes and repairs.

NATIONAL INDEPENDENT STATISTICAL SERVICE • 3601 Vincennes Road, PO Box 68950, Indianapolis, IN 46268, Tel. 317-876-6200. www.niss-stat.org — National statistical agent and advisory organization for all lines of insurance, except workers compensation.

*NATIONAL INSURANCE CRIME BUREAU • 1111 E. Touhy Ave., Suite 400, Des Plaines, IL 60018, Tel. 800-447-6282; 847-544-7000. www.nicb.org — A not-for-profit organization dedicated to preventing, detecting and defeating insurance fraud.

NATIONAL ORGANIZATION OF LIFE AND HEALTH INSURANCE GUARANTY ASSOCIATIONS (NOLHGA) • 13873 Park Center Road, Suite 329, Herndon, VA 20171, Tel. 703-481-5206. www.nolhga.com — A voluntary association composed of the life and health insurance guaranty associations of all 50 states, the District of Columbia and Puerto Rico.

NATIONAL RISK RETENTION ASSOCIATION • 16133 Ventura Blvd., Suite 1055, Encino, CA 91436, Tel. 800-928-5809. www.nrra-usa.org — The voice of risk retention group and purchasing group liability insurance programs, organized pursuant to the Federal Liability Risk Retention Act.

NATIONAL SAFETY COUNCIL • 1121 Spring Lake Drive, Itasca, IL 60143-3201, Tel. 630-285-1121. www.nsc.org — Provides national support and leadership in the field of safety, publishes safety material and conducts public information and publicity programs.

NATIONAL STRUCTURED SETTLEMENTS TRADE ASSOCIATION • 1100 New York Ave. NW, Suite 750W, Washington, DC 20005, Tel. 202-289-4004. www.nssta.com — Trade association representing consultants, insurers and others who are interested in the resolution and financing of tort claims through periodic payments.

NCCI HOLDINGS, INC. • 901 Peninsula Corporate Circle, Boca Raton, FL 33487, Tel. 561-893-1000. www.ncci.com — Develops and administers rating plans and systems for workers compensation insurance.

NEIGHBORWORKS AMERICA • 999 N. Capitol St. NE, Suite 900, Washington, DC 20002, Tel. 202-760-4000. www.nw.org — The goal of this group is to develop partnerships between the insurance industry and NeighborWorks organizations to better market the products and services of both, for the benefit of the customers and communities they serve.

NEW YORK ALLIANCE AGAINST INSURANCE FRAUD • 1450 Western Ave., Suite 101, Albany, NY 12203, Tel. 518-432-3576. www.fraudny.com — A cooperative effort of insurance companies in New York state to educate the industry about the costs of insurance fraud, the many forms it can take and what can be done to fight it.

*NEW YORK INSURANCE ASSOCIATION, INC. • 130 Washington Ave., Albany, NY 12210, Tel. 518-432-4227. www.nyia.org — Domestic and non-domestic property/casualty companies operations: lobbying.

NEW YORK PROPERTY INSURANCE UNDERWRITING ASSOCIATION • 100 William St., 4th Floor, New York, NY 10038, Tel. 212-208-9700. www.nypiua.com — Provides basic property insurance for New York State residents not able to obtain the coverage through the voluntary market. Administers the C-MAP and FAIR Plan.

NONPROFIT RISK MANAGEMENT CENTER • 204 S. King St., Leesburg, VA 20175, Tel. 703-777-3504. www.nonprofitrisk.org — Conducts research and education on risk management and insurance issues of special concern to nonprofit organizations.

NORTH AMERICAN PET HEALTH INSURANCE ASSOCIATION • 46 Shopping Plaza, Chagrin Falls, OH 44022, Tel. 877-962-7442. www.naphia.org — Group whose members work collaboratively towards establishing and maintaining universal and professional standards for terminology, best practices, quality and ethics in the pet health industry.

OPIC • 1100 New York Ave. NW, Washington, DC 20527, Tel. 202-336-8400. www.opic.gov — Self-sustaining U.S. government agency providing political risk insurance and finance services for U.S. investment in developing countries.

PHYSICIAN INSURERS ASSOCIATION OF AMERICA • 2275 Research Blvd., Suite 250, Rockville, MD 20850, Tel. 301-947-9000. www.thepiaa.org — Trade association representing physician-owned mutual insurance companies that provide medical malpractice insurance.

PROFESSIONAL LIABILITY UNDERWRITING SOCIETY (PLUS) • 5353 Wayzata Blvd., Suite 600, Minneapolis, MN 55416, Tel. 952-746-2580. www.plusweb.org — An international, nonprofit association that provides educational opportunities and programs to enhance the professionalism of its members.

PROPERTY CASUALTY INSURERS ASSOCIATION OF AMERICA (PCI) • 8700 W. Bryn Mawr Ave., Suite 1200S, Chicago, IL 60031-3512, Tel. 847-297-7800. www.pciaa.net — Serves as a voice on public policy issues and advocates positions that foster a competitive market place for property/casualty insurers and insurance consumers.

PROPERTY INSURANCE PLANS SERVICE OFFICE • 27 School St., Suite 302, Boston, MA 02108, Tel. 617-371-4175. www.pipso.com — Provides technical and administrative services to state property insurance plans.

PROPERTY LOSS RESEARCH BUREAU • 3025 Highland Parkway, Suite 800, Downers Grove, IL 60515, Tel. 630-724-2200. www.plrb.org — This property/casualty trade organization promotes productivity and efficiency in the property and liability loss and claim adjustment processes, disseminates information on property and liability issues and fosters education and new and beneficial developments within the industry.

PUBLIC RISK MANAGEMENT ASSOCIATION • 700 S. Washington St., Suite 218, Alexandria, VA 22314, Tel. 703-528-7701. www.primacentral.org — Membership organization representing risk managers in state and local public entities.

RAND INSTITUTE FOR CIVIL JUSTICE • 1776 Main St., PO Box 2138, Santa Monica, CA 90407-2138, Tel. 310-393-0411. www.rand.org — Organization formed within The Rand Corporation to perform independent, objective research and analysis concerning the civil justice system.

REINSURANCE ASSOCIATION OF AMERICA • 1445 New York Ave. NW, Seventh Floor, Washington, DC 20005, Tel. 202-638-3690. www.reinsurance.org — Trade association of property/casualty reinsurers; provides legislative services for members.

RISK AND INSURANCE MANAGEMENT SOCIETY, INC. • 5 Bryant Park, 13th floor, New York, NY 10018, Tel. 212-286-9292. www.rims.org — Organization of corporate buyers of insurance, which makes known to insurers the insurance needs of business and industry, supports loss prevention and provides a forum for the discussion of common objectives and problems.

RISK MANAGEMENT SOLUTIONS, INC. • 7575 Gateway Blvd., Newark, CA 94560, Tel. 510-505-2500. www.rms.com — Provides products and services for the quantification and management of catastrophe risk associated with natural perils as well as products for weather derivatives and enterprise risk management for the property/casualty insurance industry.

SCHOOL OF RISK MANAGEMENT, INSURANCE AND ACTUARIAL SCIENCE OF THE TOBIN COLLEGE OF BUSINESS AT ST. JOHN'S UNIVERSITY (FORMERLY THE COLLEGE OF INSURANCE) • 101 Astor Place, New York, NY 10003, Tel. 212-277-5198. www.stjohns.edu/academics/graduate/tobin/srm — Insurance industry-supported college providing a curriculum leading to bachelor's and master's degrees in business administration, financial management of risk, insurance finance and actuarial science. The Kathryn and Shelby Cullom Davis Library (212-277-5135) provides services, products and resources to its members.

SELF-INSURANCE INSTITUTE OF AMERICA • PO Box 1237, Simpsonville, SC 29681, Tel. 800-851-7789. www.siia.org — Organization that fosters and promotes alternative methods of risk protection.

SNL FINANCIAL LC • 1 SNL Plaza, 212 Seventh St. NE, Charlottesville, VA 22902, Tel. 434-977-1600. www.snl.com — Research firm that collects, standardizes and disseminates all relevant corporate, financial, market and M&A data as well as news and analytics for the industries it covers: banking, specialized financial services, insurance, real estate and energy.

SOCIETY OF ACTUARIES • 475 N. Martingale Road, Suite 600, Schaumburg, IL 60173, Tel. 847-706-3500. www.soa.org — An educational, research and professional organization dedicated to serving the public and its members. The society's vision is for actuaries to be recognized as the leading professionals in the modeling and management of financial risk and contingent events.

SOCIETY OF CERTIFIED INSURANCE COUNSELORS • PO Box 27027, Austin, TX 78755-2027, Tel. 800-633-2165. www.scic.com — National education program in property, liability and life insurance, with a continuing education requirement upon designation.

SOCIETY OF FINANCIAL EXAMINERS • 12100 Sunset Hills Road, Suite 130, Reston, VA 20190-3221, Tel. 703-234-4140. www.sofe.org — Professional society for examiners of insurance companies, banks, savings and loans, and credit unions.

SOCIETY OF INSURANCE RESEARCH • 631 Eastpointe Drive, Shelbyville, IN 46176, Tel. 317-398-3684. www.sirnet.org — Stimulates insurance research and fosters exchanges among society members on research methodology.

SOCIETY OF INSURANCE TRAINERS AND EDUCATORS • 1821 University Ave. West, Suite S256, St. Paul, MN 55104 , Tel. 651-999-5354. www.insurancetrainers.org — Professional organization of trainers and educators in insurance.

STANDARD & POOR'S RATING GROUP • 55 Water St., New York, NY 10041, Tel. 212-438-2000. www.standardandpoors.com — Monitors the credit quality of bonds and other financial instruments of corporations, governments and supranational entities.

SURETY & FIDELITY ASSOCIATION OF AMERICA • 1101 Connecticut Ave. NW, Suite 800, Washington, DC 20036, Tel. 202-463-0600. www.surety.org — Statistical, rating, development and advisory organization for surety companies.

THE ACTUARIAL FOUNDATION • 475 N. Martingale Road, Suite 600, Schaumburg, IL 60173-2226, Tel. 847-706-3535. www.actuarialfoundation.org — Develops, funds and executes education and research programs that serve the public by harnessing the talents of actuaries.

Appendices

THE AMERICAN COLLEGE • 270 S. Bryn Mawr Ave., Bryn Mawr, PA 19010, Tel. 610-526-1000. www.theamericancollege.edu — An independent, accredited nonprofit institution, originally The American College of Life Underwriters. Provides graduate and professional education in insurance and other financial services.

THE COMMITTEE OF ANNUITY INSURERS • c/o Davis & Harman LLP, 1455 Pennsylvania Ave. NW, Suite 1200, Washington, DC 20004, Tel. 202-347-2230. www.annuity-insurers.org — Group whose goal is to address federal legislative and regulatory issues relevant to the annuity industry and to participate in the development of federal tax and securities policies regarding annuities.

THE FINANCIAL SERVICES ROUNDTABLE • 600 13th St. NW, Suite 400, Washington, DC 20005, Tel. 202-289-4322. www.fsround.org — A forum for U.S. financial industry leaders working together to determine and influence the most critical public policy concerns related to the integration of the financial services.

THE LIFE AND HEALTH INSURANCE FOUNDATION FOR EDUCATION • 1655 N. Fort Myer Drive, Suite 610, Arlington, VA 22209, Tel. 888-LIFE-777. lifehappens.org — Nonprofit organization dedicated to addressing the public's growing need for information and education about life, health, disability and long-term care insurance.

UNDERWRITERS' LABORATORIES, INC. • 2600 NW Lake Road, Camas, WA 98607-8542, Tel. 360-817-5500. www.ul.com — Investigates and tests electrical materials and other products to determine that fire prevention and protection standards are being met.

WEATHER RISK MANAGEMENT ASSOCIATION (WRMA) • 529 14th St. NW, Suite 750, Washington, DC 20045, Tel. 202-289-3800. www.wrma.org — Serves the weather risk management industry by providing forums for discussion and interaction with others associated with financial weather products.

*WISCONSIN INSURANCE ALLIANCE • 44 E. Mifflin St., Suite 901, Madison, WI 53703-2888, Tel. 608-255-1749. www.wial.com — A state trade association of property/casualty insurance companies conducting legislative affairs and public relations on behalf of the industry.

*WORKERS COMPENSATION RESEARCH INSTITUTE • 955 Massachusetts Ave., Cambridge, MA 02139, Tel. 617-661-9274. www.wcrinet.org — A nonpartisan, not-for-profit membership organization conducting public policy research on workers compensation, healthcare and disability issues. Members include employers, insurers, insurance regulators and state regulatory agencies, as well as several state labor organizations.

ACE USA

ACUITY

AEGIS Insurance Services Inc.

AIG

Allianz of America, Inc.

Allied World Assurance Company

Allstate Insurance Group

ALPS Corporation

American Agricultural Insurance Company

American Family Insurance

American Hallmark Insurance Services, Inc.

American Integrity Insurance Company

American Reliable Insurance

Amerisafe

Amerisure Insurance Companies

Arch Insurance Group

Arthur J. Gallagher

Beacon Mutual Insurance Company

BITCO Insurance Companies

Canal Insurance

Catlin U.S.

Century Surety Company

Chesapeake Employers' Insurance Company

Chubb Group of Insurance Companies

Church Mutual Insurance Company

The Concord Group

COUNTRY Financial

CNA

CSAA Insurance Group

CUMIS Insurance Society, Inc.

Dryden Mutual Insurance Company

EMC Insurance Companies

Enumclaw Insurance Group

Erie Insurance Group

Farm Bureau Town and Country Insurance Company of Missouri

Farmers Group, Inc.

FM Global

GEICO

Gen Re

Germania Insurance

Grange Insurance Association

Grange Insurance Companies

GuideOne Insurance

The Hanover Insurance Group Inc.

The Harford Mutual Insurance Companies

The Hartford Financial Services Group

The Horace Mann Companies

Ironshore Insurance Ltd.

Kemper Corporation

Liberty Mutual Group

Lloyd's

Lockton Companies

Magna Carta Companies

MAPFRE USA

Marsh Inc.

MEMIC

MetLife Auto & Home

Michigan Millers Mutual Insurance Company

Millville Mutual Insurance Company

Missouri Employers Mutual Insurance

MMG Insurance Company

Motorists Insurance Group

Munich Re

Nationwide

New York Central Mutual Fire Insurance Company

The Norfolk & Dedham Group

Ohio Mutual Insurance Group

OneBeacon Insurance Group

PartnerRe

Pennsylvania Lumbermens Mutual Insurance Company

Providence Mutual Fire Insurance Company

QBE Regional Insurance

Scor U.S. Corporation

SECURA Insurance Companies

Selective Insurance Group

State Auto Insurance Companies

State Compensation Insurance Fund of California

State Farm Mutual Automobile Insurance
 Company

The Sullivan Group

Swiss Reinsurance America Corporation

Travelers

USAA

Utica National Insurance Group

Westfield Group

Willis

W. R. Berkley Corporation

XL America Group

Zurich North America

Associate Members

ANE, Agency Network Exchange, LLC

Crawford and Company

The Crichton Group

Deloitte

Farmers Mutual Fire Insurance of Tennessee

Mutual Assurance Society of Virginia

Sompo Japan Research Institute, Inc.

Transunion Insurance Solutions

The University of Alabama

Insurance Information Institute
110 William Street
New York, NY 10038
Tel. 212-346-5500. Fax. 212-732-1916. www.iii.org

President – Robert P. Hartwig, Ph.D., CPCU – bobh@iii.org

Executive Vice President – Andréa C. Basora – andreab@iii.org

Senior Vice President and Chief Communications Officer – Jeanne Salvatore – jeannes@iii.org

Senior Vice President and Chief Economist – Steven N. Weisbart, Ph.D., CLU – stevenw@iii.org

Research and Information Services

Chief Actuary and Director of Research and Information Services – James Lynch, FCAS, MAAA – jamesl@iii.org

Senior Editor – Neil Liebman – neill@iii.org

Research and Production – Mary-Anne Firneno – mary-annef@iii.org

Information Specialist – Maria Sassian – marias@iii.org

Manager – Publications and Web Production – Katja Charlene Lewis – charlenel@iii.org

Special Consultant – Ruth Gastel, CPCU – ruthg@iii.org

Publications Orders – Daphne Gerardi – daphneg@iii.org

Digital Communications

Director – Digital Communications – James P. Ballot – jamesb@iii.org

Director – Technology and Web Production – Shorna Lewis – shornal@iii.org

Manager – Digital Media – Alba Rosario – albar@iii.org

Media

Vice President – Media Relations – Michael Barry – michaelb@iii.org

Vice President – Communications – Loretta Worters – lorettaw@iii.org

Terms + Conditions blog – Claire Wilkinson – clairew@iii.org

Impact **Magazine** – Diane Portantiere – dianep@iii.org

Administrative Assistant – Rita El-Hakim – ritae@iii.org

Administrative Assistant – Lilia Giordano – liliag@iii.org

Representatives

Davis Communications – William J. Davis, Atlanta – billjoe@bellsouth.net
Tel. 770-321-5150. Fax. 770-321-5150.

Hispanic Press Officer – Elianne González, Miami – elianneg@iii.org
Tel. 954-389-9517.

Florida Representative – Lynne McChristian, Tampa – lynnem@iii.org
Tel. 813-480-6446. Fax. 813-915-3463.

O

occupational disease, 193
ocean marine insurance, 59, 61, 64, 123
older drivers
    automobile/motor vehicles crashes, 176, 177
    license renewal laws, 90-91
online sales, life/health insurance, 27
    property/casualty insurance, 25
operating results, 43, 47
other liability. *See* general liability insurance
overseas sales of property/casualty insurance.
  See foreign sales

P

personal injury lawsuits, 204-206
personal injury protection (PIP), 83, 84
personal vs. commercial insurance, 60
policyholder dividends, 43, 47
policyholders' surplus, 43, 48
premium taxes, 24
premiums, v
    average renters and homeowners, by state, 104-105
    by line, 35-40
        life/health, 35-40
        property/casualty, 60-61
    by type of insurer, 14
    direct written
        by state, 55
        leading countries, 1
        leading writers, 15, 68, 69
    growth in, 14
    life/health, by state, 39-41
    property/casualty, by state, 55, 62-66
    worldwide, 2
    See also specific lines of insurance; direct premiums
      written; net premiums written
private mortgage insurance. *See* mortgage guaranty
  insurance
private passenger cars, accidents
    automobile insurance, underwriting expenses, 74
    bodily injury, 75
    insured vehicles, 76
    property damage, 75
Private Securities Litigation Reform Act, 210
products liability insurance, 59, 61, 63, 119
profitability, 45
property crime offenses, 167
property/casualty
    by line, 59-66
    financial data, 43-58
    online sales, 25
public health risks, 195-196

Q

questionable claims, by insurance type, 200

R

rate of return, 45
real estate investments, 50
recreation, 184-187
reinsurance, 3, 54, 59, 61
    domicile of alien reinsurers, 3
    top ten brokers, global, 5
    top ten companies, global, 4, 5
        U.S., 54
renters insurance, 103, 105
residual market. *See* shared market
retirement assets, 131
retirement programs, 131-135
risk-financing options, 7-9

S

Saffir/Simpson Hurricane Wind Scale, 146
seatbelt laws, 85-86
securities lawsuits, 210
shared automobile market, 77-78
shareholder class-action lawsuits, 210
sports injuries, by sport, 186-187
state by state tables
    alcohol server liability laws, 89
    automobile financial responsibility laws, 81-82, 84
    automobile insurance expenditures, 71-73
    automobile shared market, 77-78
    automobile theft, 183
    automobile/motor vehicle deaths, 173
    coastal properties, 98, 99, 100
    cybercrime, 169
    direct premiums, 55
        by line, 62-66
    drivers license renewal laws, 90-91
    drunk driving laws, 87-88
    FAIR Plans, 101-102
    flood insurance, 112-113
    fraud laws, 201-202
    guaranty fund assessments, 58
    homeowners insurance, premiums, 104-105
    identity theft, 171
    insurance companies
        employment, 18
        number of, 23
    life/health insurance, premiums, 39-41
    liquor liability laws, 89
    population change, coastal counties, 96
    premiums, by state, 62-66
        direct written, by state, 55
    private passenger cars insured, 77-78
    seatbelt laws, 85-86
    taxes, premium, 56

tornadoes, 154
tornadoes and tornado deaths, 154
uninsured motorists, 79, 80
vehicles insured, 77-78
watercraft theft, 186
wildfires, 161
young driver laws, 93-94
stocks, 50, 51
storms, losses. *See* catastrophes; hurricanes; tornadoes
surety, 59, 61, 64, 124
surplus lines, 52-53
    top ten companies, 53

T

taxes, 24, 43, 44, 55, 106
teenage drivers. *See* young drivers
terrorist attacks, 156-157
theft, automobiles, 167, 182-184
    by state, auto, 183
    homeowners, 107, 108
    watercraft, 186
    See also burglary and theft
tornadoes, 151-154
tort liability, automobile insurance, 83, 84
tsunamis, 142

U

underwriting expenses, 43, 74, 106
    automobile insurance, 74
    homeowners insurance, 100
underwriting results, 44, 47
uninsured motorists, 78-80
unintentional injuries. *See* accidents; automobile/motor
    vehicle crashes; workplace losses

V

vehicles insured, by state, shared market, 77-78
verbal thresholds, automobile insurance, 84
voluntary automobile market, 76
    by state, 77-78

W

warranty, 130
    direct premiums written, by state, 66
water damage, claims, 107, 107
watercraft, recreational accidents, 184-185
watercraft theft, 186
wildfires, 160-161
wind and hail, claims, 107, 108
windstorm plans. *See* beach and windstorm plans
winter storms, most costly, 150
workers compensation insurance, 59, 61, 63, 117-118
    medical costs, 118
workplace
    disease, 193, 194
    losses, 191-194
    losses and deaths, 191, 193
work-related illnesses, 192, 193
world insurance market, 1-12
    by year, 2
    leading companies, world, 4-5
    leading countries, 1
    premiums, v, 1, 2
Write-Your-Own Flood Insurance Program,
    110, 112-113

Y

young drivers
    automobile/motor vehicle crashes, 176, 177
    laws, 92, 93-94